Management Guides
to Mergers & Acquisitions

Management Guides to Mergers & Acquisitions

Edited by

JOHN L. HARVEY
Partner, Arthur Young & Company, Pittsburgh

ALBERT NEWGARDEN
Principal, Arthur Young & Company, New York
Editor, *The Arthur Young Journal*

WILEY-INTERSCIENCE   A Division of John Wiley & Sons

NEW YORK / LONDON / SYDNEY / TORONTO

Copyright © 1969, by John Wiley & Sons, Inc.

All rights reserved. No part of this book may be reproduced
by any means, nor transmitted, nor translated into a machine
language without the written permission of the publisher.

10 9 8 7 6 5 4 3 2 1

Library of Congress Catalogue Card Number: 79-82978

SBN 471 35798 7

Printed in the United States of America

The editors and the publishers are grateful to the following publishers and authors for permission to include the copyright material indicated:

American Management Association, Inc., for: "Mergers and Fringe Benefits," by John L. Hawn, based on an article originally published in AMA Financial Series No. 113, *Integration Policies and Problems in Mergers and Acquisitions,* copyright © 1957 by the American Management Association, Inc.; and for "Mergers and People," by Thomas J. Riggs, Jr., originally published in AMA Management Report 75, *Corporate Growth Through Merger and Acquisition,* copyright © 1963 by the American Management Association, Inc.; and for "How to Make an Overseas Acquisition You Can Live With," by Robert L. Prince, originally published in the November 1965 issue of *Management Review,* copyright © 1965 by the American Management Association, Inc.

Business International Corporation, for material included in "Finding and Evaluating a Business Abroad," by George B. Finnegan, originally published in *Acquisitions Abroad for Growth & Profits,* copyright © 1964 by Business International Corporation.

DePaul University, for "Tax Considerations in Buying or Selling a Corporate Business," by Robert H. Monyek and Richard L. Kessler, originally published in the *DePaul Law Review,* Autumn-Winter 1966, copyright © 1966 by DePaul University.

Dun & Bradstreet Publications Corp., for "The Pitfalls of Acquisitions," by L. A. Casler, originally published in *Dun's Review,* June 1966, copyright © 1966 by Dun & Bradstreet Publications Corp.

v

Preface

THE PURPOSE of this book is to assemble, in a single volume, examples of the many kinds of information management must have to make logical decisions relating to business combinations, to describe some of the techniques that have been found useful for developing such information, and finally to explore the rationale of the key decision to merge or not to merge.

Although a number of books have been published on the subject of mergers and acquisitions—some of them good, some of them mediocre, a few of them bad—even the best of these books suffer, in our view, from one important defect: they are written from a single narrow viewpoint, whether it be that of the attorney, the accountant, the investment banker, the corporation executive, or the academic researcher. With a few notable exceptions, most successful business combinations have been the result of a *team* approach, in which the knowledge and experience of the companies' own executives has been broadly supported by the specialized knowledge and experience of a variety of outside consultants, including attorneys, bankers, CPAs, appraisers, and others with special skills related to the business of mergers.

For the first time, to our knowledge, in the literature of mergers and acquisitions we have brought together in this volume the expertise of a wide variety of merger specialists—consultants as well as corporate executives, sellers as well as buyers. The result, if we have been successful, should be a volume uniquely suited to the needs of the corporate executive whose experience with mergers and acquisitions has been limited and who is seeking some general guidance to the wide range of very specific considerations involved in effective merger planning—establishing objectives, finding and screening prospective merger candidates, investigating the more promising candidates, tax and legal aspects, alternative financing methods, personnel and labor relations considerations—the list is not endless but a very long one indeed. For much the same reason this book should be of particular value to students and teachers of business management with a more than casual interest in the subject of mergers and acquisitions. And, finally, it is hoped that the book will be of value to specialists in the various merger-related fields and disciplines it covers, in helping them to better understand the roles of other members of the merger and acquisition team.

As indicated on page v, many of the chapters in this book are based upon material originally published in such periodicals as *Harvard Business Review, Financial Executive, Mergers & Acquisitions,* and *Dun's Review,* as well as in various legal and accounting journals. Of the remaining chapters, two are condensations of material originally published in book form, and others were prepared especially for inclusion in this volume. Through the kind cooperation of their authors, most of the chapters previously published as articles have been substantially revised to reflect changes since their original publication.

HOW TO READ THIS BOOK

As is true of all "contributed" books, this volume is not designed to be read like a novel, beginning at page 1 and continuing straight through to the end. To the contrary, it is assumed that readers will skip about, choosing those sections or chapters of immediate or particular interest to them. Thus, for example, a prospective seller may read this book quite differently than a prospective buyer would; and those whose immediate interests lie in the area of international mergers and acquisitions can be expected to turn to that section of the book long before those whose interests at the present time are purely domestic. It is our hope, however, that most readers will, at some early stage in their use of the book, read the first section, "Planning and Fact Finding," in its entirety, for it is this section that explores the relationship between the specialized subject areas covered elsewhere in the book and the roles of the members of the merger and acquisition team.

Because each chapter of the book is designed to be self-sufficient, in the sense that it is not assumed that the reader will have read the preceding chapters, there is bound to be some overlapping. Though we have taken pains to minimize unnecessary repetition, some necessary repetition survives.

A few words about the organization of the book may also be helpful. Obviously no volume of this size, made up of the individual contributions of authors with a variety of different interests and fields of knowledge, could possibly hope to cover every important aspect of so large and complicated a subject as mergers and acquisitions. The material included in this volume was selected from an original group of more than a hundred articles and research studies which we reviewed carefully. The choice of what to include in this volume was based primarily on our desire to cover at least generally the major areas of premerger and postmerger planning and, within those areas, to deal more specifically with subjects which, in our opinion, have received insufficient attention in other books published in recent years. Just as an example, there are many legal problems associated with acquisitions that are outside the scope of the two legal chapters we have included. Books could be written about these other problems, but such books *have* been written; and we have included only those legal subjects that we considered to be of substantial interest to the nonlegal reader.

Finally, a note of caution, with particular reference to those chapters that deal with legal and accounting matters. Although every effort has been made to bring these chapters up to date as of the time this book was set in type, the laws, accounting principles, and governmental attitudes affecting mergers and acquisitions are always subject to change and will be particularly so, it seems clear, in the months and years ahead. The purpose of those chapters dealing in detail with such matters is to suggest the kinds of questions management should explore with its expert advisers, and not necessarily to provide timely answers to those questions. In matters of law and accounting principles there is no substitute for current counsel, and no book, including this, should be expected or relied upon to take the place of up-to-date professional knowledge.

ACKNOWLEDGMENTS

The editors gratefully acknowledge the cooperation of the authors and original publishers of the articles included in this volume. Particular thanks are due to the American Management Association, to John F. Chapman, executive editor of *Harvard Business Review,* and to Stanley Foster Reed, editor and publisher of *Mergers & Acquisitions* magazine, for their generosity in making copyrighted material available.

Almost a third of the chapters included in this book were written by partners and other associates in Arthur Young & Company. At the same time that we express our gratitude to these colleagues, we wish to emphasize that the opinions or preferences expressed by any contributor to this volume are his alone and do not necessarily reflect the views of other contributors or of the firm of Arthur Young & Company.

Others who have been most helpful in the preparation of this volume include Frank T. Weston, Salvatore A. Botte, Alan G. Clark, and Stanley H. Pantowich of Arthur Young & Company, each of whom reviewed and commented on various portions of the manuscript. To Patricia A. Quinn, who typed and retyped the manuscript, helped secure the necessary permissions, and in general kept the project moving, we are particularly grateful.

Very special thanks are due to our colleague Charles G. Gillette who, in addition to contributing several articles, reviewed the entire book in manuscript and made many valuable suggestions for improvement.

Finally, we are grateful to our wives and children, for their patience.

John L. Harvey
Albert Newgarden

New York, New York
May 1969

Contents

Management Guides
to Mergers & Acquisitions

I

Planning and Fact Finding

"Look ere thou leap."

TUSSER, *Five Hundred Points
of Good Husbandry,
of Wiving and Thriving*

The Chief Executive's Role
in Acquisition Planning

MYLES L. MACE and GEORGE G. MONTGOMERY Jr.

THE BASIC RESPONSIBILITY for charting corporate growth is an inseparable part of the chief operating executive's job. It is he who must set short- and long-term goals and outline plans for attaining them. He may draw upon the advice and counsel of the company's line and staff officers, but the ultimate responsibility is his. The board of directors, typically, does not initiate corporate plans, even though corporation law usually charges the board with the management of the corporate entity. The board clearly controls the achievement of corporate plans for growth through acquisition by its necessary vote and approval, but it usually does not create the operating plans themselves.

Once defined and outlined, a corporate plan for growth should be submitted to the board of directors for their concurrence. The requirement for this step is more a matter of sound management procedure than it is of complying with the legal requisites. Since the board of directors must vote on any proposal for acquisition, its participation in approving the plan ahead of time expedites the implementation of a corporate program.

Myles L. Mace is Professor of Business Administration at Harvard Business School. George G. Montgomery, Jr. is a partner in the investment banking firm of White, Weld & Co., New York. This chapter is based on excerpts from the authors' research study, *Planning for Growth Through Acquisition,* originally published by the Division of Research, Graduate School of Business Administration, Harvard University.

In those situations in which the president has not included the planning function as an important element of his personal concept of his job, board members have both the opportunity and the responsibility to stimulate planning by asking discerning questions about where the company is going.

ESTABLISHING OBJECTIVES

During our study we found several situations where top management executives had failed to think through their corporate objectives for growth and, caught up in what seems to be a fad for acquisitions, had spent considerable amounts of money and tremendous amounts of time in a fruitless search for what they thought would be growth opportunities.

The real danger is that, without objectives defined, a management may be induced to buy what seems to be a worthwhile and profitable venture. A basic resin company, for example, bought a plastic-boat manufacturer because this seemed to present a controlled market for a portion of the resin it produced. It soon found that the boat business was considerably different from the manufacture and sale of basic chemicals. After a short but unpleasant experience in manufacturing and trying to market what was essentially a consumer's item, the management concluded that its experience and abilities lay essentially in industrial rather than consumer-type products.

Definition of objectives requires careful analysis of what strengths and weaknesses the company has in personnel, product line, manufacturing and distributing facilities, finance, and research and development. Working with this background of experience, and with forecasts of the future market for present product lines, the president then has a basis for evaluating what if anything needs to be done to strengthen the company's position.

Once the direction of a company's growth is defined, creating criteria and implementing the program are relatively easy. Perhaps it is because constructing objectives and thinking about the future involve dealing with intangibles that some managements shy away from the task. We believe that no corporate growth program can be successful without a clear definition of objectives. It is dangerous and risky to embark on an acquisition project without this first step. The purchase of other companies without clear objectives as to the reasons for their acquisition can lead to loss of profits except under the most accidental circumstances.

The failure to define objectives seems to result in a sense of top management dissatisfaction, a feeling that something needs to be done. Under these circumstances top executives may become overanxious to buy something that looks good to them without defining what is good, and too often they embark on purchase programs later to be regretted. They think of defining objectives as an academic exercise without realizing its elemental importance. But as one vice president stated, "The need and desire for acquisition stem from topflight plans, not poor plans—nor from in-between."

DEFINING CRITERIA

Once a corporation's broad objectives have been thought through and accepted, the second step in planning growth by acquisitions is to construct a set of criteria which describes more narrowly what kinds of companies should be considered for purchase.

There are at least three reasons for establishing useful criteria:

1. As definitive guidelines for line and staff personnel involved in acquisitions.

2. For screening possible acquisitions: Once an acquisition program as a method of growth is embarked upon, candidates for acquisition can be identified both by internal staff studies and by outside agencies. Unless carefully drawn criteria have been established to screen large numbers of potential companies quickly, enormous amounts of time will be spent and largely wasted on abortive evaluation attempts.

3. For use by bankers, brokers, and board members: There are many sources of leads as to the possible availability of companies interested in selling. But if these sources do not have a fairly clearly described set of criteria, their proposals will waste the time of corporate evaluators on non-useful and diversionary studies.

It should be noted that statements of criteria must be constructed to give detailed meaning to the individual company objectives and to reflect realistically what is practicable in view of the acquirer's condition. The criteria for a company in a non-growth industry, subject to wide cyclical changes, with a low price/earnings ratio and unlisted stock, will be quite different from the criteria for a company in a growth industry with listed securities and a high price/earnings ratio. To serve the purposes indicated earlier, statements of criteria must be tailored to each company's objectives and situation.

ORGANIZING FOR ACQUISITION

With the creation of corporate objectives and criteria, the next and extremely important step is to organize for the job. That the unique nature of "the job" was not fully understood was evident from peculiar kinds of organization offices set up in some companies. Apparently in these situations the chief operating executives assumed that setting up an organization for acquisition was much like establishing a marketing or a financial function, and since no one in this area with experience was available, anyone could be assigned to the job. The results were odd on two counts:

1. The office, whether called corporate development, or plans, or acquisition, had no clear definition of authority and responsibility in the corporation;

2. The people assigned typically were castoffs who had proved incapable in carrying out their duties in other segments of the company.

Often a chief operating executive, having given intellectual lip service to doing something about an acquisition program, belied his real interest by returning to the demands of his day-to-day operating tasks.

PERSONAL INVOLVEMENT OF THE PRESIDENT

We found that in every company in which there was a successful acquisition program, the chief operating executive was personally involved. There were no exceptions. In some companies the president worked closely with another key executive, such as a vice president and general manager of a division or a vice president for plans, a staff officer for acquisitions, or in one case, vice president and general counsel, an extraordinarily capable top management executive, where the skills, capacities, and working relationships between the two enabled the joint consummation of six acquisitions in two years. This is not to say that staff groups especially organized or other functional line and staff specialists do not have significant contributions to make. They do, but the leadership and drive must come from the chief operating man or his representative with his support. We believe that the personal involvement of the president is crucial, and its absence explains the many unsuccessful acquisition programs extant today.

There are many reasons why the chief operating executive's involvement is critical in acquisitions. Some of the more important are described below.

1. He has the responsibility to plot the growth of the enterprise. If, in addition to internal growth methods, he decides to augment this growth through acquisitions, he has a powerful motivation to be sure that the program succeeds.

2. The chief operating executive, subject as noted to the board of directors, has the authority to represent the corporation in relations with others. In a sense, he speaks as the company and carries a powerful mantle of prestige and position in all negotiations.

3. Today's high interest in acquisition as an approach to company growth has resulted in what many describe as a sellers' market. Sellers' representatives, usually the president or in some cases members of the board, like to be approached by the chief operating executive of a potential acquirer. The subtle but meaningful equivalent of position has important influences on the degree of acceptance by sellers.

4. The chief operating executive usually has had line experience in the industry or has someone with him who has had line experience, and therefore either or both can talk the language of the business with executives of companies to be acquired.

5. The president with long experience in an industry becomes acquainted with his competitors and customers in the business. These friendships, built up through trade and professional associations, result in rather intimate knowledge of who is doing what in the industry and which companies might be amenable to being acquired.

6. He must convince the board of directors of the desirability of growth through acquisition.

WORKING THROUGH A SUBORDINATE

For the reasons oulined above we believe that the personal involvement of the president is crucial to the success of a company's acquisition program. We found several instances, however, where success was achieved by a senior executive who worked closely with the president. The relationship between the two top executives was characterized by complete rapport, confidence, and unity of thought and concept. When this relationship existed it was possible to increase the number of active evaluations and negotiations being carried on. But in all cases the president was fully aware of what was being done by his senior executive and participated to the extent necessary to accept or to reject the opportunity for acquisition, whichever the indicated course of action was.

ROLE OF STAFF GROUPS

In many corporations presidents have organized new and separate staff groups to be concerned with acquisitions. Typically their functions are described as:

1. Advise and counsel corporate and divisional management concerning the effect of significant outside financial, social, and economic factors on the company's plans and objectives.

2. Perform economic and financial analyses on which to base short- and long-term plans.

3. Identify, evaluate, and prepare recommendations on opportunities for growth in new areas, either by acquisition or by internal development.

We found that most staff groups of this type performed very valuable analyses and recommendations. Their principal functions were to locate promising fields for growth, internally and by acquisition, and the members of these groups developed a professional skill in doing this job.

The assignment of functional specialists to a staff group for planning acquisitions has many advantages. The processes of acquisition are markedly different from the processes of administering a going business. Acquisition involves financial and personnel evaluations quite divergent from the usual operating problems found in a company. Various concepts such as pooling of interests, tax-free exchanges, new bases for depreciation, and the integration of substantial plant and people resources are everyday facts for those involved in acquisitions, but not for those whose experience has been entirely in the customary corporate operations. Many staff executives, however, who have gone through the process once, have become immeasurable aids in subsequent negotiations and agreements to acquire. They perform the dual function of specialists on both operating and acquisition problems.

USE OF CONSULTANTS

To provide the professional and specialized services needed to carry through one or more acquisitions, some company managements have employed consultants. During our study we found that some consulting firms had done eminent and impressive jobs in helping managements construct a philosophy of growth through acquisition, had elaborated detailed criteria for the objectives, had assisted in constructing an effective organization to achieve the goals, and had performed the other important functions essential to a sensible acquisition program. But, as is the case when employing consultants for any management assistance, it is important for company executives to evaluate carefully the experience and qualifications of the individual consultants who will work on the assigned project as well as the recommendations which result from their studies.

Effective planning for growth through acquisition, then, consists essentially of establishing the company objectives, defining meaningful criteria, and assuring the personal involvement of the president. Many instances were found where neglect of these three relatively simple, basic concepts resulted in wasteful, time-consuming, and unproductive acquisition efforts.

Planning for Mergers and Acquisitions

JOHN L. HARVEY

PERHAPS THE MOST STRIKING ASPECT of corporate mergers and acquisitions is the seemingly random dispersion of the successes and failures among such combinations. For every well-publicized case of "one plus one equals more than two" there seems to be another (albeit less well publicized) in which one plus one equals, if not exactly zero, at any rate substantially less than two.

Obviously some mergers are good, and others are fatal. It would be naïve to assert that the good mergers are always the result of effective planning and the careful study of facts, while the fatal ones are invariably the result of management by inspiration. Experience does suggest, however, that there is more than a chance relationship between planning and success in coperate combinations. Smart management takes the time and effort to study each prospective combination in such detail as is necessary to permit a decision based on the brain and not on the seat of the pants. Such a study invariably begins with a clear understanding of just what it is that the company hopes to achieve through the combination in question.

DEFINING OBJECTIVES

Why are there such things as corporate mergers and acquisitions? At the risk of oversimplification, it might be helpful if we arranged some of

---

John L. Harvey, CPA, is administrative partner of the Pittsburgh office of Arthur Young & Company.

the more common reasons for business combinations into a few broad categories:

1. *Market considerations.* One frequent merger objective is to capture a greater share of the market which the company serves. A merger may make it possible for the company to offer a complete product line for the first time, or it may expand the geographic area in which the company sells its goods. Foreign acquisitions are frequently made for this latter reason.

2. *Distribution economies.* Often a single distribution system (including salesmen, jobbers, dealers, retail outlets, and, of course, transportation facilities) can handle two products having common, or at least similar, markets and distribution methods at a lower unit cost than it can a single product.

3. *Diversification.* Many companies embark on merger programs to avoid the cyclical effect of a single industry, to minimize the impact of adverse conditions in a particular market, and/or to be able to participate in new growth areas.

4. *Manufacturing advantages.* By combining two manufacturing units, weaknesses can often be strengthened, overcapacity eliminated, and overhead reduced. Seasonal problems, particularly, can often be solved in this way.

5. *Research and development needs.* R&D cost is becoming an increasingly important element of overhead in almost every field of business and industry. Common laboratories and other R&D facilities frequently result in a reduction in research cost per unit of production.

6. *Financial considerations.* The purpose of a merger is often to secure higher earnings per share and an improved image in the marketplace and consequently a higher price/earnings ratio or to achieve greater financial security and stability.

7. *Redeployment of excess capital.* Many insurance companies have millions of dollars in low-yield securities in excess of their reserve requirements. United Fruit had $100 million in cash; Ebasco Industries has $400 million in securities; there are many other examples.

8. *Personnel considerations.* This is most commonly a motive of service organizations. Frequently a merger is undertaken to provide key personnel for an organization weakened through death or through failure to plan ahead for orderly management succession.

9. *Complexity and automation.* The business world is becoming increasingly complex. A small enterprise unable to support a staff of specialists or to afford the cost savings available to larger entities through automation may seek refuge in a merger with a larger operation. Simi-

larly, two small companies, neither of which is able to afford these necessities, may join to create an organization of sufficient size to cope with the growing complexity of business life and to compete with larger operations.

A review of these considerations will at least serve to start management thinking in an orderly, logical way about the possibility of merger. Could *your* company benefit in any of the areas outlined above? If so, you have the beginning of a merger plan. This plan must be carefully developed by top management until the specific objectives of your merger program are clearly defined and understood.

FINDING AND SCREENING CANDIDATES

The next step is to find what companies that would fit your plan are available. Do you feel that the secrecy of your plan is important? If so, the problem of finding available companies becomes considerably more difficult. Most managements under these circumstances have found that secrecy is a relative term. The old cynic's saw, that two can keep a secret if one of them is dead, has a great deal of support among those who have been involved in mergers. In most cases the best approach is to throw open your doors and cry in the marketplace that you are interested in a purchase or merger. In practice this can be accomplished simply by passing the word, either personally or by advertisement, to your business friends, your lawyers, your brokers, your bankers, your CPAs.

It is generally desirable to establish two or three benchmarks against which to measure prospective acquisitions to decide whether they are worth pursuing further. Since this is a first rough screening, the criteria should be as objective as possible, and capable of simple application on the basis of readily available data. Some illustrative benchmarks are: "in the auto parts replacement market"; "a price/earnings ratio not more than 10 percent higher than ours"; or "a growth rate for the last five years of 12 percent per annum, compounded annually." Your first screening will, of course, let through some bad deals. More seriously, the application of any arbitrary criteria is likely to eliminate some desirable deals. But where there is a large number of choices, an arbitrary method of elimination is better than none at all.

ESTABLISHING PRICE CRITERIA

Determining the fair value or price of a going business is seldom a simple matter. Although this subject is discussed at greater length elsewhere in this volume, it is a key element in the merger planning process and deserves some attention here.

If a company's stock is traded regularly and a market price is established from such trading, an arm's-length value of the company exists. It must be recognized, however, that if relatively few shares are exchanged at a given market price, this may not represent a realistic price for the entire number of shares outstanding. Although "dumping" has traditionally been considered a market depressor, current statistics reveal that acquisitions of public companies tend to be at prices in excess of the previously traded price of the stock.

The technique of capitalizing earnings is frequently used to determine the value of a business—the theory being that earnings are the objective of every investment, and hence, the greater the earnings, the greater the value of the investment. The real value of a going business, however, lies in future earnings rather than past earnings, so an attempt must be made to estimate future earnings on the basis of past experience. Such a projection requires the elimination of nonrecurring items from past earnings and a careful consideration of changing conditions that might increase or decrease future earnings as compared with the experience of the past. The rate at which earnings should be capitalized depends entirely upon the degree of confidence that can be placed in the likelihood that the projected future earnings will actually be realized. Today money can be invested at over 6 percent with virtually no risk. Thus, some recognition of the risk element must be added to the 6 percent figure. This, of course, is entirely a matter of judgment. A typical risk factor is 10 percent, thus establishing a 16 percent capitalization rate (which is not uncommon). In the case of well-established and stable industries, such as utilities, a lower risk factor might be reasonable. Highly speculative ventures, on the other hand, require a much greater potential return, and an appropriate risk factor for such a venture might be 15 or 20 percent—or, in certain instances, a great deal more.

The net worth of an enterprise, as disclosed by a current balance sheet, may also be an indication of its value. It should be realized, however, that the generally accepted accounting principles upon which financial statements are based are predicated on certain conventions which may not be valid in establishing the price at which a business should be sold. Inventories, for example, may be valued at a cost, determined on a last-in, first-out basis, which is well below their current market value. Property, plant, and equipment are also carried at cost, which again (e.g., during periods of inflation) may be well below replacement value. Intangibles such as patents, goodwill, and know-how may be the most valuable assets a company owns, and yet they generally do not appear on a balance sheet. On the other hand, certain liabilities such as a portion of past service pension costs are, under current accounting concepts, often excluded from liabilities on the balance sheet.

A more general problem arises from the accounting convention that financial statements are on a "going concern" basis. This means that the statements are based on the assumption that the company will continue its present method of operation. If, in fact, a merger would mean a radical change in the company's method of operation, the conventional net-worth figure would have little validity. Inventories and plant no longer useful to the new operation would have only liquidation value to the purchaser, not the value at which they are carried on the balance sheet.

Every business is faced with uncertainties, both good and bad, which may give rise to future increases or decreases in net worth. An unsettled lawsuit may eventually be decided for or against the company. Federal income tax matters in dispute may be favorably or unfavorably settled. Product warranties may produce unexpected liabilities. Guarantees of the debt of others may or may not result in actual future liabilities. None of these contingent assets or liabilities, however, is conventionally included in the corporate balance sheet. Major contingencies are properly disclosed in footnotes to financial statements, and the effect that such items have on the worth of a business is a matter of judgment.

Two items of possible future value which are often missing from the balance sheet but which can be an important factor in business combinations are a tax loss available to offset future taxable income and an investment credit available to offset future taxes. Such contingent assets merit footnote disclosure.

Generally speaking, little importance should be attached to unadjusted book value in establishing the fair market value of a company. All book figures must be tempered by the judgment of the buyer and the seller. Each asset, recorded or unrecorded, must be considered in detail and a fair value established. Each liability, direct or contingent, must be weighed and evaluated.

If the historical rate of return is considered a significant statistic, care should be taken to see that assets and earnings are related by periods. It may be that net asset values fluctuated sharply during the period under review, with some effect upon earnings. Thus, average earnings should be compared to average investment over the same period rather than to net assets at the end of the period. And future earnings should be discounted to give recognition to the fact that any given amount of earnings today is worth more than the same amount of earnings at some future date.

All of the above information can be utilized in price setting as follows:

1. Selling price = Average adjusted earnings ÷ Rate of return.
2. Selling price = Fair value of assets, both tangible and intangible — Direct liabilities — Estimated "value" of contingent liabilities.

Theoretically, the prices derived from these two formulas should be the same. Since the components entering into both calculations represent arbitrary adjustments, it is not to be expected that the two computations will produce very close results. Nevertheless, a wide discrepancy is fair warning to re-examine one's premises. If the price based on earnings is higher than the price based on assets, it may be that there is an unrecognized asset value (perhaps goodwill), or it may be that the assets do not have the earning power to sustain in the future the earnings level used to determine selling price. If, on the other hand, the calculation based on earnings produces a lower price, it is probable that the assets do not have so high a going-concern value as has been assigned to them. If this position does not seem reasonable, consideration should then be given to the concept of "negative goodwill."

The introduction of formulas into this discussion may suggest a quality of precision about this business of valuing a company which in fact does not exist. In actual practice the valuation process is much the same, to use a hackneyed comparison, as horsetrading: both buyer and seller know, or attempt to find out, all they can about the horse, but the price at which the horse is sold is based on the relative bargaining abilities of the two parties and not on any mathematical equation.

FINANCING THE DEAL

In every business combination the various parties to the deal must receive and give up things which they believe to be of equal value. But the "things" may vary widely in their nature. They may be items of intrinsic value, such as cash, inventory, property, forgiveness of indebtedness, etc. Or they may be only "paper" items, paper representing certain rights. These include various types of stock, a wide variety of debt forms, and contracts requiring specified future action. The things exchanged depend on what each party has to begin with or can acquire, what he is willing to part with, and, frequently the most important, the tax effect of using the different things. This last is so complex a subject that we can only touch on it here in a very general way:

1. An exchange of all the common stock of one corporation for that of another is not taxable.

2. An exchange of the stock of the "acquiring" corporation for the assets of another corporation can be made taxable or nontaxable, as the parties desire.

3. An exchange of nonstock "things"—for example, cash, notes, contracts requiring future payments—for either the assets or stock of the corporation being "acquired" is taxable.

4. The measure of taxable income is the excess of the fair market value of the things received over the tax basis of the things given up.

5. The income can generally be made to take the form of capital gains, taxed usually at a rate below that applied to ordinary income.

6. A taxable transaction results in a higher asset basis to the acquiring company, and in the case of depreciable assets increases future tax deductions. In a nontaxable exchange the basis of assets in the hands of the seller becomes their basis in the hands of the buyer.

Tax considerations for both buyer and seller are discussed at length, by experts in that area, elsewhere in this volume. Suffice it here to say that, in any business combination, no financing arrangements should be considered without the benefit of expert tax advice.

Leasing also has its place in the financial picture. A company short of cash, for example, may purchase all the assets of the selling corporation except the plant. The plant may then be leased by the purchaser on a long-term basis and rental payments substituted for an initial cash outlay.

As discussed above, the purchase price of a corporation may in part be based on its future earnings. In practice this may be translated into a price consisting of a fixed amount paid down plus future contingent payments computed as a percentage of the future net profits of the business acquired. Such an arrangement is frequently referred to as a "workout deal" and is, of course, a useful financing tool, since part of the price can be paid out of future earnings.

STAYING ON THE RIGHT SIDE OF THE LAW

In almost every major corporate combination, and in a surprisingly large number of small ones as well, the major legal problem is that of compliance with the antitrust laws. Sometimes this is a problem that cannot

be resolved. Many a company pair has gone through the marriage cere-
mony only to learn later that they have been living in sin. The sin involved is broadly described in Section 7 of the Clayton Act, the "antimerger
law." A quotation from that section describes the purpose of the law:

"That no corporation engaged in commerce shall acquire, directly or
indirectly, the whole or any part of the stock or other share capital and
no corporation subject to the jurisdiction of the Federal Trade Commission shall acquire the whole or any part of the assets of another corporation engaged also in commerce, where in any line of commerce in any
section of the country the effect of such acquisition may be substantially
to lessen competition or to tend to create a monopoly."

This is a broad road, wide enough for both the Federal Trade Commission and the Antitrust Division of the Justice Department to travel
abreast.

Corporate management is often surprised at the strange situations that
are considered in Government circles to lessen competition. Are you
manufacturing cast-iron tubs, and would you be interested in acquiring a
company that manufactures steel tubs? Tread carefully; these are products that can be substituted one for the other. Are you making and
distributing your product in the East and would you like to acquire a
company doing the same thing in the South? You may not necessarily
be home free. If your industry is on the sick list and companies are
dropping out faster than others are entering, you will find the Justice
Department taking a closer look. You may be a monopoly in a few
years. Would you like to acquire one of your suppliers, with an eye to
closing this source of supply to your competitors? The odds are that
you won't even get a chance to try. A merger objective might be to get
a corner on the industry's know-how or patents. The Justice Department
will probably object to that objective. The question of a conglomerate or
diversification merger is a complex one, in which the law is in an
evolutionary state.

It is well to obtain information on the parties to any merger relating
to their relative size in the industry (sales and assets), geographic distribution areas, rates of growth (and the relation of such rates to the
industry growth rate), names of major customers and suppliers, history
of previous acquisitions, and any other information which might disclose
the effect of the combination on the degree of competition.

If there is a serious possibility of a problem, companies often go to
the Justice Department for an opinion in advance of the merger. This
is probably a good procedure, but it pays to remember that it is only

an opinion. The Justice Department never seems to be embarrassed to find that its opinions have been in error.

So much for antitrust; now let us consider another important and sometimes troublesome area of the law. Corporations are owned by stockholders, stockholders are not necessarily management, and stockholders have certain legal rights, often designed to protect them from management. Under the various state laws the requirements of stockholder approval and the rights of dissenting stockholders are complicated and are constantly changing. Consequently, there is no substitute for a good lawyer. The subject is beyond the scope of this discussion, but a few generalizations will at least serve to indicate the nature of the problems.

A statutory merger or consolidation generally requires approval by the stockholders of all the corporations involved. An exchange of stock of Company A for assets of Company B would normally require only the approval of the stockholders of Company B. An exchange of stock of Company A for the stock of Company B ordinarily would require no stockholder approval at all. Here, of course, each stockholder, in effect, is acting as an individual.

How much approval is enough? For statutory mergers this varies from one state to another, from a simple majority in many states to as high as 80 percent. Under several state laws the articles of incorporation establish the percentage, but in no case can the requirement be less than 50 percent. In most states corporations cannot sell off their assets without approval of the holders of at least 50 percent, and often more, of the total outstanding shares.

Even though a corporation may not require stockholder approval under the above rules, the stockholders may become involved because under the corporate charter their approval may be required to increase the number of shares outstanding, add to corporate powers, and so forth.

As pointed out above, these general rules are not always reliable and have in fact been set aside by court decisions. Get back to that lawyer.

Suppose you get sufficient stockholder approval but something less than 100 percent: What are the rights of the stockholders who don't like the whole idea? The remedy most generally (but not always) provided by state law to dissenting stockholders is the right to have their shares appraised and to receive cash in the amount of the appraised value. Such appraisals are generally messy, subjective things, and if you have a recalcitrant minority you may be in for a lot of trouble.

Under common law stockholders had the right to subscribe to any new stock being issued to the extent necessary to hold the same proportion of the total outstanding stock. This situation, which would create all sorts of merger problems, has, fortunately for this sort of activity, been greatly modified by statute. But it's something the lawyers should look into. Articles of incorporation often set forth the pre-emptive rights of the stockholders of that particular corporation.

Another legal obstacle: In wilder days gone by a corporation might sell all its assets, distribute the proceeds, and leave its creditors to whistle whatever mournful tune occurred to them. Today, however, there are state bulk-sales laws which are designed to protect creditors from such maneuvers. When inventories and fixed assets are sold otherwise than in the ordinary course of business, all creditors of the seller must be notified by the purchaser of the terms of the transaction. Failure to do so exposes the purchaser to the claims of the seller's creditors.

There is one other legal matter that may have some bearing on at least the form of the business combination. Under employee insurance laws covering unemployment compensation and workmen's compensation a seller's experience rating will carry over to the buyer through the purchase of stock. It will never follow the purchase of assets, however, and may be lost even in a statutory merger.

Financial institutions, public utilities, and similarly regulated companies are already painfully aware of the government approvals necessary in their operations, and business combinations generally require such approval. The Securities Act of 1933, the Securities Exchange Act of 1934, and to a lesser extent the state "blue-sky" laws, are of great importance in mergers. Suffice it here to say that these laws deal primarily with the information which must be disclosed if securities are offered publicly or if additional shares are listed on a national securities exchange.

PLANNING FOR INTEGRATION

The periods immediately preceding and following any business combination are always characterized by an abnormal amount of confusion. Both companies are shaken out of their usual routines. There will be new ways of doing things and different people doing them. The turmoil may significantly affect the efficiency of the new organization. To avoid profit reduction through excessive chaos, plans covering all phases of the integration should be prepared. Such plans should be quite specific as to items to be covered and people and departments responsible. Above all, they should include an integrated time schedule for accomplishing the objectives. Each situation is, of course, different, and the plans must be carefully tailored to the situation. The following comments, however, will give a general ideal of the areas the plans must cover and, within those areas, some objectives common to most mergers.

General

Premerger planning can, first, prevent incompatible couples from considering marriage and, if compatibility is established, do much to make the early merger period a reasonably satisfactory honeymoon.

The discovery of incompatibility must be based upon the prompt determination of relevant facts. These cover all aspects of the business. First, there are the broad general items to consider. These are the fundamentals that provide the reason for the merger, as discussed earlier. Does the merger fit into a long-range plan to increase geographic coverage, to offer a complete product line, to acquire better management, to provide research and development facilities? If the answer to these is a repeated "No," further investigation should be dropped at once. Generally, it takes more than a short-term benefit to make a marriage worthwhile.

Accounting and Finance

Financial data come next in importance. Here analyses of financial statements, including future projections, play a vital role. A determination of the accounting ground rules under which financial statements were prepared is particularly important.

Credit reports from Dun & Bradstreet as well as from banks are helpful, but it is well to remember that these are generally based only on information deliberately made available by the company.

Full information on insurance coverage and costs should be secured. The status of patent, royalty, and similar agreements should be studied. Bonuses, profit-sharing plans, pension obligations, employment contracts should be investigated.

Then certain potentially dangerous areas should be looked into. These include the following:

1. *Accounts receivable.* "Collectibility" is the key word. Study credit and collection policies and "aged" trial balances.

2. *Inventories.* This is the most dangerous area of all. Assuming that controls over physical quantities are good, the question is, what will the cash realization be and when? Slow-moving, defective, and (above all) obsolete inventories are the real danger. Watch market value.

3. *Property, plant, and equipment.* The general accounting rule is that these assets are carried at cost less depreciation. If fixed assets are

not stated at cost, the basis of evaluation should be thoroughly investigated. There are several acceptable methods of computing depreciation which produce very different net book values. This must be studied. Has maintenance been adequate? Is there any idle plant resulting from overcapacity? Is any equipment obsolete? And watch out especially for differences in book and tax basis; this can make or break the deal. Perhaps the most important *caveat* relating to fixed assets is that book value may have very little relationship to that all-important concept, the economic utility of the plant.

4. *Liabilities.* Watch out, too, for those liabilities that do not appear on the books. The search for unrecorded and contingent liabilities may be of the utmost importance. The Federal income tax liability may require the most thorough investigation of all.

At least for a manufacturing company, the four areas listed above will include most of the financial and accounting problems likely to be encountered in a merger, but there are many lesser matters to consider which in the aggregate may become significant.

Taxes

Advance tax planning is crucial. Unless there is a compatible tax plan on the part of both the buyer and the seller, the negotiations may as well be broken off in the initial stages. If, for example, it is essential for the seller to have a nontaxable transaction to avoid what would otherwise be a significant capital gain, and the purchaser must have the stepped-up basis in assets inherent in a taxable transaction, then there will be no marriage.

All of this should be considered early in the premarital period, so that an unproductive courtship can be avoided.

Production

Planning for the integration of the production operations of two or more companies that are considering corporate wedlock is based on several factors. The effect of the merger on production costs is of prime importance. This puts a tremendous responsibility on the shoulders of the cost accountant. The success or failure of the marriage may well rest on the outcome of production planning.

It is reasonably self-evident that the less similarity there is in the products and production methods of the merging companies, the greater the initial problems will be—assuming, of course, that there will be a combining of production facilities. Often, however, production methods vary significantly, even among companies manufacturing the same product. Regardless of the size and complexity of the problems, the keynote to success in this area is standardization. In the earliest planning stages, standard practices should begin to take written form: scheduling, production, material control, purchasing methods, lead times. As mentioned earlier, one of the major benefits of merger is an increase in know-how, and nowhere is this more true than in the production area. Plans should begin early to extend the best features of all production methods to the entire enterprise.

There is also a high correlation between problems and geographic dispersion if the production at various locations is interdependent. These problems extend to procurement as well as production. Again, advance planning is the only answer. Emphasis must be placed on transportation times, methods, and reliability. Knowing in advance, however, that the best of plans is never completely effective, it would be well also to plan a good communication system between locations.

Early plans must encompass the use of plants and equipment. There must be room for the new production, storage, and office needs. In many cases, plant layouts will have to be redesigned. Such basic questions as whether the floors will support added equipment or whether the air-conditioning system will accommodate an increase in personnel must be answered in advance. If they are not considered, or if they are answered incorrectly, profits during the transitional period will suffer.

Personnel

While no merger should be consummated unless the areas discussed above augur well, it is in the field of personnel that the greatest amount of planning must be carried out and the greatest risks of failure exist. Personnel plans can range from utilizing all personnel of the acquired company—that is, running it as a decentralized unit integrated only at one point (the top)—to discharging personnel, either in the acquired or in the acquiring company, wherever there is a duplication of positions. Whatever the situation, specific organization plans must be drawn up with great care and in full detail.

Usually, the personnel plan lies somewhere between these two extremes. Whenever personnel of the acquired company are needed, it becomes important to encourage them to stay with the new organization. The strategy to be employed in this regard must be started early in the game. If the management of the newly acquired corporation is to remain intact, this should be convincingly stated as soon as the merger has been agreed upon. If the merger opens new vistas of progress to executives who had reached the end of the road with the acquired company, this can be used to good effect.

Personnel integration must be approached on a person-to-person basis. Letters and executive memorandums are not substitutes for personal contact. Get the new management personnel into home office where they can meet their new associates. The devil you know is always more acceptable than the devil you don't. And if you all get together, who knows—you might even create an atmosphere of mutual trust!

Job satisfaction has some relationship to compensation. This includes not only salary but all fringe benefits. The best way to assure contentment on the part of new executives is to offer them either present or potential financial benefits in excess of those they had or expected with the old organization. If necessary, you may be able to trade heavily on the future.

Often one or more executives of the acquired company are compensated at a rate higher than their responsibilities, at least in the new setup, would seem to justify. Perhaps such an individual can be given work of greater scope in the combined operation which would justify his pay scale. In any event, it is worthwhile to exercise patience and to assume that the situation will correct itself in time. It is not worth risking organizational chaos for the sake of a salary differential.

Where the parent utilizes profit-sharing plans, some interim plan might be established for the subsidiary until a permanent plan can be established. Stock option programs should be offered to the new members of the management team on the same basis as they have been offered to established members. The same is true of pensions and deferred-compensation plans. These benefits may be delayed for a period of time and may in fact serve as an effective carrot to encourage rapid integration.

Because of the wide variety in the methods of compensating salesmen, there is little likelihood that two merged companies will have much uniformity in this area. Perhaps the best solution is not to worry much about uniformity—at least not at first. If various sales units are operating in different ways, their compensation often can differ without causing friction.

Napoleon once pointed out that to get a man to die for him he merely had to offer him a medal costing a few francs. Similarly, in a corporation men will work their hearts out for a title that often costs nothing at all. This aspect of corporate life is especially important in mergers if two executive groups are to be integrated. Make sure that everyone who had a title before has a title at least as impressive under the new organization. This will assure a harmonious marriage at the cost of only a few sleepless nights dreaming up the new tags.

A special phase of personnel planning is that which relates to union employees. Here again a great deal of information can be developed in advance to permit proper planning. What unions are involved? What are the pay-rate schedules? Are piece rates paid and, if so, on what basis? What are the seniority rules? What are the fringe benefits such as insurance, paid holidays, and vacations? Are labor relations generally good? What has the history of labor relations been like? Does the size of the workforce seem to be reasonable? Is turnover or absenteeism a problem? One of the most important areas is that of retirement and disability benefits. Even workpace, grievance procedures, shop practices, and time standards may require investigation. All such information should, of course, be obtained for all unions at all locations; local situations will differ.

The premerger planning should be as elaborate as the facts warrant. If the two companies that are coming together are in the same industry and have the same union, plans can be limited to standardizing practices and resolving small differences. There may be problems integrating small independent unions with AFL-CIO unions. If the merger involves a small company, perhaps that company will have no union. As a general rule, management can expect the union of Company A to attempt to organize nonunion Company B as soon as the acquisition has been completed.

In many mergers different industries, different unions, and different geographic locations are involved, and wide differences will prevail in the terms of union contracts. In these cases elaborate plans may be necessary. The unification of pay rates and fringe benefits can have a significant economic effect on the merger, since the unions involved may attempt to incorporate the best features (from the union's standpoint) of each separate contract into the uniform contract.

Marketing

After an idea is produced it must be marketed. In this area, too, pre-merger planning is essential. If one of the reasons for the business combination was the "market approach" described earlier, presumably some market research was conducted before the companies came very close together. Such a survey should include consideration of the effect of offering a complete product line, the effect of entering new geographic areas, and the advantages or disadvantages of a new name. It should also include consideration of what the customer thinks of the product.

Then, as the two companies approach matrimony, the questions must become more specific. What products do the companies sell? In order to answer this question definitively, annual sales dollars for each product should be developed, and these in total should agree with the published company sales figures.

Before a product can be sold it must be packaged. Can a new distribution system be used with the old packaging? Are packaging methods old-fashioned? What would be the cost of desirable changes?

Detailed information on how the product is distributed should be developed. This involves not only geographic areas but methods—that is, brokers, direct mail, etc. Preliminary judgments should be made as to the effectiveness of each phase of marketing.

Similarly, the effectiveness of the company's advertising should be judged. How well does the consumer recognize the company's brands? Time may permit a customer survey on this point.

Finally, we get back to people again. Who are the executives involved in selling? Perhaps you know them and their reputation in the trade. How do you plan to use them? What would happen if you let them go? How will the sales organization be integrated at lower levels? Plans, plans, plans.

ORGANIZING FOR MERGER

It should be apparent by now that there are so many aspects to a merger that a successful combination can be effected only by utilizing all the talent available. With very few exceptions, in-house talent must be supplemented by professionals in the merger and acquisition field—the company's CPAs, its legal counsel, its investment bankers, and to a lesser degree many others. Each corporation must develop its own merger organization, but some general observations, based on actual plans that have worked successfully, may be helpful.

We have reviewed in the preceding pages the various activities that merger planning comprises. Basically, each activity should be assigned to that member of management whose experience makes him most familiar with that activity. The following individuals or departments may play special roles.

Over-all responsibility for merger planning, if it is not assumed by the president himself, is often assigned to the executive vice president. He is responsible, first, for reviewing the broad general aspects of the proposed merger. Is the management of the new company good? Does it fit into the acquiring company's management? Are the products the ones desired? Second, he is responsible for directing and coordinating the activities of the other executives involved in the preliminary investigation and in the execution of the merger.

The financial vice president is usually assigned responsibility for obtaining all accounting and financial data, including future projections, and for translating such data into terms comprehensible to the president or the executive vice president. He is involved in establishing the purchase price on the basis of the financial data available, including stock market prices. The financing of the acquisition is also planned by his office.

Tax planning may also be the responsibility of the financial vice president, but as a practical matter the company's top tax executive should be intimately involved from the very outset. Tax considerations can affect not only the form of the merger and the method of financing but the purchase price as well.

The top personnel executive is also an important member of the merger planning team. Typically, he performs a study in depth of each level of management in the prospective acquisition, including a review of the education and experience of each executive and key employee. Evaluation of management personnel is often delegated by the personnel director to the counterpart managers in his own company.

A review of the labor situation, including a detailed study of all labor contracts, is also usually the responsibility of the personnel director.

Legal counsel must assume responsibility for preparing the formal purchase agreement, and in this role must elicit the necessary information from all others working on the merger. Counsel must work out all the details of the agreement, including not only the purchase price but also such things as warranties, representations, method of payment, and restrictions on any abnormal transactions prior to closing. Counsel must also determine whether SEC registration will be required and what other legal problems will be encountered. Are there any antitrust matters to consider? Are there patent problems? Attorneys should carefully examine all corporate records and real estate titles.

Counsel will also prepare all documents that must be signed at the closing. Since these must be reviewed by counsel for the seller, sufficient time should be allowed for this. Some companies have found that a "dry run" closing a day or two before the legal closing is helpful in identifying any loose ends that may have been overlooked.

No discussion of organizing for corporate mergers would be complete without consideration of the role of the board of directors and the relationship between the board and the management team. Since authority and responsibility for all acquisitions ordinarily rest with the board of directors, it is imperative that members of the board be kept advised of acquisition plans as they are developed, to the end that they will agree with management in the ultimate decision. This means that as soon as a corporate acquisition is contemplated, members of the board should be advised. This permits them to offer their suggestions or to voice objections to the merger before management has committed itself to any extent. The agenda of each board meeting thereafter should include a report on the status of all acquisitions under consideration. This permits the board to act promptly when the final decision is reached. Keep your board in your acquisition picture.

A final word of caution: Corporate executives are sometimes on the defensive when it comes to merger planning. They are careful to point out all the possible pitfalls so that, if all does not go well, they can protect their part in the investigation with the customary "I told you so." Any merger team that approaches its job with this attitude is of little value. The objective of each member of the merger team should be to point out what can be done with a new company, not merely to raise all possible objections. One of the most important qualities that the leader of the merger team can contribute to the merger planning process is *objectivity*.

THE MERGER TIMETABLE

Once a merger has been proposed, it is important to set up a time schedule that shows each necessary step, the individual or department responsible, and the date on which each step must be undertaken or completed. Each corporation, of course, will have its own steps, and those described here are intended merely as an example. It should also be noted that the time schedule described here covers a period of four months. This may be typical of a major merger of two public companies.

The initial phases of the work should relate to outsiders who are to become involved:

Internal Revenue Service

Apply for all necessary tax rulings—for example, tax-free exchange, preferred-stock "bailout," pension plan revisions.

Securities and Exchange Commission

Apply for any required rulings such as exemption of transactions under the 1933 Act.

Other regulatory agencies

Apply for required permissions.

Creditors

Take steps necessary to obtain consent to merger from creditors if required under debt indentures.

State authorities (all states involved)

Review applicability of "blue-sky" and bulk-sale laws, and initiate any necessary actions. Initiate steps necessary to obtain approval of merger agreement if this is required by state law.

Justice Department

Request advance opinion on merger if antitrust situation is considered to be a potential problem.

Within two or three weeks the boards of directors of *both companies* must take certain actions. The following are similar for both boards:

1. Approve and execute "housekeeping" agreement.
2. Call special stockholders' meeting, fix record date, and appoint proxy committee.
3. Approve form of proxy and other statements of explanation in preparation for stockholders' meeting.
4. Make necessary changes in transfer agent arrangements.
5. Authorize officers and directors to take all necessary actions to complete the merger.

In addition, the board of the *acquiring company* has the following chores to complete:

1. Authorize issuance of any required stock. If a new issue is involved, this will also require approval of the new certificates. A listed company issuing additional stock must file a listing application.
2. Authorize any action required by "blue-sky" laws.
3. If the surviving corporation will be doing business in any new states, authorize qualification in those states.
4. Authorize any required amendments to employee benefit plans.

The board of the *selling company* must cope with its own special problems. These include the following:

1. Authorize transfer of title to all assets, including bank accounts, real property, and securities.
2. Authorize any required writedown of assets or establishment of additional reserves.

By the end of the second month all printing should be completed, and proxies, letters of explanation to holders of debt, etc., can be mailed. The rest of this month provides a period to solicit proxies, to obtain the consent of other parties to the assignment by the selling company of its nonassignable contracts, and to commence qualification on the part of the surviving company in states in which it is not qualified to do business.

The meeting of the stockholders of both corporations will take place toward the end of the third month. Assuming ratification of the merger by both groups of stockholders, this will permit the execution of the agreement of merger by the directors and officers of the two companies and the filing of the agreement with the appropriate state officials. At the same time the effective status of the merger can be released to the press.

A few days later a letter can be mailed to both groups of stockholders advising them of the effective status of the merger. If an exchange of stock is involved, the exchange of certificates can be started at this time.

The formal closing of the deal, including delivery of deeds, bills of sale, and all necessary assignments, may take place in this same period. This is generally followed by a special meeting of the board of directors of the buying company to adopt bank resolutions and handle any other necessary matters.

The end of the fourth month of our merger timetable may be the deadline for dissenting stockholders of the selling company to make demand for payment of their stock.

To maintain a high level of employee morale throughout the acquisition period, a series of letters to employees should be included in the time schedule to keep the employees of both companies informed about the merger plans, the progress of the negotiations, and the anticipated effects of the change on their personal fortunes.

The Pitfalls of Acquisitions

L. A. CASLER

CORPORATE MERGERS AND ACQUISITIONS are one of the most rapidly growing areas of commercial activity today. An increasing number of large firms have been earning high profits for several years now, and they are looking for outlets in which to put their cash to work. As a look at any financial publication will show, the purchase of outside companies has become a favorite way of obtaining corporate growth and diversification.

But, it is safe to say, there are few business activities that offer so many pitfalls or so many possibilities for future trouble. Nowhere in business, in fact, is there need for greater care on the part of the executive.

For, as many purchasers have found to their regret, acquiring a company can be extremely tricky. The buyer must remember at all times the old rule of *caveat emptor*. For example, the seller may have held back on vital information. Or he may have found some way to "dress up" the company, and thus hide a fatal flaw in its make-up.

What, then, should an executive look for when he buys a company? And, perhaps more to the point, what are the factors that a seller most likely will be hiding in a company?

WHAT THE SELLER MAY BE HIDING

Surprisingly, the seller himself may be the biggest danger in an acquisition. Suppose that he is an owner-manager. As he says, he may truly be

---

L. A. Casler is a partner in the firm of Little & Casler, financial consultants specializing in mergers and acquisitions. He was formerly Vice President – Acquisitions of Textron Inc., Providence, R.I.

tired of having "the total responsibility for the company on my back." He may indeed want to continue what he calls "the challenge" of operating the company without the fiscal headaches he had as owner.

On the other hand, once the seller has signed a management contract with a new owner, he may intend to take life easy. The purchaser, who is now the employer, will have to honor the contract and cannot fire the erstwhile owner on the payroll. Yet there is nothing that can make this gentleman work. Management contracts are always on the side of the employee.

Worse yet, the company owner in search of a buyer may be peddling a white elephant. He may realize that his product line needs revamping but be unwilling or lack the financial resources to do the job. So he does not plow anything back, preferring to show high profits and dress up the firm for a sale.

Companies selling the bulk of their production to one or two customers are particularly vulnerable to this kind of crisis. Perhaps the owner has discovered that a customer who purchases 40 percent of his line has made firm commitments to an overseas supplier. The new contract starts 18 months from now. The owner, not unnaturally, wants to unload the company before the overseas contract becomes general knowledge.

The company heavily dependent on military contracts also may have a hidden danger for the buyer. One such firm, let us say, has had a preferred position as a vendor of a semi-proprietary product to the Government. The owner obtained that position any way he could, perhaps even to the extent of engaging in certain illegal business practices. These practices have come to light. The owner's company is on the blacklist, and its preferred position is no more. The owner knows that he has to find a buyer for his company before the next round of contracts. Naturally, he cannot be expected to advertise his fall from Government grace.

Sometimes the unknown factors so closely guarded by the would-be seller are less dramatic than that, but they can be just as damaging to the unwary purchaser. A key employee may be about to leave, taking many of the company's best customers with him. The union may be planning to fight for heavy, overdue wage increases. The big new product may be inferior, despite the early record of high sales, with many units being returned by dissatisfied customers. In a situation like this, of course, there is always the added possibility of lawsuits for personal damage.

Another and increasingly common danger: The company may have been informed that it will have to comply with new and stringent air- or water-pollution standards. Here, the cost may be so high that it will do away with profits for several years.

By the law of averages, of course, it is only logical to assume that the owner of a company seeking to sell has some kind of problem. But this is not necessarily a reason to avoid buying the company. The trick comes in determining if the problem that is causing the owner to sell is one that can be solved by the purchaser.

Some of these problems may be more difficult than others. If the company has no second-line management worthy of the name, the purchaser may well have trouble supplying it himself. If the company has been too highly leveraged, the profits may look fine—but they will fade rapidly when the business outlook takes a dip. If the sales policies have been unrealistic, the entire customer-based underpinnings of the firm may be ready to collapse.

Even the company with an outstanding product line may have more to its operations than meets the eye. Simply put, the product line, as excellent as it may be, may be too limited; as a result, the company has been unable to push the line as hard as it should have, because it could not afford the costs more easily absorbed by a company with a broader line of products.

On the other hand, the product line may be *too* broad and varied. Sales may have been built to a high level by giving customers an unrealistic variety of products. Customers, it is true, speak highly of the company. But they have been spoiled. The seller cannot continue to support the large line of products—and he is going to have many unhappy customers when they realize it.

Consider an area of the company's activities that might seem less important than sales: employee benefits. This problem arises when a company has been overly paternalistic with wages, benefits, insurance, and pensions. In these cases there may be hidden obligations, such as unfunded past service pension costs, which may amount to many millions of dollars. Or perhaps a large number of employees are about to retire, raising the company's commitment to insurance for retired workers to an extremely burdensome level. The company may have an unreasonably high salary level, a built-in weakness which cannot be rectified without demoralizing the organization. It goes almost without saying that if a man is overpaid, you cannot simply slash his salary.

Other problems can come from employee relations. The company may be self-insured in the health field, for example, possibly because of the nature of its industrial activities. In the future, however, it may well face a huge liability for health damages to employees.

All such considerations must be studied if the acquisition-minded firm is to make an addition that will be a healthy and contributing one to the corporate family. At Textron, incidentally, we believe that the major part of any corporation's growth must be generated from within. We do not believe that a corporation that grows only by grafting on new companies can be in an essentially strong position.

In short, we do not believe that you can buy profits. Each new acquisition should itself be capable of important future development—self-generated.

Thus a potential acquisition must be looked at as a long-range investment and in the widest possible perspective. The economic condition of a company's industry and its prospects are as important as the particular details of its operation.

Let us say a company is in a field that has had fast, strong growth but relatively light profits. Now it is on the crest of a wave such as all industries experience from time to time. The question is whether it is going to be carried forward on that crest or plunged down to the depths. There may be new companies about to crowd the field and turn the prospect of high profits sour. I am sure that we all remember how this happened at one point to the aluminum, electronics, and titanium industries.

Knowledge of basic currents and movements in the field of the prospect company is vital. Consider another type of company: one in a fast-growing field, with a high-profit record. Let us say that the firm we are looking at is essentially a converter. There are signs that the suppliers of the basic material in this industry are going to have trouble with overcapacity. The owner of the converting firm looks into the future and sees that the supplier companies are going to be buying up converters to build a captive market for their output. Remembering what happened in the paper industry a few years ago, he knows that converters without their own source of basic materials will be in a profit squeeze; they will be unable to compete in price with companies that can profit from the margins on both raw materials and the converted product.

The buyer must remember that in almost any industry the surface may appear calm but trouble can be brewing underneath. To see it in still another light, consider an extremely successful supplier of parts for a large systems manufacturer. There are straws in the wind indicating that the systems firm has the cash and space to cut its own costs by making some of the parts furnished by the supplier. The only way the parts-maker can stay in business is to drastically cut his prices, which may not be feasible, or to become a manufacturer of the whole system. If he chooses the former, he will have to compete with the people he is trying to sell parts to. If he follows the latter course, he may well end up in even worse straits.

The reasons why a company is up for sale can be complex in the extreme. And if the would-be buyer is wise, he will take the trouble to unwind the complexities. Ideally, before he makes a decision on a particular proposition, the buyer will know at least as much about the company as he would had he been an employee. Of course, he may not know every executive by his first name, but he will have a picture in depth of the firm, its management, the details of its operation and its prospects.

Then, if he still is intent on making the acquisition, he can feel somewhat secure that it is a wise move. But he still must remember the admonition of General Motors' famed Charles ("Boss") Kettering: "Who is interested in his welfare except himself?"

Getting the Facts:
The Acquisition Investigation

CHARLES G. GILLETTE and JOHN L. HARVEY

ACT-FINDING is an obviously important part of the acquisition planning process; it is also a frequently neglected part. This neglect may be attributable to any of several causes:

☐ **In some cases there is a naïve assumption that the information presented by the seller represents the truth, the whole truth, and nothing but the truth.**

☐ **Sometimes real or assumed deadlines or time pressures lead to the dangerous conclusion that there simply is not enough time to get the facts.**

☐ **In other cases, acquisition decisions are based on the intuitive business judgment of two chief executives, and none of their subordinates is prepared to suggest that they are not so brilliant that they don't need the facts.**

Whatever the reasons, any acquisition decision based on inadequate information is an invitation to disaster. There is considerable evidence that 50 percent or more of all corporate acquisitions are so poor that in due course the managements of the acquiring companies regret that they were ever made. In other cases, even though the transactions as a whole may be regarded as having been worthwhile, there have been

Charles G. Gillette, CPA, is a partner in the home office of Arthur Young & Company in New York. He is responsible for coordinating the firm's services to clients in connection with mergers and acquisitions. John L. Harvey, CPA, is administrative partner of the Pittsburgh office of Arthur Young & Company.

unpleasant surprises after the wedding. Some of the facts which come to light in the postmerger period might have affected the price if they had been anticiapted; others, if anticipated, might have been dealt with in such a way as to effect a smoother or less costly transition.

FOUR CASES IN POINT

In his discussion of technological obsolescence later in this volume [1] Dr. Johan Bjorksten describes some dramatic examples of failure to get the facts on technology in the acquired company's field. Let us pause a moment to consider four other horrible, but factual, cases in point. The facts have been disguised, and in each case the buyer is identified as Groom, Inc. and the tempting seller as Bridal Veil (with the emphasis on "Veil").

Case 1

Groom, Inc. entered into a tentative agreement to acquire all the outstanding stock of Bridal Veil for $5 million, with a planned closing date in ten days. The investigative team descended on Bridal Veil. Bridal Veil had told Groom that its tax returns were presently under examination and it anticipated only insignificant adjustments from disallowances of certain officers' expenses.

A member of the investigating team requested and received permission to meet with the revenue agent. The revenue agent opened with, "Before I discuss the matter, I want to present my credentials." His credentials showed that he was a "Special Agent," and this information alerted the investigator to the fact that a possible fraud was suspected.

On the basis of this information, the transaction was renegotiated. In the revised terms, the assets were acquired and the liabilities, *other than income tax liabilities,* were assumed. The price was reduced to $3.2 million. Subsequently, tax liabilities and penalties were assessed against Bridal Veil in the amount of $2.5 million. Thus the ten-day investigation produced a saving of $4.3 million on what was to have been a $5 million purchase.

Case 2

Groom Inc. entered into a letter of intent to acquire the outstanding stock of Bridal Veil subject to a favorable market survey by the Groom,

[1] "A Sure Guide to *Un*successful Mergers," p. 309.

Inc. marketing staff and an audit by Groom, Inc.'s certified public accountants.

The market survey indicated that Bridal Veil had reached its probable maximum sales and that future growth was highly questionable. The audit revealed that, as a result of inadequate inventory controls and cost accounting, there was an overstatement of inventory which exceeded the reported profit for the year. The acquisition was never consummated.

Case 3

Groom, Inc. was interested in acquiring Bridal Veil Ferry Lines but arranged for an investigation before entering into a contract. Bridal Veil's business consisted of shipping a single commodity between two port cities. It had a profitable history. The investigators learned that the railroads which operated between these same two ports had filed with the Interstate Commerce Commission a request for a new tariff. The investigators obtained a copy of the proposed new tariff and noted that the proposed rail tariff was lower than Bridal Veil's cost. The acquisition was never consummated. Subsequently Bridal Veil Ferry Lines sank into bankruptcy.

Case 4

Groom, Inc. acquired Bridal Veil on the basis of its management's representations, including unaudited financial statements. There was no on-the-scene investigation. Bridal Veil's business involved long-term contracts. Of the nine contracts in progress, eight were substantially completed and one was not. Groom, Inc. acquired the business, excluding the eight substantially completed contracts. Since it was assuming responsibility for only one contract, and since the information submitted by Bridal Veil indicated that all nine contracts were profitable, Groom's management believed that it was assuming only minimal risk. It was particularly reassured by the fact that the indicated profit on the one contract was almost as much as the purchase price of the business.

Completion of this contract produced no profit. New contracts entered into immediately after the acquisition produced substantial losses. Subsequent investigation revealed that, in each of the past several years, Bridal Veil had reported a loss for income tax purposes and had been able to report a profit for book purposes only by setting up as assets some questionable claims for price adjustment. This acquisition proved to have a value below zero.

In the following pages we will try to suggest how to achieve the successes of cases 1, 2, and 3 and avoid the anguish of case 4. First we will discuss the fact-finding approach from an organizational viewpoint, then we will describe some illustrative mechanics of the fact-finding process in the area of our particular concern, accounting.

ORGANIZING FOR INVESTIGATION

Satisfactory fact-gathering requires an orderly plan of attack. The principal ingredients of a good plan are a timetable, an identification of the facts to be obtained, and a competent team with defined responsibilities. The timetable must realistically reflect both the need to get the job done with minimum delay (sometimes to meet contractual deadlines) and recognition that not everything can be done overnight.

One of the reasons why people sometimes regrettably conclude that they haven't time to get the facts is that they have an exaggerated notion of how much time is required. This notion may be based on their previous experience with the amount of time required for a recurring annual audit, but this is not an appropriate guideline. An acquisition investigation is not an audit "in accordance with generally accepted auditing standards." It is more comprehensive than such an audit, and yet, on the other hand, it may exclude many steps which would be considered a necessary part of such an audit. Such exclusions may be based on the fact that there has recently been an audit on which the buyer is willing to rely, or they may be based on the willingness of the buyer to accept certain risks of error which an auditor would not be entitled to accept if he were required to express an opinion on financial statements. As a typical example, an annual audit almost always includes verification procedures with respect to a company's bank balances, but an acquisition investigation almost always excludes such procedures. Circumstances drastically alter cases but, typically, the elapsed time for an acquisition investigation runs from two to four weeks. Anyone who is being pressured to make an acquisition decision faster than this should be sure that the reasons for the pressure are substantial and should be convinced that the deal is so good that he won't regret it even if he gets a few nasty surprises.

Our second planning ingredient is to decide what questions need to be answered. The wisdom and skill that go into this process will determine whether we get the facts we need and whether we effectively meet our time commitments.

A number of organizations have checklists of one sort or another which are used in the investigative process.[2] Such lists, if available, should also be used in the planning process. Not all the items on any such list are necessary for any given investigation, and some of them may be impracticable to accomplish within the allowed time. The planning process requires that the general checklist be converted into a specific checklist by making extensive deletions and by adding items of special interest in the particular situation.

It is rare that an acquisition investigation is or should be the work of one man. There should be an investigative team reflecting a broad spectrum of skills. It should be a team of men, not boys. It may include, and usually should include, both officers and key staff members of the acquiring company and professionals from outside the company. Depending on the circumstances of the particular case, it may include specialists in marketing, engineering, industrial relations, appraisals, or manufacturing processes. It should always include a lawyer, and it should always include an auditor. It should also include a tax specialist, who may or may not be the aforementioned lawyer or auditor.

When the tailored checklist of required facts has been developed, the team should cooperatively review it for two distinct purposes which can be fulfilled concurrently. The talents of the entire team should be brought to bear on the question of the completeness and appropriateness of the checklist. Each member should be thinking about the questions that should be answered in his area of specialization and be sure that they are all on the list. At the same time the items on the list should be assigned to the respective specialists so that there will be no duplication of effort and no omission of performance. Careful attention to these assignments will establish the beginnings of cooperation within the team. Just as an example, the auditor will be interested in the payroll from the viewpoint of product costs, and the industrial relations specialist will be interested in the same payroll from the viewpoint of rates. The allocation of work should be such that the fact-finding of one member will be used in the analysis of the other.

There is another member of the investigating team who has not yet been mentioned. This "invisible" member of the acquisition team is the staff of the company being investigated. A shrewd and experienced

[2] Such checklists can vary in length and detail from a one- or two-page document to a manual of fifty or a hundred pages. For an example of a relatively brief checklist, see the "Go/No Go" list of FMC Corporation on pp. 277-279 of this volume.

acquisitions investigator will at the outset prepare a list of materials which he asks the acquiree company to submit to him. Frequently this material can and should be assembled and submitted before the team does much direct investigation. If these requests are skillfully prepared, much of the data will be largely self-checking, in that they will have to tie in with other information, and quite limited sampling can satisfy one as to their accuracy. There are several advantages to this process. The data are assembled by those most knowledgeable of the subject matter; the harassment of the acquiree's personnel by the investigator is minimized; the investigator saves time (both man-hours and elapsed time); and, finally, the level of competence and integrity reflected in the data may furnish useful insights into the competence and integrity of the acquiree's organization.

THE ROLE OF THE AUDITOR

In the typical case the principal objectives of the auditor as a member of the investigative team are: (a) to develop reasonably accurate net income figures for the past several years and identify any material and unusual items reflected in either income or retained earnings; (b) to determine the net asset value of the company; (c) to determine any significant values not reflected in the books; (d) to determine the accounting principles reflected in the financial statements and the possible impact of alternative accounting principles; and (e) to identify any significant contingent liabilities.

The thrust of the auditor's work must be influenced by what will be significant to the acquisition decision. If the company is a financial institution, for example, the balance sheet may be of paramount importance. In the more typical acquisition of a commercial or industrial company, a clear earnings history may be of greater significance.

The auditor may very well find himself cast in the role of data developer for the other members of the investigative team. Thus, the initial audit work may be aimed at obtaining a general knowledge of the company to serve as a framework within which the other investigative work can be performed. In this situation, a descriptive memorandum would be prepared covering the products or services, the methods of manufacture and distribution, research and development activities, and other subjects as appropriate. Since the primary usefulness of historical information is to permit projections into the future, changes in operating methods or the nature of the business during the period under review are especially important. These changes might be part of a short history of the business. Such data should, of course, be promptly shared with the other members of the team.

A review of the articles of incorporation, the corporate charter and by-laws, and minutes of stockholder, director, and executive committee meetings should be made and unusual items noted. This review should cover major subsidiaries as well as the company itself.

If audit reports are available they should be reviewed, along with the accompanying financial statements. Any exceptions taken by the company's auditors or inconsistencies in accounting noted by them should receive special attention. Attention should be given to the competence and independence of the acquiree's auditors, as this will have a bearing on the amount of verification which must be done in connection with the acquisition audit. Not only should inconsistencies in reporting from one year to another be noted but also (and this may not be fully determinable until additional work has been done) inconsistencies between the accounting practices of the company and those of the prospective purchaser. Detailed historical financial information must be obtained. Statements of cost of goods sold, selling expense, general administrative expense, other income and expense, and the like may reveal unusual situations existing in prior years.

If the company is subject to the Securities Exchange Act, additional historical information can be obtained from its annual reports to the SEC and from proxy statements.

Moving from the past through the present into the future, the auditors should review current monthly and year-to-date operating figures and then examine the company's future profit plans, including budgets for operations and capital expenditures, in as much detail as is available.

Once a general concept of the company has been obtained, investigation of specific balance sheet and income statement captions can begin. The following brief comments cover only a few such captions.

Inventories

Inventories are often the most important area of investigation. The usual approach is to obtain a schedule breaking down inventories into the various categories of raw materials, work in process, and finished goods. If inventory represents construction in process, the degree of completion and the cost to complete are important. The basis of recording inventories must be ascertained. Is the basis for determining tax profits the same as the book basis? The method of costing should be described and the relation of cost to market should be studied.

The need for the auditor to physically observe inventories will depend on the responsibility he has been asked to assume and the time available. Generally, a team of experts from the acquiring company, often accompanied by the auditor, should at least inspect the inventory and make limited tests of quantities to determine the reliability of the records. Perhaps the most important and difficult investigation is that of value. Obsolete, defective, and slow-moving inventories are a favorite asset of companies which are for sale. Many a corporate marriage has been marred by the post-ceremonial discovery that inventory valued at cost had not been written down to realizable value. The auditor must look into the future. Are there any purchase or sales commitments that the company would rather not have entered into?

Receivables

Notes and accounts receivable are often extremely important, and a major portion of the investigation may relate to this caption. The most important matter to consider is the collectibility of the receivables. Collectibility can be substantiated by a review of the company's bad-debt experience, the study of an aged trial balance of all receivables in conjunction with applicable trade terms (and whether such terms were recently extended), and a review of cash collections subsequent to the date of examination. Emphasis should, of course, be placed on major accounts.

In addition to ascertaining that adequate provision has been made for bad debts, provisions for returns and allowances and for discounts should also be reviewed.

Nontrade receivables are sometimes important. These may be due from directors, officers, and employees, from affiliated companies, or from others with whom the company does not normally trade. It may be appropriate to make special contractual provisions for dealing with these items.

An effort should be made to determine whether any accounts or notes have been discounted and whether the company has any contingent liability.

It is important in a merger investigation to develop information on all major customers, especially where a few customers represent a disproportionate amount of sales. This information relates more to the objectives of the marketing members of the team than to the principal objectives of the auditor, but it is usually convenient for the auditor to develop the data in connection with his other work on accounts receivable. For all major customers the sales volume for the last several years should be obtained. Then the basis of the relationship with these companies should be explored. Perhaps there is a personal relationship or common-stock ownership that might not continue after the merger. Current financial statements for such companies should be obtained. Regular as well as all special trade terms should be reported.

Whether or not accounts receivable are to be confirmed will be based on such considerations as the adequacy of internal control, the practice and experience of the regular auditors, and, possibly, the time available.

Property, Plant, and Equipment

In most acquisitions the buyer should be more concerned about the economics of productive facilities than about their historical cost. He should be concerned about whether they will be useful in the ongoing business, whether they are adequate, and, if they need to be replaced, what he can realize on disposal. He should not, however, neglect their accounting and financial aspects. The auditors should develop sufficient detail that the buyer's management can evaluate the significance of differences between economic value, book value, and tax basis. In many cases, it is also appropriate to develop data on the reporting impact of alternative methods of depreciation.

Liabilities

Moving from the asset side of the balance sheet to the liability side, the auditor's prime concern shifts from a study of what is recorded to an investigation leading to a determination of what has not been recorded. The search for unrecorded liabilities will include steps determined by the circumstances and by the ingenuity of the auditor. Trade accounts payable, for example, can be verified by reference to invoices received and disbursements made subsequent to the balance sheet date. Major debts can be readily confirmed with creditors. In addition to the terms of the debt information on collateral, sinking-fund requirements and restrictions as to working capital, dividends, and the like should be obtained and studied.

The reasonableness of accrued liabilities can often be determined by a knowledge of the business. Have accruals been made for vacation and holiday pay? Through what date have state and local taxes been paid?

Commitments and Contingencies

The search for unrecorded liabilities can lead into many areas. Government sales may result in unrecorded refunds arising from renegotiation. Many companies give guarantees or warranties with respect to their products or services. These may require a provision for future adjustments applicable to past sales. The company's lawyers must be consulted to obtain information on any pending law suits.

Commitments both favorable and unfavorable must be identified and reviewed. Employment contracts with both union and salaried employees are important. Are there pension and/or profit-sharing plans? What are the major leases to which the company is a party? Has the company entered into any royalty or franchise agreements?

Income Taxes

The matter of income taxes is usually so significant that it requires special attention. The review of prior-year tax returns and revenue agents' reports is a good starting point. Tax contingencies should be discussed. If there are loss carryovers, they should be scheduled by year. If any tax matters are in litigation, the lawyers involved should be consulted. The alert auditor may spot danger areas unsuspected by the company or methods of achieving tax savings of which management was not aware. He should study the reconciliation of book income and taxable income and be alert to the significance of major differences.

Operations

In the typical acquisition, earning capacity is the key issue. Historical earnings are a major indicator of future earnings. Thus, the auditor must devote considerable attention to the income statements covering a period of years.

The starting point is, of course, a review of income statements in as much detail as is available over, say, a five-year period. Pertinent operating ratios are often valuable. If the company is a multiproduct one, then profit (or at least sales) by major product lines is important. The auditor should determine changes in product or production methods, changes in the methods of distribution, changes in research. If only a portion of the business is being acquired, the methods of allocating costs to that portion must be considered.

If the company has prepared projections of income for future years, the figures and the assumptions on which they are based should be reviewed critically in the light of past performance, current conditions, and probable future changes.

Financing

The auditor may also prove to be a helpful member of the financing team. Projections of earnings, equity, and cash flow under various financing alternatives can help in deciding the best route to follow. Determining and explaining the tax consequences to both the buyer and seller of the several ways of effecting and financing corporate combinations are often the responsibility of the certified public accountant.

The above are just a few examples of what the auditor might do. An acquisition investigation calls on the total spectrum of his regular audit skills and places a special premium on flexibility and ingenuity.

REPORTING ON THE INVESTIGATION

The form and completeness of reporting on an acquisition investigation are necessarily influenced by the time pressures. Subject to time limitations, it is most desirable that all significant findings be expressed in writing. This does not mean that the report should be cluttered with detail. Generally, the time pressures on those preparing the report are no greater than the pressures on those who read and act on the report. The report should be a succinct statement of findings, not a rambling recitation of the processes the investigators went through to arrive at their findings. It is also desirable, though not always feasible, for the work of the several fact-finding specialists to be integrated into one report.

Finally, even the best-written report will not convey the full flavor of the investigators' observations, and reports written under the typical time pressures of an acquisition investigation are not always "best-written." It is most desirable, therefore, that when the report is being reviewed all members of the investigating team be present to explain, justify, and elaborate upon their findings.

A certain executive of our acquaintance has on his wall a placard which reads: "Management is the art of making decisions on the basis of inadequate information." There is truth in this statement, but it should not be used as an alibi; it should be recognized as a warning.

II

Legal and Accounting Considerations

"They say, in wiving and thriving,
a man should take counsel of all
the world, lest he light upon a
curse while he seeks for a blessing."

HENRY SMITH, *Sermons* (1866)

Corporate Expansion
and the Law

ROBERT L. WERNER and JOHN D. HILL

T HE AMERICAN CONCEPT of the sanctity of small business and the need to protect it has for years been both a political and a legal philosophy. Commencing with enactment of the Sherman Act near the close of the last century,[1] and followed by Teddy Roosevelt's trust-busting activities early in this century, the crescendo of attacks on the growth of big business because of the alleged threat it presents to traditional small business has mounted both in frequency and in intensity.

It is not our purpose here either to agree or to disagree with the supposition that little business provides the backbone of our economy and is always good, and that big business is inherently a peril to little business, tends toward wicked monopoly, and is always suspect. Our purpose rather is to discuss certain legal aspects of corporate expansion and to outline the development and application of general rules which currently reflect the Government's and the courts' attitude toward corporate expansion.

There are two ways in which a corporation can expand. It can become larger through internal growth, or it can become larger by merger or acquisition.

[1] 26 Stat. 209 (1890), 15 U.S.C. §§1-7.

Robert L. Werner is Executive Vice President and General Counsel of RCA, New York. John D. Hill is Staff Vice President and Trade Regulation Counsel of RCA.

EXPANSION BY MERGER OR ACQUISITION

Before 1950 Section 7 of the Clayton Act, the provision of the law which specifically covers corporate acquisitions and mergers, covered only mergers by stock acquisition.[2] As a consequence, most corporations participating in mergers took the route of asset acquisition.

In 1947, in the *Columbia Steel* case, the Government attempted to prevent Columbia Steel Company, a subsidiary of U.S. Steel, from acquiring the assets of Consolidated Steel, a competitor. The Justice Department filed suit, alleging violation of the Sherman Act. The Government lost the case.[3] It is clear, however, that if the law in 1948, when *Columbia Steel* was decided, had been the same as it is today the Government would have had no problem in preventing the merger.

What then has happened to bring about this change?

Clayton Act Amendment of 1950

The answer lies in the fact that in 1950 the Congress amended Section 7 of the Clayton Act.[4] This amendment broadened the reach of the Act to cover acquisition of assets as well as acquisition of stock. In addition, the amendment substituted a new test of illegality, requiring only a showing that the probable effect of the acquisition would be substantially to lessen competition or tend to create a monopoly in any line of commerce in any section of the country.

The Senate and House committees, reporting on the proposed new legislation, said its passage should prove an effective measure to "limit further growth of monopoly and thereby aid in preserving small business as an important competitive factor in the American economy."[5]

The terms of the amended law placed new tools in the hands of the Justice Department and the Federal Trade Commission both to block and to undo mergers and acquisitions. And the scope of the 1950 amendment was such that attacks could be made not only on horizontal mergers (those between corporations engaged in competing businesses) but also on vertical mergers (those between a supplier corporation and its actual or potential customer) and additionally on conglomerate mergers (those between corporations engaged in unrelated businesses).

[2] 38 Stat. 731 (1914).
[3] *United States v. Columbia Steel Co.,* 334 U.S. 495 (1948).
[4] 64 Stat. 1125 (1950); 15 U.S.C. §18.
[5] S. Rep. No. 1775 & H.R. Rep. No. 1191, 81st Cong., 2d Sess. (1950).

Initial FTC and Justice Department Action

Pillsbury Mills, the first case under revised Section 7, was filed by the Federal Trade Commission in June 1952. The suit was an action against Pillsbury, the second-largest flour miller, for an order requiring it to divest itself of the stock and assets of two other millers it had acquired. The FTC won.[6]

The Commission concluded that the new law called for a case-by-case examination of all relevant factors bearing upon the economic consequences of a merger. The Commission also ruled that if such examination indicated a reasonable probability that a substantial lessening of competition in the relevant market would result, then a violation was present.

In finding that these conditions were met, and that a violation had taken place, the Commission considered such factors as the prior pattern of acquisitions in the industry generally, and by Pillsbury particularly; a trend of increase in the market shares enjoyed by the major flour millers; a decline in the number of mills; a lack of new entries into the business and an industry movement toward oligopoly.

Since *Pillsbury,* the FTC has brought more than 75 additional cases challenging corporate mergers and acquisitions. It has been successful in most of them. In many not only has it prevented an imminent merger or dissolved a past one, but it has also obtained orders forbidding future mergers or acquisitions without its or a court's consent.

The Department of Justice was off to a slower start in its use of the new law. The Antitrust Division filed its first merger case under revised Section 7 in 1955. This was a suit against Schenley, to require it to divest itself of a competing distiller and liquor importer, Park & Tilford. The suit was settled by a consent decree under which Schenley agreed that for ten years it would not acquire another whiskey distiller without prior approval of the Division or the Court.[7] Schenley was permitted to retain Park & Tilford, but only because, following the acquisition, that company had lost the most profitable part of its business, its principal import customers.

Although subsequent cases filed by the Justice Department have not been so numerous as those brought by the FTC, each agency has been active in the field. Of the many cases brought, some are of more than usual interest because they reached the Supreme Court.

[6] F.T.C. Docket 6000; 57 FTC 1274 (1960).
[7] *United States v. Schenley Industries, Inc.,* 1957 CCH Trade Reg. Cases ¶68664.

Significant Supreme Court Cases
Under Revised Section 7

The first such case is *Brown Shoe*.[8] Here the Supreme Court considered the acquisition in 1956 by Brown, the fourth-largest manufacturer of shoes, with about 4 percent of industry production, of G. R. Kinney, which operated the largest family-style retail store chain in the country, with about 1.6 percent of the total retail market. The case had both horizontal and vertical aspects, since Kinney also had manufacturing facilities and Brown had both owned and franchised retail outlets.

The Court fixed the entire United States as the relevant geographic market for the vertical aspects, since most shoe manufacturers sell on a nationwide basis. It fixed all cities with a population of more than 10,000 as the relevant geographic market for the horizontal aspects, since these were the principal localities in which Brown and Kinney had retail operations.

Although the percentages of 4 for Brown and 1.6 for Kinney were in themselves unimpressive, the Court found that their joinder, in light of conditions existing in the shoe industry, was sufficient to violate the law. These conditions were that, despite the fact that domestic shoe manufacture was spread over approximately 800 manufacturers, a relatively small number of them—the top four, including Brown—produced 23 percent of the national total.

In addition, the Court found that there had been a definite trend among shoe manufacturers to acquire retail outlets "to supply an ever-increasing percentage of their needs, thereby foreclosing other manufacturers from effectively competing for retail accounts."

The *Brown Shoe* case shows that, in applying the law, market percentages must be viewed in light of the particular structure of the industry at the time and the probable effect which a merger will have on that structure. Thus even small market percentages, such as in *Brown Shoe,* can be decisive.

Another important Supreme Court case is *Philadelphia National Bank,* which dealt with the proposed 1961 merger between the Philadelphia National Bank and the Girard Trust Corn Exchange Bank.[9] Philadelphia and Girard were, respectively, the second- and third-largest of the 42 commercial banks located in the Philadelphia metropolitan area. Philadelphia had about 20 percent of total commercial deposits for the area

---

[8] *Brown Shoe Co. v. United States,* 370 U.S. 294 (1962).
[9] *United States v. Philadelphia National Bank,* 374 U.S. 321 (1963).

and Girard about 15 percent. The merger would have created the largest commercial bank in the area.

Evidence was introduced by the Justice Department to show that the standings of the two banks were, at least in part, the result of prior mergers; also, that there was a general trend towards concentration of commercial banking in the Philadelphia area. The Supreme Court held these facts alone sufficient to indicate a threat to competition. The 35 percent was considered unreasonable on its face, and the proposed merger was enjoined.

In *Continental Can* the Justice Department sued to stop Continental, the second-largest producer of metal containers, from acquiring Hazel-Atlas Glass Company, the third-largest producer of glass containers.[10] The lower court held that metal containers did not compete with glass containers and denied an injunction. The Supreme Court reversed.

The Supreme Court found that competition did exist between the two types of containers and that there was potential competition in other container lines made by the two companies. It also held that the addition of the Hazel-Atlas share of 3 percent of the combined metal and glass container market to the 22 percent held by Continental would probably substantially lessen competition in the industry.

In *Penn-Olin* the Supreme Court, for the first time, had before it the question of whether revised Section 7 covered a joint venture.[11] Here the Justice Department sought dissolution of the Penn-Olin Chemical Company, a new corporation formed and jointly owned by Pennsalt Chemicals and Olin Mathieson to produce and market sodium chlorate in the Southeastern section of the country. Neither Pennsalt nor Olin had previously been in this business.

The Supreme Court held that Section 7 of the Clayton Act covered joint ventures. It also held that if there was a reasonable probability that either Pennsalt or Olin, in the absence of the joint venture, would have built a plant for the manufacture and sale of sodium chlorate in the Southeastern market area, while the other remained a significant potential competitor, this alone was sufficient to establish a violation. Accordingly, it sent the case back to the District Court to consider and determine this question of fact. After receipt of further testimony on the question, the lower court decided that there was not sufficient evidence to show that in the absence of the joint venture either company would have established

[10] *United States v. Continental Can Co.,* 378 U.S. 441 (1964).
[11] *United States v. Penn-Olin Chemical Co.,* 378 U.S. 158 (1964).

its own plant in that area, and dismissed the complaint. On appeal by the Government, the Supreme Court, equally divided, upheld without opinion the decision of the lower court.

The significance of the case is not lessened by its dismissal, which turned upon a question of fact. It sets a landmark for the Justice Department by establishing the principle that joint ventures clearly fall within the ambit of the antimerger law.

In *Consolidated Foods Corp.* the FTC sought to compel Consolidated to divest itself of Gentry, Inc., which it had acquired several years before.[12] Consolidated was a major grocer and Gentry a prominent producer of dehydrated onion and garlic. Consolidated was a substantial purchaser of products from food processors who in turn purchased dehydrated onion and garlic in their business. At the time of the acquisition Gentry had about 32 percent of the dehydrated-onion and -garlic market. The particular significance of this case is that it dealt with a conglomerate merger, involving the issue of reciprocity and the relationship of that issue to probable lessening of competition.

There was evidence to indicate that Consolidated had unsuccessfully attempted to exercise reciprocity by having its suppliers purchase dehydrated onion and garlic from Gentry.

The Court pointed out that when, as here, the acquisition was of a company that commanded a substantial share of a market, a finding of the probability of reciprocal buying was sufficient. Divestiture was ordered.

Mention should also be made of the Supreme Court's 1966 decision in the *Von's Grocery* case, because it is a further manifestation of the Supreme Court's concern with industry concentration and its desire to protect small business.[13] Von's, the third-ranking food chain in the Los Angeles area, acquired Shopping Bag, the number six company in the area. Together they became the number two company. Both companies had impressive records of growth by internal expansion in the ten-year period prior to the merger. During this same period the number of single grocery stores in the area had declined by more than 20 percent, whereas the number of chains had increased by more than 50 percent. The grocery business was thus being concentrated into the hands of fewer and fewer owners through absorption of small companies by larger firms. On these facts the Supreme Court reversed a decision of the lower court and ruled the merger illegal.

---

[12] *Federal Trade Commission v. Consolidated Foods Corp.*, 380 U.S. 592 (1965).
[13] *United States v. Von's Grocery Co.*, 384 U.S. 270 (1966).

In applying Section 7 of the Clayton Act the Supreme Court took the broad grocery field as the applicable line of commerce and the Los Angeles metropolitan area as the section of the country affected.

Justice Black, writing for the majority, said that the basic purpose of amended Section 7 of the Clayton Act "was to prevent economic concentration in the American economy by keeping a large number of small competitors in business."

In *Procter & Gamble*, decided in 1967, the Supreme Court again enlarged its interpretation of the application of Section 7. The case involved a suit by the FTC to compel Procter & Gamble, the country's leading seller of soaps, detergents, and household cleansers, to sell Clorox Chemical Company, the leading manufacturer of household liquid bleach, which it had acquired in 1957.[14] This case is particularly significant because it contains the first specific ruling by the Supreme Court that Section 7 applies to all mergers, whether horizontal, vertical, conglomerate, or other, and that all are to be tested by the same standard—their probable effect upon competition in any line of commerce in any section of the country.

The FTC had characterized the acquisition as a "product extension merger," to distinguish it from the pure conglomerate type, since household liquid bleach and packaged detergents are complementary products made with similar facilities, and usually marketed through the same channels and advertised by the same media. The Commission found that the acquisition violated the law and ordered divestiture. On appeal, the Court of Appeals reversed and directed dismissal of the complaint. On further appeal by the FTC, the Supreme Court, without any Justice casting a dissenting vote, sustained the Commission.

Supporting the findings of the Commission, the Supreme Court held that the merger involved serious anticompetitive effects because substitution of P&G, with its huge assets and advertising discount advantages, for Clorox, and the availability of these advantages to benefit Clorox, would tend to dissuade new entrants from coming into the liquid-bleach field. The Court said that the great economic power of P&G would discourage smaller firms from aggressively competing for fear of retaliation, thereby leading to still greater concentration in an already concentrated liquid-bleach industry. In addition, the Court pointed out that the merger diminished potential competition, since there was likelihood that Procter would have entered the complementary household liquid-bleach business if it had not acquired Clorox.

[14] *Federal Trade Commission v. Proctor & Gamble Co.*, 386 U.S. 568 (1967).

Foreign Acquisitions and Joint Ventures

There are as yet no court decisions under the revised Clayton Act dealing directly with the legality of acquisitions by U.S. corporations of foreign corporations or joint ventures participated in by U.S. and foreign corporations. However, decisions under the Sherman Act hold quite clearly that the American antitrust laws reach all commercial agreements, no matter where or with whom made, if such agreements have a direct and substantial effect upon the domestic or foreign commerce of the United States. Therefore a completed foreign acquisition or joint venture which has the effect of unreasonably restraining our foreign or domestic trade in any commodity can be successfully attacked under the Sherman Act.

The Clayton Act was passed to provide a means to enjoin incipient restraints, and thereby avoid the necessity of waiting until actual restraints have taken place. Accordingly, it is only reasonable to believe that the courts will hold that the Clayton Act can be used to prevent or dissolve a foreign merger or joint venture. Such an injunction would result from a showing that the foreign merger or joint venture would probably substantially lessen or interfere with the foreign or domestic trade of the United States. On the other hand, if it is likely that the effect of the merger or joint venture would be upon local trade in a foreign area, there seems little likelihood that it will be attacked by the Government.

Recently, the Justice Department found an acquisition in the foreign area which it apparently decided to use for a test case. In February 1968 it filed suit in the Federal District Court in Boston to require Gillette Co. to divest Braun A.G., a company of West Germany which it acquired in 1967. Braun is the third-largest European manufacturer of electric razors, while Gillette is the largest American producer of safety razors and blades. The Government's complaint alleges that Gillette's acquisition of Braun will have the effect of eliminating potential competition between the two companies in the shaving-instrument market in the United States.

EXPANSION THROUGH INTERNAL GROWTH

The Courts, the Department of Justice, and the Federal Trade Commission take a much milder and more constructive position with respect to expansion through internal growth.

In December 1966 a top Antitrust Division official said:

"I have been asked to speak on the antitrust approach towards growth through internal expansion as compared to growth through acquisitions and joint ventures. The short answer is that the antitrust approach is favorable to internal growth. One might even say that 'surely one premise of an antimerger statute such as Section 7 [of the Clayton Act] is that corporate growth by internal expansion is socially preferable to growth by acquisition'."[15]

Nor is size alone an offense against the law. However, size does carry with it an opportunity for abuse, and this the courts will not ignore when the opportunity is proved to have been utilized in the past.

The leading case involves Aluminum Company of America's alleged monopoly of aluminum ingots. Although decided in 1945, the law it established remains unchanged today. In its opinion, holding that Alcoa had violated the Sherman Act, the Court said:

"The only question is whether it [Alcoa] falls within the exception established in favor of those who do not seek, but cannot avoid, the control of the market. It seems to us that that question scarcely survives its statement. It was not inevitable that it should always anticipate increases in the demand for ingots and be prepared to supply them. Nothing compelled it to keep doubling and redoubling its capacity before others entered the field. It insists that it never excluded competitors; but we can think of no more effective exclusion than progressively to embrace each new opportunity as it opened, and to face every newcomer with new capacity already geared into a great organization, having the advantage of experience, trade connections, and the elite of personnel."[16]

In general, however, expansion by internal growth, absent the exercise of monopoly power, does not by itself give rise to legal problems.

Department of Justice Guidelines

On May 30, 1968, the Department of Justice issued policy "guidelines" for its enforcement of Section 7 of the Clayton Act. In the guidelines the Department stated its intention to preserve and promote market structures conducive to competition and to challenge any type of merger, whether horizontal, vertical, or conglomerate, which alters market structure in a direction likely now or eventually to encourage or permit noncompetitive conduct. The guidelines indicated the Department's special concern with mergers involving a large company holding a sizable share of the market.

---

[15] Address by Lionel Kestenbaum, Chief, Evaluation Section, Antitrust Division, Justice Department, before Practising Law Institute Forum, December 2, 1966.
[16] *United States v. Aluminum Co. of America,* 148 F. 2d 416, 431 (2d Cir. 1945).

As to horizontal mergers, the Department said that it accords primary significance to the size of the market share held by both the acquiring and the acquired firms. Among the examples of the types of horizontal mergers the Department said it would expect to challenge are those made in a highly concentrated market in which the four largest firms share 75 percent or more and each firm has 4 percent or more of the market, or where the acquiring firm has 15 percent and the acquired firm 1 percent or more. As to less highly concentrated markets, the Department indicated that it would expect to challenge mergers where each firm holds 5 percent or more or where the acquiring firm holds 25 percent and the acquired firm 1 percent or more.

The Department also pointed out that it would expect to challenge horizontal mergers, irrespective of market share, where the acquisition is of a competitor which is a "particularly disturbing, disruptive, or otherwise unusually competitive factor in the market," or where a merger involves a substantial firm and a firm which possesses an unusually competitive potential or has an asset that confers an unusual competitive advantage.

As to vertical mergers, the Department said that it intends to prevent mergers that tend significantly to raise barriers to entry in either market or to disadvantage existing nonintegrated or partly integrated firms in either market in ways unrelated to economic efficiency, and will ordinarily challenge a merger between a supplying firm accounting for 10 percent or more of the sales in its market and one or more purchasing firms accounting for 6 percent or more of the total purchases in that market.

As to conglomerate mergers, the Department said that it will take enforcement action against any type of conglomerate merger which on specific analysis appears anticompetitive and that, with respect to mergers involving likely market entrants, it will ordinarily challenge a merger between one of the most likely market entrants and (a) a firm with approximately 25 percent or more of the market or (b) a firm with less than 25 percent of the market if the market is substantially shared by a limited number of firms. As to mergers creating the danger of reciprocal buying, the Department indicated that it will ordinarily challenge any merger undertaken to facilitate the creation of reciprocal buying arrangements.

The new administration in 1969 appointed a new Assistant Attorney General in charge of the Antitrust Division of the Justice Department. He has expressed the view that many mergers of a somewhat "purer" conglomerate nature than have been ruled on by the Supreme Court have a dangerous potential for substantial lessening of competition. He has indicated that he will be examining mergers of this type, particularly those involving larger corporations, and expects to move promptly on some of them. He has also cautioned that businessmen cannot rely on the former Merger Guidelines in this area and that "we may sue even though particular mergers appear to satisfy those Guidelines."[17]

On April 14 of this year the Antitrust Division filed suit for an order requiring Ling-Temco-Vought, Inc., fourteenth-largest industrial corporation in the nation and a conglomerate with a history of many acquisitions, to dispose of its 63 percent stock interest in Jones & Laughlin Steel Corporation, the nation's sixth-largest steel producer, and to prevent LTV from attempting to acquire the remaining shares.[18] Two weeks later the Division filed suit against International Telephone and Telegraph Corporation, the nation's twelfth-largest firm and another conglomerate with a long history of acquisitions, for an order requiring ITT to divest itself of its interests in Canteen Corporation, a leading food and vending service company which it had acquired.[19]

These appeared to be the new administration's opening attacks upon conglomerate mergers and its first test cases seeking judicial clarification on the application of Section 7 of the Clayton Act to such mergers. Since a large number of LTV's suppliers, customers, and subsidiaries are users of steel and a large number of ITT's suppliers, customers, and subsidiaries are users of food services, we can expect the potential for reciprocal dealing to be one of the cardinal points at issue.

Additionally, the suits are expected to present to the Court the question of whether entry by a large conglomerate company into a new line of business through an acquisition violates the Clayton Act when such acquisition may substantially lessen competition in that line of business.

FEDERAL TRADE COMMISSION NOTIFICATION

On May 6, 1969 the Federal Trade Commission issued an order requiring all firms with assets of $250 million or more to give advance notification to the Commission of any acquisition or merger involving 10 percent or more of the stock or assets of another corporation whose assets total at least $10 million, and all firms with assets of between $10 million and $250 million to give notice of any acquisition or merger which will result in combined assets of $250 million or more.[20]

---

[17] Address by Richard W. McLaren, Assistant Attorney General, Antitrust Division, Justice Department, before National Industrial Conference Board, March 6, 1969.
[18] Department of Justice release, April 14, 1969.
[19] Department of Justice release, April 28, 1969.
[20] 34 Fed. Reg. 7592.

Notification to the Commission is required to be given within 10 days following an agreement in principle to merge or within 10 days following accumulation of 10 percent or more of the voting stock of the corporation being acquired and in no event less than 60 days prior to consummation of the proposed acquisition or merger.

Special reports on forms furnished by the Commission are required to be filed by firms whose assets exceed $250 million at the time notification is given. These reports call for detailed information on the industries involved, product sales, and past acquisitions. Notifications will become a part of the public records of the Commission, but special reports containing detailed company information will be treated in confidence subject to disclosure to the Congress, the Department of Justice, and other Government agencies upon request.

GENERAL RULES

A study of what the Supreme Court has said and done in merger cases, of statements by Government antitrust enforcement officials, and of the Department of Justice guidelines indicates some general principles that a large American corporation would be well advised to consider in connection with any program of expansion it may contemplate:

1. Wherever feasible, expansion of any line of business should be accomplished through internal growth.

2. Acquisition of a significant interest in another domestic company engaged in a business in which the acquiring corporation also is significantly engaged will probably be attacked by the Government and condemned by the courts.

3. Acquisition of a significant interest in another domestic company from which the corporation makes significant purchases or to which it sells, and which company is a significant source of supply or source of outlet for the corporation's competitors, will probably be attacked by the Government and condemned by the courts.

4. A conglomerate-type acquisition where (a) the acquired company is a potential entrant into a business in which the acquiring company is engaged or (b) such acquisition produces a large disparity in size between the merged companies taken as a whole and the largest remaining companies engaged in competitive business is likely to be challenged by the Government and declared illegal by the courts.

5. A conglomerate-type acquisition which will provide an opportunity to exercise any significant amount of reciprocity will probably be attacked by the Government and condemned by the courts. A conglomerate-type acquisition by a large corporation with little or no opportunity

for the exercise of reciprocity is less likely to be attacked, but the law has yet to be clarified in this area.

6. Whenever a conglomerate- or product-extension-type acquisition is made by a large integrated company, use of income or resources derived from other business of the corporation to support the business of the acquired company to the detriment of that company's competitors can constitute an abusive and illegal use of the power of integration.

7. A product-extension-type acquisition by a large company having a prominent position in the sale of a particular line of products, through acquisition of a company engaged in the sale of a product or line of products complementary to that of the acquiring company, presents a serious risk of being challenged by the Government and condemned by the courts. The probability of such a result is substantially increased if the acquired company is one of the principal companies in an already concentrated industry.

8. Foreign mergers and joint ventures will probably not be attacked if they appear to have no substantial effect on the domestic or foreign trade of the United States. However, joint ventures or mergers between large U.S. companies and major foreign companies can present risks, since such mergers or ventures might have just that effect.

9. Any of the above situations which constitutes a violation of law can also give rise to private litigation by injured competitors, with resultant damage claims.

CONCLUSION

In determining whether it may be wise under questionable circumstances to risk an acquisition or a merger or a joint venture, an illuminating observation was made by an eminent Supreme Court Justice in a 1966 case in which the majority of the Court held that a merger should be undone. In his dissenting opinion, Mr. Justice Stewart said:

"In a single sentence and an omnibus footnote at the close of its opinion, the [Supreme] Court pronounces its work consistent with the line of our decisions under Section 7 since the passage of the 1950 amendment. The sole consistency that I can find is that in litigation under Section 7, the Government always wins."[21]

Quite possibly the day will come when the Government finally will lose a Section 7 case before the Supreme Court. But at least in the present mood of the Court, an acquisition, merger, or joint venture by a large corporation should be approached with caution and its legal aspects carefully examined before the final determination to go ahead is made.

[21] *United States v. Von's Grocery, supra,* at 301.

An SEC Primer

ROBERT M. ELLIOTT

WHEN A CORPORATE MERGER OR ACQUISITION affects the rights or interests of public investors, it is likely that these rights or interests will be afforded certain protections under the Federal securities laws. Although this legislation does not guarantee that only mergers beneficial to all parties will be negotiated nor provide assurance against financial loss by public stockholders, it is designed to insure that all the facts are made available for public evaluation and to guard against fraud. In order to understand fully the application of the Federal securities laws to the merger and acquisition phenomenon, it might be helpful at the outset to take a brief look at the origin and jurisdiction of the Securities and Exchange Commission, the Federal agency responsible for administering the securities laws.

ORIGIN AND JURISDICTION OF THE SEC

The final impetus for legislation was provided by the stock market crash in October 1929, and the Great Depression which followed. A highly speculative atmosphere compounded by fraudulent and unethical practices in the sale of securities led the way to the crash which made the distribution of corporate securities a national problem overnight. Investor confidence, vitally important to the maintenance of strong capital markets, was badly shaken. Today investor confidence has long since

---

Robert M. Elliott is a partner in the law firm of Shepherd, Elliott and Shepherd in Litchfield, Conn. He was a member of the SEC's Division of Corporation Finance from 1962 to 1966.

been restored, public investment participation is the broadest in our history, and the SEC's "full and fair disclosure" concept is widely accepted throughout the securities industry.

The first piece of corrective legislation, the Securities Act of 1933, placed a responsibility on corporate managements to provide the investing public with the material facts regarding new issues of securities. Congress felt that full publication of the facts surrounding potential investment would prevent most fraudulent security offerings and would provide maximum investor protection with minimum interference with legitimate business transactions. Thus "disclosure," not "regulation," became the basic tenet on which most of the securities legislation was premised. It follows that the Securities and Exchange Commission has no authority to evaluate a proposed security offering or to judge its merits, but only to require disclosure of information necessary for the protection of investors.

The second piece of corrective legislation, the Securities Exchange Act of 1934, established the Securities and Exchange Commission. The Commission administers six statutes: the Securities Act of 1933, the Securities Exchange Act of 1934, the Public Utility Holding Company Act of 1935, the Trust Indenture Act of 1939, the Investment Company Act of 1940, and the Investment Advisors Act of 1940. The SEC also has additional advisory functions under Chapter X of the Bankruptcy Act. Statutory provisions affecting mergers and acquisitions are found throughout the Securities Act of 1933 (Securities Act) and the Securities Exchange Act of 1934 (Exchange Act).

Securities Act of 1933

The Securities Act has two principal objectives: (a) protection of investors by requiring adequate and accurate disclosure regarding securities distributed to the public, and (b) prevention of misrepresentation, deceit, or other fraudulent practices in the sale of securities. It must be remembered that the Act is a piece of Federal legislation and derives its strength from constitutional provisions. Thus a distribution of securities is within the jurisdiction of the Act if the mails or instruments of interstate commerce are used at any step in the distribution.

The procedure that ensures that the investor *will* be provided with sufficient disclosure on which an intelligent investment decision may be based is known as the "registration process." Briefly, Section 5 of the Act provides that a security may not be *offered* for sale until a registration statement has been filed with the SEC, and the *sale* of a security may not be actually consummated until the statement is effective. The registration statement must include a "prospectus" which contains significant information about the issuer and the offering. A copy of the prospectus must be furnished to each purchaser at or before the sale or delivery of the security.

Securities Exchange Act of 1934

Although the Securities Act deals primarily with the initial distribution of securities, the Exchange Act is concerned with postdistribution trading, both on the national securities exchanges *and* in the over-the-counter market. The Exchange Act, as amended by the Securities Act Amendments of 1964, places registration responsibilities upon the managements of all companies which have securities listed for trading on national securities exchanges and all over-the-counter companies with total assets in excess of $1 million and more than 500 shareholders.

First, Section 12 of the Act requires each such company to file a registration statement with the Commission. This statement, which is placed in the Commission's public files, contains essentially the same type of information that is required in a Securities Act registration statement. Section 13 requires that current information be made available to the public through the filing of annual, semiannual, and current reports. Section 14 subjects all proxy solicitations by these companies to the Commission's proxy rules. Section 16 prevents officers, directors, and shareholders who own more than 10 percent of any class of equity security from profiting from purchase-and-sale or sale-and-purchase of the company's stock within any six-month period. The object of this insider trading prohibition is to prevent the insider—an officer, a director, or a controlling stockholder—from using inside information to profit at the expense of the public shareholders. Finally, Section 10 and Rule 10b-5 thereunder, the Commission's broadest antifraud weapon, proscribe misrepresentation, deceit, and other fraudulent devices and practices in connection with the purchase or sale of *any* security. Rule 10b-5 applies not only to companies and insiders but to the activities of "any person."

Let us now direct our attention to when and how these provisions of the Federal securities laws affect mergers and acquisitions.

"MERGERS" AND "ACQUISITIONS" DEFINED

For the purposes of this discussion the term "merger" generally includes the following types of transactions: (a) a statutory merger, in which the acquired corporation becomes part of the acquiring corporation and the stockholders of the acquired corporation receive stock in the acquiring corporation in exchange for their former holdings in the disappearing company; (b) a statutory consolidation, similar to a statutory merger except that a new corporation is formed to acquire both merging companies and the stockholders of both disappearing companies receive stock in the new corporation; and (c) a stock-for-assets acquisition, the so-called "practical merger," in which the acquiring corporation issues its securities to the acquired corporation in exchange for all or substantially all of the assets subject to the liabilities of the acquired company. To complete the "practical merger" the acquired corporation is usually dissolved and the securities of the acquiring company are passed on to stockholders in liquidation.

The term "acquisition," as used in this discussion, is generally limited to the acquisition directly from the stockholders of all or substantially all the stock of the acquired company, its legal existence remaining intact, in exchange for stock or other securities of the acquiring corporation or cash or other assets.

MERGERS

Exemptions from Securities Act Registration

The task of putting together a merger typically includes gaining the formal approval of stockholders of the company to be acquired and the issuance of new or additional securities of the acquiring company upon completion of the transaction. This raises a Securities Act problem which must be dealt with at the outset: Does the presentation of a merger plan to shareholders of the corporation to be acquired and the subsequent issuance of securities of the acquiring company to them require *registration* under the Securities Act? In most cases the answer is "No," but it should be stressed that this "No" has definite limitations.

Although the Act is probably broad enough to subject such activities to the registration requirements, the Commission has long taken the position, expressed in its Rule 133, that this and similar transactions are exempt from the registration process. Rule 133 of the General Rules and Regulations under the Securities Act provides in effect that for the purposes of Section 5 of the Act no "sale," "offer," "offer to sell," or "offer for sale" is involved insofar as the stockholders of a corporation are concerned where, pursuant to state law or the corporation's certificate of incorporation, there is submitted to stockholders a plan or agreement for a statutory merger or consolidation or reclassification of securities or a proposal for a reorganization through the transfer of assets, and where the vote of a required favorable majority will bind all stockholders of the corporation except for the appraisal rights of dissenting stockholders.

This "no sale" rule is derived from the theory that the corporation, in presenting a plan of merger to shareholders for approval, is not so much offering a security for sale as it is consummating a corporate act in accordance with state law. The shareholder, in voting on the merger, is acting more in his capacity as a corporate functionary than in the role of an *investor* making an investment decision. This theory is borne out by the fact that, once the holders of the requisite number of shares have given their approval, the new securities are issued in accordance with the merger plan without regard to decisions made by *individual* shareholders.

One important limitation in the use of the exemption from registration provided by the "no sale" rule deserves special attention. Suppose the controlling stockholders of the acquired company wish to liquidate their stock interests in the acquiring company for cash. Since the sellers want cash, they arrange, with or without the help or knowledge of the acquiring company, to effect a public sale of the stock which they receive. Since the requisite shareholder approval for the plan was obtained, the *initial* distribution of shares to the stockholders of the acquired company was exempt from registration. The question now is this: Will this stock *continue* to be exempt from registration? Is this stock now under *secondary* distribution so-called "free" stock? The answer is an emphatic "No!"

Back in the mid-1950s the Commission found that the "no sale" rule was being used as a device to evade registration and to effect widespread public distributions of unregistered securities. The *Great Sweet Grass Oils* case (37 SEC 683 [1957] 256 F.2d 893 D.C. Cir. 1958) illustrated the need for the protection of the Act in such a situation. Great Sweet Grass Oils and Kroy Oils Limited (the subject of a companion case) were both Canadian corporations with stock listed on the American Stock Exchange. Both companies were under the common control of one individual. The Commission found that an unregistered public offering of 3,750,000 corporate shares had been made as part of an over-all scheme engineered by the controlling stockholder to effect an illegal distribution.

This is how it is reported to have worked. A large number of shares of Sweet Grass and of Kroy were issued to dormant corporations controlled by the individual and his associates in exchange for oil and gas properties. The acquisition of properties by Sweet Grass and Kroy in exchange for stock were corporate acts authorized by shareholders. The stock, however, did not come to rest in the hands of these corporate vehicles. In fact, most of the 3,750,000 shares involved were distributed to the public by means of an intensive sales campaign. Through the efforts of the controlling stockholder, his cohorts, and several broker-dealers, the public investors paid over $15 million to finance the acquisition by Sweet Grass and Kroy of properties worth a great deal less. In addition, substantial underwriting commissions were paid to the brokers at the expense of the investing stockholders.

Both companies claimed that Rule 133 had made the stock "free" from registration in connection with the subsequent distributions by the dormant corporations. The Commission instituted proceedings against both companies and ordered the stock of both companies to be delisted from the American Stock Exchange. The Commission in its opinion made its view very clear that Rule 133 applies *only* to the initial issuance of securities to shareholders pursuant to a merger plan and not to subsequent or secondary distributions to the public. Although *casual* resales by noncontrolling stockholders do not contravene the statutory provisions nor violate the spirit of the "no sale" doctrine, the rule should be carefully scrutinized before any member of a controlling group resells. It should also be remembered that Rule 133 by its terms provides an exemption *only* from registration and not from the antifraud provisions of the Securities Act.

Where you *have* a situation in which a subsequent distribution is to be made and in which the issuer has solicited proxies under the Commission's proxy rules with respect to the merger transaction, the Commission has developed a simplified registration procedure whereby a special registration form (Form S-14) may be used. When this form is used, the proxy statement employed earlier plus a few required additions constitutes the "prospectus" for the subsequent distribution.

Solicitation of Proxies

Investor protection generated under the Securities Act depends solely on whether or not a "public offering" of securities is involved.

Although most mergers are exempt from Securities Act registration, as a practical matter stockholders of listed companies and stockholders of unlisted companies with total assets of $1 million and at least 500 shareholders receive substantially the same disclosure protection under the Exchange Act when faced with a merger decision. Let us examine the type of disclosure that the SEC requires management to furnish to shareholders when soliciting proxies in connection with a proposed merger.

The proxy itself must offer the shareholder an opportunity to vote "Yes" or "No" on *each* matter solicited. The proxy statement must contain the information required by Schedule 14A, which is found in Regulation 14 of the Exchange Act. Briefly, the proxy statement must include an informative description of the business and properties of each company involved in the proposed transaction, an explanation of the merger agreement, the shareholders' rights (including dissenters' rights), and the recommendations of the board of directors with respect to the transaction. The merger exchange ratio as well as the market values over a two-year period of the securities involved must also be furnished. If the transaction involves the election of directors, the proxy statement must furnish information about the proposed directors, their principal occupations for the past five years, their stockholdings in the company, the amount of their total annual remuneration if it is more than $30,000, and their interest in any material transaction with the company. Most important, the proxy statement must contain extensive financial statements and other financial data as described later in this article. In short, shareholders must be apprised of all material facts available so that they can make an intelligent decision on the basis of the information in the proxy statement.

Although the Commission has no jurisdiction over *when* the stockholders meeting is held, the rules specify that the preliminary proxy soliciting material must be furnished to the Commission's staff *at least ten days* before such material is mailed to shareholders. It is the practice of the staff to examine the preliminary material and promptly to furnish the company with a letter of comments describing any deficiencies in the material. Companies are cautioned to defer the printing of the definitive material until the comments of the staff have been received and considered. The staff generally gives priority to merger proxy material, but because of its heavy workload often is unable to furnish a comment letter within the ten-day period. *Because this letter typically may request additional information and because the proxy statement will sometimes require one or more revisions, it is advisable for a company to file its first preliminary material three or four weeks before the desired mailing date.* Any major problems which are contemplated should be brought to the attention of the Commission's staff *before* the filing of the first preliminary draft. This procedure is particularly helpful to both the company and the staff when financial statement requirements are involved.

Occasionally, a merger proxy solicitation will develop into a proxy contest when a group of stockholders who are dissatisfied with the proposals of management solicit proxies to oppose the merger. Under the proxy rules, anyone can solicit proxies but *all* solicitations must be made within the SEC's investor-protective purview. Thus the "opposition" must submit a preliminary proxy statement to the SEC staff in the same manner as management, and the disclosure on both sides must remain accurate and complete. In addition, when a merger involves the election of directors, all participants in a proxy contest, management and the opposition, must file public statements with the Commission on Schedule 14B announcing the degree of each person's participation and including a complete statement of each person's personal background.

Violation of the proxy rules can lead to court action instituted either by the Commission or by interested stockholders. A suit may be brought to enjoin the use of false and misleading proxy solicitation material, to contest the validity of the proxy vote, or for other appropriate relief. In connection with a stockholder suit attacking a *merger* which was allegedly effected through the use of false and misleading proxy statement, the Supreme Court held in 1964 that a Federal court may grant "all necessary remedial relief" to redress proxy rule violations *(J. I. Case Company v. Borak,* 337 U.S. 426). Thus, in a recent case a Federal court decr ed an accounting and restitution to stockholders of a company which v as acquired by merger where the proxy statement used in connection with the merger transaction was held to be false and misleading in violation of Rule 14a-9 of the proxy rules *(Gerstle v. Gamble-Skogmo, Inc.,* USDC, Eastern Dist. N.Y., 3-7-69).

Disclosure Protection for Minority Stockholders

What protection (in the absence of fraud) does the Exchange Act provide for public stockholders when management holds enough shares that a proxy solicitation is unnecessary?

The answer until recently was "None." However, Congress in 1964 amended the Act to impose upon management the responsibility to provide stockholders in such cases with information substantially similar to that required under the proxy solicitation strictures. To implement this provision the Commission adopted Regulation 14C which has applied to shareholder meetings held since March 15, 1966.

ACQUISITIONS

Securities Act Registration

Now let us consider acquisitions which generally do not involve shareholder approval or the solicitation of proxies unless required by stock

exchange rules. Some acquisitions are subject to the registration requirements of the Securities Act and others are not. It should be remembered
that the Securities Act applies to all companies, regardless of size, and
that the basic test is whether securities are being offered for sale to the
public.

Consider an acquisition in the form of an exchange of stock in one
company for stock in another. Suppose, for example, that Rockets, Inc.
wants to take over Space, Inc. (both fictional companies). Rockets
wants to issue its stock in exchange for Space stock. The exchange offer
is made to Space shareholders *individually*. This constitutes an offering of
Rocket securities and (absent an exemption—discussed below) comes
under the purview of the Securities Act.

The Registration Procedure

When registration *is* required in an acquisition, a registration statement
must be filed on the prescribed form (usually Form S-1). The largest
part of this registration statement is the basic selling document—the "prospectus." It must contain the terms of the offering, descriptions of the
business and properties of *both* parties, information about management,
financial statements, and comparative financial data (as described later
in this article). In short, all material facts necessary for the investor
(the stockholder of the company to be acquired) to make an intelligent
investment decision must be supplied.

Once the registration statement is filed, the Commission staff makes its
initial examination and issues a letter of comment describing deficiencies
and often requesting supplemental information needed to enable the staff
to complete its examination. Generally, the comment letters are issued
within one month after the registration statement is filed. Deficiencies in
the statement are corrected through the filing of amendment(s). Once
the requirements have been met, the registration statement may become
"effective." At this point in a typical exchange offer, copies of the prospectus would be mailed for the first time to the shareholders of the company
to be acquired, and the acquiring company may begin to "sell" its shares.

Exemptions from Securities Act Registration

The Securities Act provides for several exemptions (in addition to Rule
133) from the registration requirements. Among them are the intrastate
offering exemption; the small-issues exemption, better known as "Regulation A"; and the so-called "private offering" exemption.

The intrastate "local offering" exemption is available only when the
offering is made *and completed* entirely within the state in which the

issuer is incorporated and where it carries on its principal business. This narrow exemption applies to an exchange offer only where *all* of the shareholders of the company to be acquired are residents of the state in which the acquiring company is incorporated and doing business.

The "Reg A" exemption is available only for offerings of $300,000 and under. It requires the use of an "offering circular" somewhat similar to a full registration "prospectus," one notable difference being that the financial statements in a Reg A offering circular need not be certified.

It is important for corporate executives to understand the proper basis for reliance on the "private offering" exemption, because a great many unregistered securities offerings, including offerings for corporate acquisitions, are made in dependence on this exemption. Section 4(2) of the Act states that the registration provisions shall not apply to "transactions by an issuer not involving any public offering." Although it cannot be denied that the number of persons *to whom the offering is to be made* is a major determinant of whether a public offering exists, there is no "magic number." Of equal importance are the nature of the group, the degree of investor sophistication its members possess, *and* their relationship to the issuer.

The Commission states in its Securities Act Release #4552 that "whether a transaction is one not involving any public offering is essentially a question of fact and necessitates a consideration of all surrounding circumstances, including such factors as the relationship between the offerees and the issuer, the nature, scope, size, type and manner of the offering." The Supreme Court in *SEC v. Ralston Purina Co.,* 346 U.S. 119, 125 (1953), held that "the applicability of [this exemption] should turn on whether the particular class of persons affected need the protection of this Act."

The private-offering-vs.-public-offering question can be illustrated by the situation where Rockets, Inc. wishes to acquire stock of Space, Inc. by offering Rockets stock to all of the Space stockholders, who happen to total 30 individuals. Let us say that of the 30 there are three who effectively control the company through ownership of 30 percent of the stock and who act as the company's management team. Rockets realizes that, in order to be successful in its bid, Space's three controlling stockholders must be prevailed upon to accept the offer. In arriving at its decision to accept Rockets' offer, particularly with respect to the exchange ratio, the management of Space participates in extensive negotiations with the management of Rockets, during which it examines the books and records of Rockets and becomes familiar with the business and operations of that company and with its management personnel. It is clear that these three persons, who have access to all material facts about the offering, do not need the protection provided by registration. It is not so clear, however, with respect to the remaining 27 offerees, who, despite their relatively small number, would be accepting the offer primarily on the basis of their management's recommendation rather than on the basis of first-hand knowledge of the facts. It would appear, in the language of the Supreme Court, that this "particular class of persons affected needs the protection of the Act."

In addition to the number and nature of the offerees, the issuer must consider where the securities offered are to come to rest. Suppose, for example, that the three shareholders owned 100 percent of the stock of Space, Inc. They accepted Rockets' "private offering," but upon receiving their Rocket stock they immediately reoffered it to many other persons. Since the original offerees were merely conduits for a much wider public distribution, the private offering exemption would not be available. Because of this problem it is often the practice for an issuer relying on the private offering exemption to secure from the initial purchasers "investment letters" representing that they are acquiring the securities for investment and not with a view to distribution. Since such a letter is not conclusive as to the actual intent of the purchaser, additional precautions are often taken by the issuer, such as placing a restrictive legend on the stock certificates and issuing stop-transfer instructions to the transfer agent.

Acquisitions by Tender Offer

Suppose, to use our previous illustration, that Rockets, Inc. makes an offer to acquire Space, Inc. shares for cash or other assets not involving Rockets securities. Is registration under the Securities Act required in such a transaction? The answer is "No." The Securities Act applies exclusively to the *sale,* not the *purchase,* of securities. Thus, traditionally, cash tender offers and similar takeover bids not involving the offer for sale or the sale of securities of the acquiring company have been outside the disclosure protection of the securities laws except for the antifraud provisions of the Exchange Act.

However, amendments to the Exchange Act which were effective on July 29, 1968, have placed future acquisitions by tender offer under full SEC jurisdiction. Now stockholders of the acquired company will have access to significant information respecting the proposed takeover when making the investment decision of whether to accept the offer.

Basically, the new statutory amendments provide that the acquisition of or solicitation for the acquisition of more than 10 percent of a class of equity securities registered under the Exchange Act, which includes listed companies and over-the-counter companies with more than 500 stockholders and $1 million of assets, are subject to disclosure requirements which are written into the statute and which in time will undoubtedly be fully developed by SEC rules and regulations.

OTHER DISCLOSURE REQUIREMENTS RELATING TO ACQUISITIONS AND MERGERS

All companies subject to the reporting requirements of the Exchange Act must file with the Commission a current report on Form 8-K reporting any material acquisition or merger. Such report must include a recent certified balance sheet of the acquired company and certified income statements for three years. Generally, an acquisition is "material" if either the assets or gross revenues equal 15 percent of the assets or gross revenues of the acquiring company, although under a proposed amendment to the form these tests would be lowered to 10 percent.

Additionally, when a company first comes under the Exchange Act reporting requirements, recent significant acquisitions should be reported in its initial registration statement filed under Section 12 of the Exchange Act.

Finally, in the prospectus of a Securities Act registration statement the staff will often require disclosure of a significant, recently acquired business. Financial statements are required for any business *to be* acquired or which *was* acquired after the date of the latest balance sheet furnished for the issuer.

MERGERS AND ACQUISITIONS—AND FRAUD

In addition to the disclosure protections, the Federal securities laws provide the investing public with protection against *fraud* in securities transactions. Section 10 of the Exchange Act and Rule 10b-5 promulgated by the Commission are the general antifraud provisions. Rule 10b-5 prohibits the use of any device or scheme to defraud, any misrepresentation, and all other fraudulent acts in connection with the purchase or sale of any security. It is important to remember that the application of this provision does *not* depend on the size of the company or the number of stockholders involved. It applies to "any person" and to all securities transactions. Section 17 of the Securities Act is similar in scope to Rule 10b-5 except that it applies only to *sales* of securities and not to purchases.

Rule 10b-5 applies to mergers and acquisitions in at least two ways. First, mergers and acquisitions involve either a "purchase" or "sale" of securities, or both. Thus, proxy statements and prospectuses used in connection with a merger or acquisition transaction are subject to scrutiny under Rule 10b-5. In the recent *Gamble-Skogmo* case (previously referred to), the Court found misrepresentations in a merger proxy statement to be in violation of Rule 10b-5 as well as the SEC proxy rules. Second, the purchase or sale of a security by an individual, in the open market or privately, prompted by "inside information" about an impending merger or acquisition not yet announced could result in a recovery under Rule 10b-5.

In recent years Rule 10b-5 has been relied on with increasing frequency by private litigants as a basis for civil actions against corporate fiduciaries. The Commission has also increased its activities in the Rule 10b-5 area in the past few years, as illustrated by the following case.

Widespread publicity was given to the Commission's civil action against Texas Gulf Sulphur Company *(SEC v. Texas Gulf Sulphur Co., et al.,* 258 F. Supp. 262, aff'd in part, rev'd in part, 401 F.2d 833, CA-2, 1968). It is essential that the legal implications of this case be understood by corporate executives involved in a merger or acquisition situation.

The allegations in the Commission's complaint related the following events: During November 1963 Texas Gulf Sulphur Company began test-drilling on company property near Timmins, Canada. The results of the initial tests were highly promising. For several months, pending additional land acquisition and further testing, the company withheld information about the potential new mining area. The Commission alleged that, during that time and on the basis of that information, certain directors, officers, and key employees of the company purchased shares of the company's stock and recommended the stock to friends who also purchased it. The insiders also bought calls entitling them to purchase the shares later and received stock options from the company.

The District Court found that on April 9, 1964, the value of the mineral discoveries was fully ascertained by the company's insiders. Between April 9 and April 16, when the company issued a press release announcing a major ore discovery, more stock purchases were made. After the public announcement the price of the stock soared.

The statutory basis for the Commission's suit was the alleged violation of the general antifraud rule. Rule 10b-5 prohibits *misrepresentations* in connection with the purchase or sale of any security. Misrepresentations include the *failure* to state material facts *as well as* the making of untrue statements.

The District Court held that before April 9, 1964, there was no abuse of inside information, since the information available to the corporate insiders up to that time did not constitute "material" facts. The stock purchases which had been made upon "hopes" and "educated guesses" were not in violation of Rule 10b-5. The purchases made between April 9, when the inside information became "material" and April 16, when the public announcement was issued, were held by the lower court to be in violation of Rule 10b-5.

On August 13, 1968, the Second Circuit Court of Appeals handed down its decision, in large part reversing the District Court. The appellate court affirmed that the purchases made after April 9 were in violation of Rule 10b-5. However, the higher court did not accept what it called the lower court's "narrow definition of materiality" and held that all transactions in Texas Gulf Sulphur stock by individuals apprised of the drilling results commencing in November 1963 were in violation of Rule 10b-5. The court held that outside investors should have the benefit of the same information which motivates insiders to engage in transactions in their company's stock.

The principles of corporate responsibility underlying the Texas Gulf Sulphur action were discussed by Hamer H. Budge, then a member and now chairman of the SEC, in an address before the New York Chapter of the American Society of Corporate Secretaries, New York City, November 18, 1965. Commissioner Budge stressed that corporate officers and directors are in fiduciary positions with respect to their company's shareholders and should not capitalize on inside information for personal profit by trading in their company's securities. Although corporations should make full and accurate disclosure of all information of material importance to shareholders and the investing public, the Commission recognizes that under certain circumstances there are legitimate business reasons for a corporation temporarily to withhold significant information from the public. In fact, in the *Texas Gulf Sulphur* case the Commission did not allege that the company's silence was wrongful. Thus the cardinal rule is that, when circumstances necessitate the delay of an important corporate announcement, insiders should refrain from trading in the company's stock until a full and accurate announcement is made.

The problem of when information becomes "material" exists when merger or acquisition negotiations are in progress. By applying the principles set forth above it can be seen that the terms of a merger should be announced as soon as possible. However, if there are legitimate reasons for delaying an announcement, corporate insiders should stay out of the market during any serious negotiations and should refrain from passing their inside information on to their friends and associates.

SHORT-SWING TRADING

In addition to Rule 10b-5, stockholders of companies subject to the Exchange Act's reporting requirements receive protection against the unfair use of information by insiders from Section 16(b) of that Act. Any profit realized by an officer, director, or a more than 10 percent stockholder from purchases-and-sales or sales-and-purchases within any six-month period inures to the company; and a stockholder's derivative suit may be instituted to effect recovery.

Under Section 16 an exchange of stock in a merger is considered to be both a "purchase" of the stock of the surviving company and a "sale" of the stock of the disappearing company. An exemption is provided for an exchange in a merger between a company and its 85-percent-owned subsidiary. The impact of Section 16(b) in corporate mergers is also mitigated somewhat by a Commission rule which exempts the disposition of a security pursuant to a merger if the security was purchased by exercising an option acquired more than six months earlier or acquired pursuant to the terms of an employment contract entered into more than six months before the exercise of the option.

Generally, however, profits realized by insiders in short-swing trading, in which one end of the transaction was exchange of stock in a merger, are subject to divestment back to the company. Thus, officers, directors, and 10 percent stockholders of a company being acquired by merger should avoid any purchases in their company's stock within six months before the merger date. In addition, if such a person is to become an officer, director, or 10 percent stockholder in the surviving corporation, he should avoid any sales in the stock of that company within six months before or after the merger.

FINANCIAL STATEMENT REQUIREMENTS

The Securities and Exchange Commission has broad statutory authority to prescribe the form and content of financial statements prepared for inclusion in filings with the Commission. This authority would permit the Commission to apply a rigid standard of uniformity in accounting procedures and in the classification of accounts for these filings. Historically, however, the Commission has stressed fair and adequate disclosure rather than strict uniformity, and it has relied heavily on the public accounting profession to aid in the maintenance of high standards of financial reporting. The reliance on the accounting profession has been primarily founded upon the independence of the public accountants and certified public accountants who issue their opinions as to the fairness of the financial statements filed. The profession has been primarily responsible for adopting and continuously re-examining the "generally accepted accounting principles" on which these opinions are based.

The Commission, however, does provide a framework within which the profession must operate. The statutes, rules, and forms establish what financial statements are required. Regulation S-X provides (a) the guidelines for preparation of the financial statements, (b) the test for independence of the certifying accountants, and (c) certain requirements as to the accountant's certificate. The Commission's Accounting Series Releases represent the Commission's opinion and position upon particular problems of importance. Finally, the daily schedule of conferences, conversations, and correspondence between the Commission's staff and registrants and independent accountants often provides a great deal of insight into staff views.

The financial statement and other financial data required to be included in a merger proxy statement and in an exchange-offer prospectus are essentially the same, although there is more flexibility in the proxy statement requirements. Generally, the Commission attempts to provide the shareholders of each company involved, acquiring and acquired, with sufficient financial data to enable them to observe how each company has performed in the past, the present financial condition of each company, and what effect the proposed merger or acquisition will have on their separate interests as stockholders.

More specifically, the registrant is required to furnish for each company a certified balance sheet as of the end of the last fiscal year, certified income statements for each of the three years prior to the balance sheet date, and a five-year summary of earnings which need not be certified although certification is always desirable.

In situations in which the most recent certified balance sheet available is more than 90 days old (or, under certain circumstances, more than six months old) at the date of filing, a more recent unaudited balance sheet is also required to be furnished. In these situations an unaudited income statement must be furnished for the recent interim period and for a comparable prior-year period.

In addition to the foregoing historical financial statements, certain so-called "pro forma" financial statements, prepared under the assumption that the merger or acquisition has already been completed, are required to show the financial condition of the combined entities. A pro forma combined balance sheet is necessary as of the date of the most recent historical balance sheet. The requirements for a pro forma combined summary of earnings depend on the basis used in accounting for the merger or acquisition. If the transaction is a "pooling of interests", the pro forma summary of earnings must be furnished for the entire five-year period corresponding to the historical summaries. If "purchase" accounting is used, the operations of the two companies are combined on a pro forma basis only for the most recent twelve-month period and any subsequent interim period. (For a discussion of the accounting aspects of poolings and purchases, see p. 86 of this volume.)

The other financial data which one may expect to find in a merger proxy statement or exchange-offer prospectus include the following: (a) a tabular presentation of the current capitalization (long-term debt and stockholders' equity) of each company and the combined pro forma result; (b) a table showing the per-share earnings of each company and the pro forma combined result (five years for a "pooling of interests" and one year and interim period for a purchase); and (c) the current per-share book values of each company separately and in combination to show the effect of the combining transaction.

Accounting to Merge By

JOHN L. HARVEY

I F A REVIEW of recent business combinations reveals nothing else, it clearly suggests that success in corporate marriage, as in matrimony generally, is a sometime thing.

Although no amount of precaution can guarantee that the married pair will live, as the fairy tales have it, happily ever after, the chances of a business combination's achieving its objectives can be substantially improved by careful investigation, in advance of negotiations, of all related factors. Many of these factors—the effect of larger markets; economies in distribution, manufacturing, and research; the benefits of increased staff specialization; and the effect of combining personnel, for example—are beyond the scope of this discussion. Much of the investigation, however, does involve accounting. Pro forma financial statements should be prepared to show the effects of the merger on the financial position and on the future earnings of the combined companies. The purpose of this discussion is to consider two areas of accounting that should be familiar to anyone who plans to become involved in a business combination.*

* The term "business combination" is used in the literature of accounting to describe the transaction in which two or more business entities are brought together for the purpose of carrying on their activities under a common management. The term includes combinations effected in any of several ways: a statutory merger or consolidation, the acquisition of shares of one corporation in exchange for cash or

John L. Harvey, CPA, is administrative partner of the Pittsburgh office of Arthur Young & Company.

The first of these areas has to do with the comparability of financial data. Although accounting has been correctly described as the universal language of business, it is spoken in a variety of dialects which need to be studied to be completely understood.

The second area relates to the accounting principles or rules that must be followed in accounting for business combinations under various circumstances. These circumstances determine whether, in accounting jargon, the combination is a "pooling of interests" or a "purchase," the accounting for each of which is different.

MAKING ACCOUNTING DATA COMPARABLE

Corporation executives are generally most familiar with the accounting practices followed in their own company, and as a result they may fall into the error of assuming that all companies, including companies with which they are contemplating merger, perform their accounting on the same basis. This, of course, is not necessarily so. An early step that must be taken in planning any corporate combination is to develop pro forma data to indicate the results that might be anticipated from the merger. For this to be done in a meaningful manner, historical accounting information prepared on a comparable basis must be obtained from each company involved. Generally, the basis will be that used by the acquiring company. Some of the matters that must be considered in establishing comparability of accounting data are discussed below.

Inventory and Asset Valuation

While the broad accounting rule relating to the value of inventories is that they be carried at the lower of cost or market, there are different ways of determining both of these measures. Cost, as we know, may be

---

for shares of another, or the acquisition of the net assets of one corporation in exchange for cash or for shares of another. For convenience, the terms "merger" and "acquisition" are used interchangeably in this discussion to refer to business combinations of all types. For information as to the accounting guidelines, see Accounting Research Bulletin No. 48, *Business Combinations,* issued in January 1957 by the Committee on Accounting Procedure of the American Institute of Certified Public Accountants, and subsequent amendments in Accounting Principles Board Opinion No. 6 (paragraph 22) and Opinion No. 10 (paragraph 5). For more extensive discussions of the subject, see Accounting Research Study No. 5, *A Critical Study of Accounting for Business Combinations* (1963), and Accounting Research Study No. 10, *Accounting for Goodwill* (1968), published by the Accounting Research Division of the AICPA.

arrived at under a number of concepts, including FIFO, LIFO, averages, or standards. The most confusing to the executive who is not familiar with these concepts is likely to be the so-called "last in, first out" (LIFO) approach. This method, in effect, values the inventory on hand at each year-end at the original cost of the same quantity of inventory at the beginning of the year—thus perpetuating, in some instances, costs of twenty years ago. The universality of inflation is well recognized; and any inventory purchased twenty years ago would almost certainly cost more today. Thus, when different inventory methods are in use, it may be necessary to make special studies to state inventory costs on the same basis for use in merger discussions. This can be a complicated and lengthy process.

"Market" is a more stable term than cost, but even here some caution is advisable. Are we talking replacement market, as we usually are in connection with raw materials, or sales market, as we usually are in connection with finished goods? If we are talking sales market, the inventory should reflect disposable value less cost of disposal. And just what is "cost of disposal"? There is considerable leeway in the answer to this question. Some companies reduce inventory value further to permit a normal profit on the eventual sale of the inventory. This is permissible, under certain conditions, but it is not mandatory. *You have to find out how the language is spoken in the company with which you are contemplating merger.*

The treatment of supplies inventories varies from one company to another. Some companies expense supply items, while others carry them in inventory. Similar variations will be found in the treatment of spare parts, small tools, and other such items.

The distinction between capitalized expenditures and repair and maintenance costs is often a matter of judgment. Some companies follow the so-called "conservative" policy of charging off many marginal items at the time of purchase. Full or partial indirect costs may be added to direct costs incurred by the company in constructing and installing its own fixed assets. Major repairs may be expensed, even though the life of the asset is extended beyond the life originally estimated. This approach is "conservative" in all respects except in the computation of future earnings, which have been relieved of the depreciation charges otherwise applicable to such future periods. Other companies, in an effort to increase current earnings at the expense of future earnings, may capitalize the marginal items expensed by the company with which they plan to merge.

No discussion of fixed-asset accounting, as it relates to mergers, would be complete without reference to the need to determine the tax as well as the book basis of fixed assets. Obviously, assets with low tax bases are less valuable because of their reduced ability to decrease future income taxes through depreciation deductions. Deferred tax accounting should have been followed in these circumstances.

While we are on the subject of fixed assets it might be well to note that the method of amortizing the cost of fixed assets to expense may vary. Depreciation in many cases is also a matter of judgment. What is the useful life of an asset or group of assets? Physical life may be accurately estimated on the basis of past experience, but the end of usefulness, which depends on such unpredictable factors as obsolescence of both machine design and machine use, defies accurate determination. Even when the useful life of an asset or group of assets is accurately determinable, the annual depreciation expense may vary as a result of the various depreciation methods which are presently permissible under generally accepted accounting principles. Straight-line depreciation, the sum-of-the-years-digits method, and the double (or 150 percent) declining-balance approach are some of the ways of determining what amount of fixed-asset cost is to be charged to expense in any accounting period. *The answers indeed come out different.*

Research and Development Costs

Expenditures in this broad area may be expensed or capitalized depending on individual circumstances. In theory, since R&D costs are incurred to benefit future earnings, they should be capitalized on the balance sheet and amortized over the future years in which those earnings will be realized. But the very nature of R&D activity is such that it is difficult to know with any degree of certainty what the future benefits, if any, will be. Consequently, many companies write off this type of expense as incurred. *You have to get down to cases.*

Pension Plans

There was in the past a wide range of alternatives that affected pension costs. Some companies provided each year only enough to pay the actual pensions disbursed ("pay as you go") or to fund the present value of pensions which became vested during the year. Other companies provided current service costs (that is, benefits "earned" during the year) or current service costs plus interest accrued on the unfunded past service costs. Still others added to current service costs an amount designed to amortize past service costs over a period of years, the length of which might vary widely. And some companies reduced pension costs (either current service, past service, or both) when the market values of securities held in pension funds increased during the year.

Opinion No. 8, *Accounting for the Cost of Pension Plans,* issued in November 1966 by the AICPA Accounting Principles Board, greatly reduced the number of acceptable alternatives in pension cost accounting, but there remains, nevertheless, considerable latitude in the determination of periodic pension expense. It might be noted in passing that, at the time Opinion No. 8 was issued, many companies made retroactive adjustments to conform their pension accounting to the new guidelines.

The problem for anyone conducting a premerger investigation is that of developing pension expense data for different companies on a comparable basis. These pension data must be developed from actuarial reports, and if such reports are not available their preparation will entail considerable time and expense. Certain actuarial assumptions—the amount of future income that will be generated by pension funds, employee turnover rates, mortality and accident probabilities (based on various experience tables available to actuaries), etc.—will affect pension costs, and these assumptions will also need to be studied if comparable figures are to be obtained.

Of course, if a different pension plan will be in effect after the merger, this will have to be considered in estimating future earning potentials. Such a projection should reflect pension expenses computed under the method that will survive the merger.

Executive Incentive Plans

In some companies cash bonuses are paid, and these involve direct charges to current earnings. In other companies, stock option plans are used as incentives. Qualified stock option plans normally conserve cash and have no direct effect on income; they tend, however, to reduce per-share earnings and dilute stockholders' equity. Nonstatutory stock option plans conserve cash but may have an adverse effect on income.

Income Taxes

There are a number of accounting problems which relate to the reporting of income taxes. These arise principally when significant items entering into the determination of taxable income are not included in the income statement or when significant items affecting the income statement do not enter into the determination of taxable income. Generally accepted accounting principles may require a provision for possible future losses that is deductible for tax purposes only when the losses occur. Good accounting requires that income for any given accounting period be reduced only by that income tax expense which can be properly allocated to it. Where the tax expense in any period differs from the tax payable, the difference is recorded as deferred tax.

Suppose that certain start-up costs are deferred for book purposes but deducted currently for tax purposes. Proper accounting requires a liability for the income taxes that will be payable on future income as a result of the current tax deduction. The offsetting deferred tax expense augments the reduced tax currently payable in the current year so as to produce the tax expense allocable to the reported income. The deferred tax will be restored to income through reduced income taxes in future years when the deferred charges are amortized against income, with no reduction in current income taxes—thereby, again, producing an income tax expense that is properly allocable to the reported income. In the case of estimated liabilities recorded on the books but not deductible currently for tax purposes, the accounting is similar to that described above but, of course, in the opposite direction. In all tax allocation decisions, including the decision as to when allocations are necessary, there is an element of judgment which may distort the comparability of financial data.

If the deferral of taxes is for a long period, it may be appropriate for evaluation purposes to discount the future tax payments, on a compound interest basis, to their present value. It should be noted, however, that the Accounting Principles Board has not sanctioned such accounting in financial statements, pending further study of the broad subject of present-value accounting.

Revenue agent examinations may require adjustment of prior-year income tax expense. Such adjustments may be included in the current income statement if they are not material. If the amounts are material enough to distort current income they may be charged or credited to surplus as a prior-period adjustment.

The loss carryover provisions of the Internal Revenue Code also create reporting problems. The prior-year taxes refundable as a result of the carryback of a current loss should be included in the income statement of the loss year. When, however, the loss is carried forward, the benefit cannot usually be recognized until the future year in which profit is earned and the tax thereon reduced as a result of the loss carryforward. In order to make these two situations more comparable for premerger investigation purposes, it may be helpful to take advantage of hindsight and restate the tax benefit from loss carryforwards to the year of the loss rather than the year of the benefit.

In those cases in which the company to be acquired is, or has been, part of a group which has filed consolidated tax returns, or part of a group which has done financial reporting on a consolidated basis, it must be recognized that neither the taxes paid nor the tax provisions recorded on the books are necessarily indicative of the taxes which will be applicable to its future operations, under new ownership. Any pro forma financial statements should substitute for the recorded tax provision a provision appropriate to the postmerger corporate situation.

While this discussion has dealt with the development of meaningful historical tax data, one purpose of such data is to permit a determination of tax expense in the postacquisition period. The historical data must, of course, be modified to reflect the altered tax posture resulting from the merger.

Extraordinary Items

One of the more perplexing problems in accounting relates to the treatment of extraordinary items in the determination of net income. Typical of such items are the following:

☐ **The disposal or sale of a substantial portion of the fixed assets.**

☐ **A substantial gain or loss on the sale or disposal of investments or securities.**

☐ **The sale or other disposition of a subsidiary, affiliate, or division.**

☐ **The effect of a significant change in the valuation basis of inventories, investments, and fixed assets (for example, to conform to a "tax" basis).**

☐ **Substantial foreign exchange adjustments.**

☐ **Nonrecurring plant expenses.**

☐ **Items applicable to prior years, including both those accounted for directly and those involving a correction of provisions made in prior years.**

Although Opinion No. 9 of the AICPA Accounting Principles Board, *Reporting the Results of Operations,* issued in December 1966, has established the rule that the effect of extraordinary events and transactions, properly segregated, must be included in the determination of net income, this treatment was made mandatory only for fiscal periods beginning after December 31, 1966. Reports on prior periods may show extraordinary items in retained earnings, in income, or in a gray area between the two captioned "Special items." Even under Opinion No. 9 certain prior-period adjustments may be recorded properly as adjustments of the opening balance of retained earnings.

Generally speaking, companies contemplating merger are more interested in net income as a measure of future earning capacity than in historical earnings. Consequently, all extraordinary or unusual items should be segregated and given separate consideration in any merger evaluation. An attempt should be made to restate prior years to reflect subsequently recorded adjustments in such years.

In seeking out unusual items in net income, it is necessary to review the regular items of income or expense, any special section of the income statement used especially for extraordinary items, footnotes to the financial statements, and even the president's letter or financial review. For earlier years "Special items" and retained earnings must also be reviewed.

POOLINGS AND PURCHASES

For accounting purposes business combinations are generally classified as either (a) poolings of interests or (b) purchases.

The principal characteristic of a pooling of interests is that substantially all the equity interests in the predecessor corporation continue in the surviving corporation without significant change. The major business activities of each of the predecessor corporations should continue in the surviving corporation, and, ideally, the management of each of the predecessor corporations should continue in the surviving corporation. If this principal characteristic is not present, then the combination is considered a purchase.

In its simplest and purest form, a pooling takes place when Company A exchanges its common stock (either treasury or unissued shares) for the common stock held by the stockholders of Company B. A pure purchase occurs when Company A buys the common stock of B for cash or its equivalent. In real life, however, business combinations often are neither simple nor pure. Some of the sophisticated "real life" variations will be described after we have considered the accounting generally accepted as being appropriate in each of these two types of business combination.

Basic Accounting Treatment

In the case of a pooling of interests, the accounting is based on the premise that the companies come together into a single reporting entity but otherwise remain unchanged. Assets, liabilities, equities, revenues, and expenses that were once reported separately are now simply added together to produce a single accounting report, without change except for the capital accounts. Thus, for example, fixed assets are still carried at their cost to the predecessor companies. Earnings retained in the business are the sum of the earnings that had been retained by each of the separate corporations.

The accounting for a purchase reflects the fact that the life of the purchased company has ended and only the acquiring company has a continuing existence. The purchased assets are recorded on the books of the acquiring corporation at their cost; a new basis of accounting is established. Purchased intangible assets may have to be recorded. The purchased company is gone, and with it all of its retained earnings. Reported retained earnings are those of the acquiring company only.

Some Special Problems in Poolings

As indicated above, corporate mergers are often complicated affairs, and it sometimes becomes a difficult matter to determine whether a business combination is a pooling or a purchase. The first requirement for a pooling is that the owners retain approximately the same interests in the new setup that they had held previously. Suppose, however, that a minority group of shareholders did not approve of the merger and demanded to be bought out for cash—does this invalidate the pooling concept? Since amounts in these situations have historically been small, the answer has generally been "No." What would be the answer, however, if larger amounts were involved? In other situations, a company may have acquired partial ownership for cash and then subsequently acquired the remaining stock through an exchange of stock. Did the original cash deal make it impossible to account for the second transaction as a pooling? Generally, accountants have felt not. Then the question was raised: Is a time lag necessary between the first part of the acquisition and the second in order to use pooling accounting? There did not seem to be much logic in requiring such a lag. It was situations such as these that resulted in the formulation of the concept of the "part pooling–part purchase." Under this approach, a single transaction may be accounted for as a pooling to the extent that the pooling requirements are met and as a purchase for the rest of the acquisition. If both common stock and cash were being exchanged, the value of the stock to the total consideration would determine the percentage of retained earnings of the acquired company that could be carried forward into the new entity. The same percentage would be applied to fixed assets to determine the amount that would be carried forward into the combined enterprise at historical cost. The remaining fixed assets would be carried at current value under the purchase concept.

In other situations a pooling may be desirable but some of the shareholders may need immediate cash. Suppose that such shareholders were to sell their shares to outside parties shortly after the pooling had been completed—would this invalidate the pooling, since shareholder equity interests had changed? The accounting profession and the Securities and Exchange Commission have set up an informal "25 percent rule" as the practical limit to any such selloff. How long must any sales in excess of

25 percent be delayed after the pooling? Obviously it would be impractical to say that shareholders could never change. There must, on the other hand, be some limitation in the absence of a change in circumstances. No definite time period has developed as yet in practice, although some accountants feel that the sale of a second 25 percent within the second year does not invalidate the pooling.

One of the corollaries to the continuity-of-ownership requirement for a pooling is that minority interests should not be created. As a practical matter, however, minority interests of up to 5 percent may not disqualify a transaction as a pooling if it can be shown that a genuine effort is being made to reduce the percentage. Another change in ownership which may occur without disqualifying a transaction from full pooling treatment is the sale to the company for cash of some portion of stock by elderly stockholders in a family-owned corporation whose management has been turned over to the younger generation.

The continuing-equity-interest requirement for poolings must be kept in mind when securities other than common stock are issued. Neither stock purchase warrants nor debt securities, even when convertible into common stock, meet the continuity-of-interests requirement. Ordinarily, nonvoting preferred stock does not qualify; but, in some cases, it may be qualified by appropriate convertibility features. Callable preferred stock generally does not qualify unless it can be shown that a call is extremely unlikely. Voting preferred stock may qualify if there is a reasonable pro rata division of voting power in proportion to economic interest.

It may safely be concluded that most pooling problems relate to the issue of continuity of ownership. The matters of continuity of management and continuity of business, however, cannot be overlooked entirely. If the management of one of the combining companies is eliminated or made disproportionately small, a purchase may be indicated. There does not need to be, however, any written contractual obligation with respect to the continuity of management. If the top executives of each constituent corporation are brought into the combination in capacities comparable to those they previously held, there will be no continuity-of-management problem.

If a significant portion of the business of one or more of the companies entering into a merger is sold or abandoned shortly after the transaction, the pooling treatment may not be appropriate. This is the substance of the continuity-of-business rule. There have been cases, however, where a business and accounting entity has properly combined in a pooling even though related components of a larger corporate complex were disposed of for reasons unrelated to the pooling.

Some Special Problems in Purchases

As described above, the accounting for a full pooling is accomplished by adding together the figures in the financial statements of the component corporations. In the case of a purchase, however, there are some special accounting problems that should be considered. The assets must be valued at cost to the purchasing company, which is determined by adding together the consideration given and the liabilities assumed. Sometimes the value of the consideration given is difficult to determine. This might occur, for example, when a new issue of preferred stock is used. Even the liabilities being assumed, if they include such items as provisions for product warranties, pending legal suits, or income taxes in dispute, may be difficult to evaluate. In such cases it may be appropriate to arrive at the cost by using the current market value of the stock of the company being purchased. The cost of the assets purchased must be determined by applying sound judgment to all available data.

The second problem relates to allocating this total cost to the separate assets being purchased. This is a specialized aspect of the general problem of any "basket" purchase. Assets such as cash, marketable securities, accounts receivable, and prepaid expenses have fairly fixed dollar values that are not subject to judgment determinations. The costs allocated to these assets are their cash realizable values.

One word of caution: The cash realizable value of cash equivalent items may not be their book value. Marketable securities may be carried at cost, which could be substantially greater or less than cash realizable value. Accounts receivable must be reduced by the estimated amount that will not be collected from the debtors. On the other hand, items carried at no value on the books may, in fact, have a very real value and hence should be included in the basket. Supplies, small tools, patents, trademarks, blueprints, and a host of other items fall into this category. Deferred debits and credits as well as reserves should be carefully reviewed; only if they represent benefits or liabilities to the purchaser should they be added to or deducted from the "basket."

The allocation of costs to inventory can be made only by considering the salability of the stock, costs to complete, market values, and so forth. The use of FIFO, LIFO, average, or other cost concepts may affect the answer. Fixed assets are generally valued through appraisal, and the sum of the various asset values is then compared to the total cost. If the total cost is greater, it indicates that something else was purchased: perhaps a going concern, "know-how," reputation, or some other intangible asset. This is then recorded and described in some appropriate manner. Perhaps the best caption would simply be "Excess of total consideration over cost assigned to net tangible assets acquired."

If, on the other hand, the total cost is less than the value assigned to the tangible assets, we have what is referred to as a "bargain purchase." In such circumstances the accounting treatment should be based on the factual situation in each particular case. Perhaps the "basket" cost was low because of an impending loss that should be provided for. Possibly an unrealistic depreciation policy in prior years requires a reduction in fixed-asset costs. In certain situations inventories may be restated to LIFO costs below current costs. If, on the other hand, the bargain purchase was created because of the prospect of low future earnings, the most appropriate accounting would be to record the excess of assigned values over cost as a balance sheet credit so described, and to amortize the amount to income over the period of anticipated low earnings. The once-permitted practice of recording the credit at the time of the purchase in capital surplus is no longer possible under generally accepted accounting principles.

Advantages and Disadvantages

In a pooling, comparative prior-year figures are reported as though the component companies had been combined in such prior periods. This requires a restatement of all historical information. In a purchase, comparative prior-year figures are the historical figures of the acquiring company only, and operations of the purchased company are included only from the date of its acquisition.

In a purchase, depreciation and amortization are based on the purchase cost, which might differ from the depreciation of the acquired company. Since current costs are generally higher than historical costs, a purchase will in most cases result in higher depreciation for the merged operation than the combined historical depreciation of the component companies. This is a fact that cannot be overlooked in projecting future earnings. It is, in fact, the desire to avoid these higher depreciation charges that has made the pooling concept so popular.

When purchase cost exceeds the value of tangible assets, the result (as described above) is the creation of some sort of intangible asset. Such assets are divided into two types: those which have a limited period of usefulness (patents, copyrights, leases, licenses, fixed-term franchises) and those which have no determinable life (general goodwill, going-concern value, trade names, secret processes, subscription lists, perpetual franchises, organization costs). Assets of the first type must be amortized by systematic charges in the income statement over their useful lives.

Assets of the second type need not be amortized but may be amortized, at the discretion of the company, on the ground that no asset will really last forever. The creation of intangibles and the need to amortize such assets (often without tax benefit) is a second common reason for companies to strive to create a pooling rather than a purchase.

We have considered some disadvantages of treating a business combination as a purchase. In certain circumstances, however, there may be serious disadvantages to pooling. The first of these is commonly described as "dilution." Since a pooling requires the issuance of additional stock, the earnings per share and stockholders' equity per share may be reduced. This, of course, will not happen in every case. If the earnings of the acquired company are greater than the product of the number of shares issued and the earnings per share of the acquiring company, the earnings per share for the acquiring company's stockholders will increase. The use of convertible securities may result in increased immediate earnings per share through leverage, but substantial potential dilution may be inherent in the conversion terms. Also, if the merger creates efficiencies in operations that did not exist in the separate companies, this may reduce any "dilution" effect. A similar pattern can be visualized with respect to stockholders' equity.

A second disadvantage of poolings is that the acquiring company cannot generally obtain for tax purposes the higher current-cost basis for the fixed assets acquired. This in turn means that future tax depreciation charges will be lower and income taxes higher. One major problem in this whole area is that the tax interests of the buyer and the seller may be diametrically opposed.

RESIDUAL SECURITIES

One of the important practical considerations for a company contemplating the issuance of securities in an acquisition is the expected effect on earnings per share. This depends in part on whether the securities will be considered "residual securities." If a security is residual, the interest of its holders in the corporation's earnings must be taken into account in determining earnings per common share.

As this is being written the question of what constitutes a residual security and some of the questions that arise in making per-share calculations are being studied by the Accounting Principles Board of the American Institute of Certified Public Accountants. The Board discussed residual securities in its Opinion No. 9, issued in 1966, which it may soon revise. In Opinion No. 9, the Board stated: "When more than one class of common stock is outstanding, or when an outstanding security has participating dividend rights with the common stock, or when an outstanding security clearly derives a major portion of its value from its conversion rights or its common stock characteristics, such securities should be considered 'residual securities' . . . ."

The Securities and Exchange Commission discussed residual securities in a statement (Release No. 4910, Securities Act of 1933; Release No. 8336, Securities Exchange Act of 1934) issued in June 1968. In the Release the Commission stated: "In general, *if at the time of issuance of a convertible security in an acquisition,* the terms are such as to result in immediate material dilution to pro forma earnings per share, assuming conversion, then that security should be considered a residual security whether or not a majority of its value may be derived from its conversion rights."

The question of whether a security is residual and, if so, the effect on earnings per share must be considered in weighing the advantages and disadvantages of the use of alternative securities in mergers and acquisitions, as well as in other financial transactions.

CONCLUSION

Although successful corporate mergers are a result more of art than of science, the degree of certainty that such a combination will be a success can be significantly increased by extensive investigation and planning before the marriage is consummated. Many groups should participate in such work. Marketing, personnel, production, research and development, corporate counsel, the corporate secretary, and (perhaps most important of all) top management, all must make their contribution. Without in any way intending to minimize the importance of these contributions, it has been the purpose of this discussion to suggest the vitally important part that the accountant plays in any plans involving business combinations. In addition to having a good general background, the accountant assigned to the merger team must have specialized knowledge in accounting for poolings and purchases. Only then will he be able to provide the technical know-how necessary to develop pro forma balance sheets and earnings projections on which the decsion to merge or not to merge, and subsequent decisions as to what form the combination should take, must ultimately be based.

III

Financial Considerations

"Remember, it is as easy to marry
a rich woman as a poor woman."

W. M. THACKERAY, *Pendennis*

How Buyer and Seller
Look at a Merger

CHARLES G. GILLETTE

BUYING A USED BUSINESS is more complicated than buying a used car; there is more involved than the condition of the commodity and its price. To effect a merger of businesses is to build an agreement between the motivations and objectives of the seller and the motivations and objectives of the buyer. These influences, both corporate and personal, may separate the seller from the buyer more than any gulf of dollars. It is from the perspective of their individual motives and goals that a buyer and a seller will judge and value each other. A merger transaction occurs when the differences between these motives and goals are understood and bridged by negotiation.

Though it is not sufficiently recognized in the literature of mergers and acquisitions, the managements of publicly held companies are motivated by quite different concerns from those which motivate the owner-managements of privately held companies. I am not referring here to the fact that hired-management interests may differ from owner-management interests; I mean that the *owners* of publicly held companies have different motivations from those of the owners of privately held companies. To understand how these different motivations, in combination with a variety of mathematical, psychological, and corporate political

---

Charles G. Gillette, CPA, is a partner in the home office of Arthur Young & Company in New York. He is responsible for coordinating the firm's services to clients in connection with mergers and acquisitions.

influences, may affect a merger negotiation, let us examine the approach of a typical buyer, a publicly held company, and the very different concerns of a privately held seller.

THE BUYER'S VIEW

Generally speaking, the stockholders of publicly held companies are interested in having the highest possible price placed on their stock in the public marketplace. Usually the stockholders can rely on the managers of their company, whether or not they are also stockholders, to reflect this interest faithfully in their day-to-day management of the business, including the conduct of the company's acquisitions program.

This compelling interest in a high stock price is not characteristic of all publicly held companies, but it is characteristic of those publicly held companies which seek to achieve growth through acquisitions. And there are sound reasons for this interest. Publicly held companies usually use their common stock, or securities convertible into their common stock, as the currency with which to buy other companies. The higher the price of their stock, the fewer shares they need issue to pay for a given acquisition. The fewer shares issued, the greater the percentage of equity which remains in the hands of the original shareholders.

The Glamor Stock as a Money Machine

Consider as well that the smaller the total number of shares outstanding after an acquisition, the higher will be the earnings per share. This increase in earnings per share from an acquisition with a high-price stock provides a double-barreled advantage. First, with a steady price/earnings ratio, the price per share goes up in proportion to the earnings per share. If the P/E ratio is 20, the price goes up $2 for each additional dime of earnings per share. Secondly, since a P/E ratio is favorably influenced by a rising earnings trend, if the acquisition produces an improvement in earnings per share, other things being equal, it is reasonable to expect an increased P/E ratio. The combined impact of increased earnings per share and an improved P/E ratio is a sharp increase in the price of the stock.

The two hypothetical cases shown in Exhibit 1 illustrate the different effects of acquisition with a low-priced stock and with a high-priced stock. The higher-priced stock of publicly held acquirer "High" achieves a high price/earnings ratio from the merger. If you can visualize acquirer "High" making another acquisition, this time with its $26 stock (up from

Exhibit 1. Effects of Acquisition with Low-Priced vs. High-Priced Stock

	Before Merger	After Merger	Before Merger	After Merger
ACQUIRED COMPANY				
Earnings	$500,000		$500,000	
Sale price	$5,000,000		$5,000,000	
Shares required to acquire	500,000		250,000	
	Acquirer "Low"		*Acquirer "High"*	
PUBLIC COMPANY				
Earnings	$1,000,000	$1,500,000	$1,000,000	$1,500,000
Shares	1,000,000	1,500,000	1,000,000	1,250,000
Earnings per share	$1.00	$1.00	$1.00	$1.20
P/E ratio	10	10	20	22
Price per share	$10.00	$10.00	$20.00	$26.40

$20) with similar economic gains, and then another and another—each with such results—it appears that a successful acquisition program is a money machine. Of course, the situation is not that simple, particularly from the viewpoint of a new stockholder—whether he buys his stock or receives it in a merger. To the new stockholder such an acquisition program bears some resemblance to a chain letter: If he comes in early in the chain of events, he gains, but if he comes in just before the chain breaks he will lose. This is not to say that all of the chains will break. Some of them will break.

This compelling interest in stock price and price/earnings ratio places a serious constraint on the acquisition flexibility of a publicly held company. Most publicly held companies feel that they cannot afford to acquire a company even with the most excellent long-term prospects if the effect over the next two years would be a reduction in earnings per share. Thus Charles R. Allen, vice president and chief financial officer of TRW (a significant acquirer of companies), declared, "The price of the acquisition must be such that it will not dilute earnings per share on a fully converted basis *now* or in the future."[1] (Emphasis supplied.)

[1] In a speech before the National Association of Investment Clubs' "How to Invest" Show, Chicago, Ill., November 8, 1967.

Who Is the Buyer Who Can Wait for Earnings?

This point of view is typical and, for the business reasons just discussed, sound and rational. However, its practical effect is to impose limitations on the kinds of businesses which can be acquired by most publicly held companies. There are healthy and potentially profitable businesses which are unattractive to these buyers because the exploitation of their profit potential requires a period of product development or market development before they can report significant earnings. Such a company should not expect to make a profitable deal with a publicly held company, because, in the words of Mr. Allen, it will dilute earnings *now,* and this fact will cause a heavy discounting of any *future* earnings potential.

The seller of a business offering primarily future potential should recognize this fact of the marketplace and seek a different kind of buyer. This different kind of buyer will generally be a private investor or a privately owned company not concerned with the immediate market value of its securities. This will mean that the buyer will not have a publicly marketed stock to offer. Therefore the seller will probably end up taking cash in a taxable transaction rather than getting a marketable stock. The seller of a low-earnings, high-potential business who is so obsessed with the idea of a tax-free exchange that he will not accept a cash transaction is likely to be unable to dispose of his business or to have to dispose of it at a price far below its intrinsic value, thereby losing more in the sale price than he saves by avoiding the capital gains tax.

The Importance of Intrinsic Values

Thus far I have emphasized the importance of current earnings in preference to long-term potential earnings. Though this concern is justified by the practical pressure on most managements to maintain current earnings, it does not mean that long-term potential is ignored. Not only must a company protect and improve current earnings but, for the same reasons, over a longer view, it will seek a continuing trend of earnings growth. Furthermore, a management which is truly responsible to its shareholders must be interested in the intrinsic value of the business acquired as well as the short-term effect on stock prices.

Present Value of Discounted Cash Flow

Carrying the idea of intrinsic value to its ultimate logic leads one to the "present-value" concept—that is, the present discounted value of future values. There are all sorts of practical difficulties in the application of this concept, but it is still worthwhile as one technique for determining whether a business is really worth the price proposed to be paid. At the least, its application forces the buyer to face some fundamental issues that might otherwise be ignored or overlooked.

Very briefly, the present-value concept involves taking all of a company's future net cash flow and discounting it at some determined rate compounded at reasonable intervals, such as annually. (Anyone who makes such a calculation using a rate such as 6 percent is probably making a gross error. Business equities should involve a considerably higher yield, generally ranging from 10 percent on up.)

Theoretically, one should look to the cash flow for the infinite future, but as a practical matter there is a point not too far in the future where the present value is so small and the uncertainties of realization are so great that cash flow beyond that point can be ignored. Just as an example, using 10 percent compounded annually, a dollar ten years in the future is worth only 39 cents today. At 15 percent, the 1979 dollar is worth 25 cents and the 1989 dollar only 6 cents today. It follows that estimating a company's cash flow for the next ten or fifteen years should disclose most of the value of the business, except in those few cases which involve truly massive accumulations of noncash wealth.

The first practical difficulty in applying this concept is in determining the interest rate to be used in discounting future values to their present value. The question of the true cost of capital is a complex and controversial subject. Some of the difficulties are these:

☐ **A fair return or price for equity capital is higher than the cost of borrowed capital.**

☐ **It is not clear whether what is considered a fair return for the cost of equity capital is applicable when high-P/E-ratio stock is used in an equity transaction. An acquirer with a P/E ratio of 50 (from one point of view, a 2 percent return on equity capital) might justify an acquisition with a 5 percent return for the "money machine" reasons discussed earlier.**

☐ **It is far from clear whether the interest or discount rate applied to an acquisition for stock should be discounted completely on the basis of the cost of equity capital. In many such transactions, the acquired company adds to the acquirer's borrowing base and thereby permits further expansion of the business (without additional equity) to an extent which would have been impossible in the absence of the acquisition.**

More serious than the difficulties involved in choosing an interest rate is the very practical problem of making a reasonably accurate projection of the future operations of the business to be acquired. Nevertheless, this is often a worthwhile undertaking for the prudent buyer. No one should buy a business on its historical record without an opinion as to its future performance. The buyer should have an opinion as to whether future performance will be the same as, better than, or worse than past performance. In forming this opinion he should consider both cash flow and earnings. He should be able to reduce his opinion to approximate numbers. If he cannot reduce his opinion to approximate numbers, it may be that he is not very clear about what he really thinks.

A thorough present-value approach will culminate in an integrated set of projected annual financial statements, including income statements, balance sheets, and cash flows. Sometimes it may be necessary and appropriate to shortcut this process by estimating the cash flow without the integrated financial statements, but this approach increases the risk of error. For example, a projection which involves substantial growth in earnings probably has included in it a growth in sales, with the attendant inventory and receivables funding requirements. This can cause a heavy lag in cash flow. In other words, a 20 percent per annum growth rate does not mean a 20 percent per annum increase in cash flow; it may even mean a negative cash flow, continuingly negative until such time as the growth stops.

The Leverage-Minded Buyer

The subject of cash flow leads directly into the question of leverage. One of the major reasons why an acquisition of a small company by a large company frequently makes business sense is an improvement in the utilization of equity capital. Many a small-business man is proud of the day when he finally gets his company out of debt. The sophisticated, leverage-minded acquirer, however, is ashamed if his company is out of debt, and quickly looks for investment opportunities to tie up additional funds—not *his* funds, of course, but borrowed funds. He regards it as his managerial duty to make a profit on the difference between an entrepreneurial return on invested capital and a lower rate which he pays for borrowed money. This is "leverage."

The leverage-minded buyer *always* evaluates the leverage potential of a proposed merger. The seller may be underleveraged, overextended, or just right. The buyer also may be underleveraged, overextended, or just right. Thus, there are nine different combinations possible in regard to the leverage situations of the seller and the buyer. If the buyer is relatively limited in his resources for obtaining and using capital, he will be attracted by a seller whose leverage situation is the opposite of his own; for instance, the merging of an underleveraged company with an overextended company will produce a combination closer to "just right."

The more flexible (and perhaps more successful) buyer will not limit himself to this balancing kind of a match, but will assume that he can always find, through a variety of other transactions, ways and means to adjust his leverage, up or down. In evaluating a possible acquisition, he will simply add to his projected cash flow the unrealized borrowing potential implicit in the balance sheet of the underleveraged seller or subtract from cash flow the cash requirements of the overextended seller. This relatively simple calculation can be crucial to the acquisition decision of a sophisticated buyer. In many cases involving an underleveraged seller the true net purchase price—that is, the price or the net asset requirements of the acquired businesses—computes out to be only a small fraction of the sale price which appears in the contract between the parties, because the buyer will turn around and borrow the rest of the money on the basis of the seller's relatively debt-free balance sheet.

Caveat Emptor

In discussing cash flow I observed that the buyer must have an opinion as to the future performance of the selling firm. In this connection, he must be aware that his opinion is no more than an opinion. He may, from bitter experience, know that the most reasonable and careful projections never quite match the future as it unfolds, and that sometimes there is no resemblance at all between forecast and actuality. The buyer must consider his risks. He must consider his risks not only mathematically but also psychologically and politically. The psychological and political considerations will cause many buyers to be more cautious than they would be from a purely mathematical pricing of the risk.

One risk that pervades every acquisition derives from the fact that the seller knows his business in a way that the buyer can never hope to know it—until it is too late. There is always the possibility of some impending disaster well known to the seller but hidden from the buyer. The buyer will attempt to protect himself from such a disaster by making his investigation as thorough as possible, but he should be aware that the deck is stacked against him.

One general thing the buyer can do to minimize his risk is to examine closely the seller's reason for selling. Unless he can satisfy himself as to the validity of the seller's stated reason for selling, he should either intensify his investigation or walk away from the deal. Also in this connection, he will be concerned about the character, integrity, and business reputation of the seller. Investigation of character is important to a buying decision, even if the seller is not going to be a continuing part of management.

The specific risks which the buyer should consider are too many and varied to be covered in this article. However, the more deeply the buyer digs into the seller's business, and the better a business man the buyer is, the more risk factors he will think of investigating. Just a few of the more common risks that should be evaluated in almost every situation are emerging competition, product obsolescence, nonrenewability of leases, plant obsolescence, pending claims and litigation, overstated inventories, understated tax liabilities, antitrust difficulties, inflated operating history, impending labor difficulties, loss of key personnel, and the effect of the proposed acquisition on the motivation of key personnel.

Laying Off the Risks

Many a merger negotiation has failed because of a disagreement between the parties regarding questions of risk which cannot be reconciled. To avoid this impasse, the buyer can do two things:

1. Specifically identify and appraise as many of the risks as possible.
2. Offer a form of transaction that leaves with the seller those risks which the seller claims to be trivial or nonexistent.

Broadly speaking, there are three ways of leaving the risks with the seller:

☐ **The scope of the transaction may be limited to exclude areas of risk.**
☐ **Warranties or guarantees may be obtained from the seller.**
☐ **The price may be made contingent on future results.**

The principal method of limiting the scope of a transaction to exclude risks is to acquire the assets of the company rather than to acquire the stock. This type of transaction frees the assets of all the liabilities or contingent liabilities of the acquired company. Of course, it is frequently impractical to acquire the assets without assuming *any* liabilities, but it is quite practical to acquire the assets subject only to those liabilities reflected on the balance sheet of the acquired company or those liabilities specified.

The technique of limiting risk by obtaining warranties or guarantees from the seller is used quite often. There are two general approaches: (a) obtain specific warranties or guarantees with respect to all the contingencies that buyer's counsel can think of or (b) obtain broadly stated warranties or guarantees as to the future earnings of the company or the absence of undisclosed liabilities. There are, of course, many possible permutations and combinations of these two approaches.

The contingent-payout contract is an important device for avoiding the greatest uncertainty in a typical acquisition—the future earning power of an acquired company. Under this arrangement, the seller receives a minimum amount of cash or stock at the time of the closing of the sale and then receives additional payments contingent on the amount of earnings during a specified period, usually three to five years. Though this device is effective, it does have problems. The disadvantage for the seller is that the final sale price is uncertain and can be adversely affected by the management decisions of the buying company. The disadvantage for the buyer is that the arrangement is expensive and the payments earmarked for the seller reduce the amount of profits left to the buyer. However, the contingent-payout contract can be a key to reconciling the seller's optimism with the buyer's fears.

Two and Two Don't Equal Four

Thus far we have been considering evaluation from the point of view of the economic value of a business considered as a separate entity. But corporate life is not really that simple. A business combination can change many things, both in the buyer's business and in the seller's business:

☐ **In the strictly financial reporting area, the earnings which the seller brings into the buyer may not be the same as their effect on the buyer's consolidated financial statements.**

If the acquisition is accounted for as a "purchase," the acquired assets will have a new carrying value, with little necessary relationship to the seller's carrying value. This, in turn, will have an effect on the determination of the income of the acquired business. The effect may sometimes be beneficial, but more often it will be adverse, and sometimes it will be fatal to an otherwise attractive-looking deal.

If, on the other hand, the transaction is a "pooling of interests," there will not be a complete new accounting basis. But even in this type of transaction there may be some adjustments in the seller's accounting to eliminate accounting practices inconsistent with those of the buyer.

☐ **If the transaction is a taxable transaction, there will be a new basis for the assets for determining income taxes, and this will change the income taxes which have to be paid and may change the reported after-tax earnings.**

☐ **Aside from financial reporting considerations, the buyer must consider whether the acquisition really represents a step toward his corporate goals.**

Does it contribute to marketing strength, production efficiency, economic stability, etc.?

☐ Also, the buyer must consider the impact of his business on the seller's business. Will the buyer's labor union cause an upsurge in the seller's payroll costs? Will the buyer's pension plan be expanded to include the seller's employees? Will the buyer's competition with the seller's customers hurt the seller's sales? Will the buyer's use of the seller's product enhance the seller's business? Does the seller have excess plant capacity, or excess engineering capabilities, which the buyer can use—or vice versa? If the seller is a "seat of the pants"-managed business, will the buyer's elaborate reporting and control systems make the seller more efficient, or will they simply cause high overhead and low morale? If the two are in radically different types of business, are the buyer's management systems adaptable to the seller's industry?

The Importance of People

The buyer must consider the demands on his management inherent in a combination of businesses. Almost all buyers include in their stated acquisition ground rules a requirement that the seller must have adequate management. This is quite reasonable, because adequate management is one of the scarcest and most valuable commodities of business today. On the other hand, almost every acquisition imposes demands on the buyer's management, sometimes heavy and sometimes light.

Buyers are not all saying and thinking the same thing when they state they will buy only a business with "adequate management." Their meaning varies with their resources—and with their rashness. Capability and willingness to devote management to an acquisition cover the spectrum, from companies which operate substantially as holding companies to those which can hardly wait to send in a new president and new chief financial officer to completely reorganize and "straighten out" the acquired company. In spite of these resource differences it remains true that buyers are interested in the depth and quality of the seller's management and will place a much higher value on a selling company which appears to have a self-sustaining management than on one with management deficiencies. A real premium is paid for the selling firm with management talent beyond its needs that can be utilized by the buyer. It is not unknown for a major company to make an acquisition in order to get a new president.

Recently a major public company gave brief consideration to an acquisition of an apparently attractive company almost its own size. After a quick survey, the investigation was dropped for this clearly stated reason: "This company has a need for managerial and financial controls over a group of entrepreneur scientists. Neither their president nor their chief financial officer is capable of doing the job, and we cannot fill this need without detracting from our ability to cope with our own problems." Even though the companies were a good fit, the buyer dropped its plans before the company being considered even knew that the buyer was thinking about a business combination.

That Valuable Corporate Image

Let us return for a moment to the case of the company with a high price/earnings ratio (acquirer "High" in Exhibit 1) which increased its earnings ratio by using its stock to acquire a company with a low P/E ratio. There was an unstated assumption in that hypothetical case— one that was necessary if the buyer was to achieve its objective of an increased P/E ratio. It was assumed that the marketplace would give the buyer at least a proportionate plus for its improved earnings and would not give it a minus for a deteriorated image. This assumption is sometimes valid and sometimes invalid, depending on various considerations. The most important of these considerations is the nature of the industry or industries of the buyer and the seller. If, for example, an electronics company acquired a steel company approaching its own size, it might well get a black mark in the marketplace for a change in its image. If the P/E ratio of the seller's industry is one-half that of the buyer's industry, the buying company may suddenly face a sharply reduced ratio, causing its "money machine" to run in reverse gear. In Exhibit 1, for example, if the P/E ratio of "High" is only 15 after the merger, the price of "High's" stock is reduced to $18. The apparent bargain purchase of earnings is offset by spoiling the P/E ratio.

THE SELLER'S VIEW

Let us now shift our viewpoint from the buyer to the seller. The principal question in the mind of the typical seller is: "How much can I get for my business?" To answer that question the seller should consider all of the things that the prudent buyer considers. Only when he has analyzed his company from the buyer's point of view can he negotiate intelligently and confidently; only then can he avoid either selling too cheaply or pricing himself out of the market.

At the outset the seller should evaluate his business from the point of view of buyers in general. When he reaches the point of talking with a particular buyer, he should try to evaluate that buyer's position and the specific effect of the transaction upon *that* buyer's affairs. It is often very helpful, for example, for the seller to try to construct pro forma combined financial statements for the combined business. In doing this the seller should not overlook the leverage which the buyer may achieve, either in the acquisition or based on it.

Of great concern to the seller is the value of his business in the general market (if there be such a thing). Though no two businesses are strictly comparable, there are price ranges, expressed principally as price/earnings ratios, for various industries and categories of companies, and the seller should try to evaluate his company objectively against the general industry pattern. In this evaluation, he should exercise a reasonable amount of humility. He may not look quite as good to others as he looks to himself. A well-established, publicly held growth company with a management team in depth commands a higher P/E ratio than a privately held Johnny-come-lately with only one substantial manager, age 70. If the seller's starting point is to take the price/earnings ratio for his industry from *Standard & Poor's 425 Industrials,* he should apply several successive discounts for (a) lack of history, (b) lack of market, and (c) lack of management. It may also be in order, depending on the case, for the seller to apply further discounts for prospective product obsolescence or for dependence on a single customer.

What Does the Seller Really Want?

Other considerations for the seller derive from his motivation for selling and from what he intends to do for the rest of his life. Some sellers want to retire and go fishing. Some sellers want jobs for their sons. Others are most anxious to continue their present careers. Some of them want to expand their present careers by playing in a bigger league. An occasional dynamic young seller will want to cash in his first successful business in order to get funds to start all over again.

Other sellers will want only to achieve a diversified and conservative investment portfolio for themselves or their heirs. Some sellers seeking portfolio security are not concerned about investment diversification. A fortunate few have enough other assets to be quite content with the securities they receive in exchange for their business.

Some sellers are concerned with the future careers of all or some of their employees. Others give only lip service to this concern, and still others do not even pretend such a concern. Some sellers take great pride in their business and the reputation they have achieved, and are very concerned with the quality of the organization into which they merge. The reaction of their club associates after the merger announcement appears in the local newspaper may mean more to such sellers than 20 percent of the sale price. Others feel that one man's money is as good as another's. Some are interested in a good cash flow in the years following the sale. Some want nothing but capital gains, and some cannot bear the thought of paying any taxes.

Depending on his objectives, the seller may prefer the stock of a stable blue chip or a company with speculative growth potential. He may prefer a company with strong management or a company that needs *him* in management. He may be concerned about or he may be indifferent to the buyer's policy on autonomy of divisions and subsidiaries. He may or may not be willing to sign a letter saying he is taking buyer's stock for investment. He may or may not be reluctant to back his projections of fugure growth by taking a contingent payout.

Sometimes the seller is a single individual or a small group with a common purpose, but it can be dangerous to assume this. As often as not there are diverse economic interests among the selling owners or between the owners and key employees who can influence the deal. Out of the many possible interests and motivations, the prudent seller, or his prudent counsel, will distill an explicit statement of the seller's objectives. This is no easy task, because some objectives are of such a nature that the seller won't even admit them to himself.

Whether or not the seller seeks diversification, he must look to the real value of any securities he is to receive. This involves more than reading a stock quotation. He may need advice from a securities analyst.

It is probably a reasonable generalization that the approach of sellers to evaluating transactions is more diverse than that of buyers, because sellers represent a greater diversity of objectives.

Tax Phobia

Many sellers take a strong position that they will accept only a non-taxable transaction. In some cases this position is justified. In many other cases, however, it is shortsighted and presents an unnecessary obstacle to a desirable deal. Many sellers' objectives are best met, if they receive stock, by the sale of a major part of the stock they receive. In these cases the tax avoidance achieved by the tax-free deal is temporary, and they need not have bothered. If they want diversity of investment, they usually have to pay capital gains tax to achieve it. Even in those cases in which capital gains tax is not in the offing, the seller who turns down a million dollars in cash to take $700,000 in stock is charging himself at least $50,000, and probably more, for the pleasure of thwarting the Internal Revenue Service. He should not delude himself with the thought that there is an offset in the appreciation potential of the stock he gets. On the average, he should be able to achieve at least as great an appreciation by taking his cash and freely investing it in a portfolio appropriate to his particular investment needs. Also, since he then has a stepped-up tax basis, he will be relatively freer to make alternative investment decisions in the future.

THE BRIDGE

This discussion of the motivations and objectives of the publicly held buyer and the privately held seller may give the impression that the differences between them are essentially a matter of objectivity versus subjectivity. That, however, is not the case. The influences on both parties are a mixture of personal and corporate, private and public. Personalities can be as great an obstacle to effecting a merger as balance sheets.

For both buyer and seller, therefore, the journey toward a successful merger begins with two important steps: (a) an awareness of one's own objectives and motivations and (b) an appreciation of the other party's objectives and motivations. Such understanding will help to build the necessary bridge between the often substantially different interests of buyer and seller.

Financing the Acquisition:
An Overview

ROBERT SPITALNIC

T HE FACTORS that influence the financing of a corporate acquisition
are many, various, and sometimes conflicting. They are also notoriously subject to change—changes in the money market; changes in the
regulations and guidelines imposed by government agencies, securities
exchanges, the courts, the accounting profession, and other interested
bodies; and changes in the attitudes of the investing public.

Some of these factors, such as legal, tax, and accounting considerations,
are dealt with elsewhere in this volume. Others are so highly susceptible
to change that to discuss them at any length in a book of this sort would
be an exercise in planned obsolescence. As its title suggests, the purpose
of this brief "overview" is not to explore in depth the subject of acquisition
financing but to identify some of the major alternatives that a prospective
acquirer should consider, and some of the more important questions that
he must answer if an intelligent financing decision is to be made.

A review of the financing techniques used by Ling-Temco-Vought
(LTV) in its acquisition program suggests the complexity and variety of
acquisition financing. Some of the instruments used by LTV include
cash, notes, debenture and warrant packages, convertible debentures,
and convertible preferred as well as common and preferred stock. Other
financing devices used to support this program include overseas borrow-

---

Robert Spitalnic is a manager in the home office of Arthur Young &
Company, New York.

ing, short-term notes, and recapitalization. One form of recapitalization which LTV has used is the issuance of a new convertible preferred stock that provides stock dividends in exchange for outstanding preferred and common shares, both of which pay cash dividends. Recapitalization can also take the form—as it did in LTV's acquisition of Wilson & Company—of splitting the acquired company into three companies, each with its own common stock and each assuming a portion of the debt that LTV had assumed in its purchase of Wilson.

Valuable as a knowledge of other companies' approaches may be, however, the experiences of other companies are not, in and of themselves, a really sound basis for acquisition planning. Before any company can meaningfully consider the financing aspects of an acquisition program it must carefully identify and evaluate its own strengths and weaknesses. This requires an analysis of the long-term trends of the company's business or businesses, as well as a review of the available sources of short-term and long-term financing.

SOURCES OF CAPITAL

If an aggressive acquisition program is to be pursued, among the first steps that may be necessary are increasing the authorized number of common shares and authorizing a new convertible preferred issue. Cash for such a program might also be acquired by issuing new common stock, perhaps through a rights offering to present stockholders. Other potential sources of cash include:

- ☐ **Short-term financing—bank loans.**
- ☐ **Long-term borrowing—public or private placements.**
- ☐ **Foreign sources—Eurodollars.**

Time spent with an insurance company, bank, or other financial institution will often provide a range of the amount of short- and long-term financing that is feasible. In addition, a review of projected cash flows will give some general idea of the level of debt that can be supported.

A detailed analysis of all the company's assets will often reveal other potential sources of cash. For example, excess assets might be sold. Unprofitable divisions or divisions that do not fit into the company's long-term plans might also be sold. Although the decision to sell a previous acquisition which has not worked out is never an easy one for management to make, sometimes it must be made.

The leasing of assets, as opposed to outright purchase, should also be considered as a source of funds. One such technique is sale-and-leaseback financing, in which the usual arrangement is for an institutional investor to buy up property from a company or build to the company's specifications and then lease it back to the company.

It is important that good lines of communication be established with all potential sources of capital. Periodic communications with stockholders, lending institutions (including foreign lending institutions), and investment banking houses will be of long-term value to the company. If cash is needed quickly, these established communication lines can greatly facilitate the lending operation.

The potential acquirer must also look at its current price/earnings ratio. If its P/E ratio is comparatively high, companies with a lower P/E ratio can be acquired without initial dilution in per-share earnings after the merger. However, a large acquisition may result in a re-evaluation of the acquiring company's P/E ratio. In addition, if the acquired company's earnings do not grow as fast as those of the acquiring company, there will eventually be a dilution in earnings per share.

An acquirer with a low P/E ratio might have to make use of cash and debt in order not to substantially dilute its earnings and perhaps reduce the market price of its stock. This, of course, applies to acquisitions large enough to have an effect on earnings per share after the merger. Another factor to consider, especially if the dividends on its common stock are high, is the net cost of debt to the company. This cost may be less than the cost of using stock, since interest is tax-deductible whereas dividends are not. Of course, interest charges result in lower reported earnings. However, there will be no decrease in postmerger earnings per share if the debt charges are paid out of the acquired company's earnings. In addition, retained cash flow—that is, cash flow remaining after the payment of both dividends and interest—will be higher if debt is used, and the after-tax interest cost is less than the dividend requirement on an equivalent dollar amount of stock.

In light of the above, consideration should be given by the potential acquirer to the purchase of its own stock on the open market or from large holders to use for subsequent acquisitions. In this case, the reporting requirements of the SEC and the major exchanges must be thoroughly explored.

Although in most instances we have discussed the use of the various types of securities individually, they can, and often are, used in combination with one another. For example, a combination of convertible preferred stock and cash, or of preferred stock and common stock, might be used as a package to provide a specified dividend to selling stockholders.

EQUITY FINANCING

The primary advantage of an equity transaction to the seller is its tax-free nature provided that certain requirements are met. The advantage to the buyer is that such a transaction may be handled as a pooling, resulting in no goodwill being placed on the balance sheet due to the excess of the purchase price over the book value of the acquired company. In addition, the acquirer often finds it easier to issue stock than use other means of financing.

Common Stock

In considering the use of common stock, some important questions to be answered are these:

☐ Will the issuance of additional common shares result in an increase or decrease in postmerger earnings per share? How much?

☐ If there is dilution in per-share earnings, given projected growth for both companies, when (if at all) will dilution be eliminated? What is the probability that the assumed earnings growth will be realized? (One useful technique is, with the aid of a computer, to generate a range of postmerger earnings per share and the probability of achieving each, under various earnings assumptions.)

☐ Will dividends on additional shares be covered by the net income or cash flow of the acquired company? What is the effect of dividends on the total retained cash flow (cash flow less dividends and interest) of the new company? Would the use of some debt financing provide a better retained cash flow for the acquirer?

☐ What effect might the merger have on the acquiring company's P/E ratio? How will this affect future acquisition financing?

Convertible Preferred Stock

Convertible preferred stock, like all convertible issues, has the advantage of usually selling at some premium over the market price of the common stock into which it is convertible. In other words, fewer common shares will have to be issued and equity dilution is reduced.

Some key questions concerning the use of convertible preferred stock are these:

☐ What are common earnings per share on a nonconverted and a 100-percent-converted basis? Here we confront the question of residual securities or "common stock equivalents." In considering the issuance of any type of convertible securities, it is important to be aware of the latest reporting requirements. The Accounting Principles Board's Opinion No. 15 requires that convertible preferred be considered the equivalent of common stock in computing primary earnings per share if it has a cash yield based on market price *at issue* of less than **66-2/3** percent of the current prime rate.

☐ **How will the conversion of the preferred into common be controlled? If there is a delay before the preferred can be converted into common, the preferred may sell at a discount from its conversion value. What will the call provisions be?**

☐ **What will be the effect of a substantial convertible issue on the acquiring company's common stock? How will it affect price, P/E ratio, and yield? How will it influence the financing of future acquisitions?**

☐ **Can the new acquisition's earnings cover the preferred dividend requirement with its own net income or cash flow? If there is dilution in earnings because of the preferred dividend, can a lower-yield preferred be issued, or a combination of preferred and common?**

☐ **What will be the effect of the preferred dividend on the premium it will command? When a preferred stock initially comes out it is usually supported by the dividend. In other words, the conversion value is less than the investment value. As the common stock rises in price, the conversion value of the preferred, and therefore its market value, also rises. As a result, the dividend yield on the preferred is smaller. Assuming an eventual increase in the common dividend, the dividend on the converted common shares will ultimately exceed the dividend on the preferred. This will generally have the effect of encouraging the conversion of the preferred into common shares. One way to delay conversion is to have a participating preferred, where the preferred dividend increases proportionately with the common dividend.**

If the acquiring company wishes to conserve cash, consideration might be given to a convertible preferred stock that is convertible into an increasing number of common shares each year. For example, we might have a preferred that is convertible into one share of common the first year, 1.03 shares of common the second year, 1.0609 shares the third year, and so on. (This may create a tax problem for the shareholder.)

Preferred Stock

Straight preferred stock—that is, nonconvertible preferred—requires a higher dividend than convertible preferred. Currently, these securities are not being widely used in acquisitions since the cost to the issuer of dividend payments is usually higher than the cost of using debt, common stock, or convertible securities. Some questions concerning the use of preferred stock are:

☐ **What will be the common earnings per share after the merger?**

☐ **On the basis of current yields, what type of dividend will have to be paid?**

Should consideration be given to a participating preferred? This will often reduce the amount of the current dividend that has to be paid.

☐ Can the new acquisition's earnings cover the preferred dividend requirements? What is the dividend requirement as a percentage of those earnings? If there is substantial dilution in postmerger earnings or poor coverage of the dividend requirement, consideration might be given to using cash or common, or even convertible preferred, for a portion of the purchase price.

☐ How will the use of preferred stock influence future financing considerations?

Warrants

Many within the financial community feel that the use of warrants as a means of financing acquisitions will increase. The same factors that encourage the use of convertible securities—primarily the reduced equity dilution as compared with the effects of issuing common stock—also encourage the use of warrants. In addition, warrants require no dividend or interest payments and when exercised may provide additional funds. In analyzing the use of warrants in acquisition financing, some key questions include:

☐ What are postmerger earnings per share before and after conversion of the warrants? The Accounting Principles Board's Opinion 15 requires that warrants (and options) be treated as common stock equivalents; however, they are not to be reflected in the computation of primary or fully-diluted earnings per share if their effect is not dilutive. The treatment required is a treasury stock approach—that is, the cash received should the warrants be exercised is assumed to be used to purchase treasury stock. However, when the total number of shares of common stock obtainable upon the exercise of warrants and options exceeds 20 percent of the common shares (excluding common stock equivalents), the treasury stock method applies only to the first 20 percent. The remaining warrants and options are treated as if the proceeds from their exercise were first used to retire debt and then invested in government securities or commercial paper. The above will result in a new net income figure which takes into account the reduced interest expense and the increased interest income, if any, on an after-tax basis. The issuing company must be aware of what effect its particular capitalization will have on reported earnings per share as it issues warrants in excess of the 20 percent figure.

☐ What will be the effect of a substantial warrant issue upon the issuing company's common stock? Regardless of the reporting requirements, a substantial amount of outstanding warrants cannot help but have some effect on the price of the company's common stock.

☐ **How will the timing of conversion into common stock be controlled?** Usually, the higher the exercise price over the current market price, the greater the delay before exercise of the warrant. However, this situation results in a lower price for the warrant. On the other hand, if the exercise price of the warrant is higher than the market price of the common, it would not be reflected in the earnings-per-share figure, since to do so would cause an increase in reported earnings per share. The whole matter of pricing warrants is a very difficult subject, and it is usually best to obtain the advice of experienced investment bankers when new warrants are to be priced. In many cases the warrant may be exercisable for a specified period of time—e.g., five or ten years. LTV has a warrant outstanding which gives it the option to lower the exercise price for a limited period of time and thereby encourage conversion.

☐ **Will the warrant when exercised—that is, when converted into common stock—be a source of funds?** In some cases warrants are attached to debentures and a portion or all of the par value of the debenture may be applied instead of cash.

CASH AND DEBT FINANCING

Often the cash used in a particular acquisition will come from some form of borrowing—long-term, short-term, or both—by the acquiring company. In other cases, as mentioned previously, the acquiring company has excess cash or sources of cash within its own operation. The same conditions may apply to the acquisition candidate. Recently the use of debt financing has come under fire. Representative Mills has proposed that only a portion of the interest paid on these securities, or on bank loans, be made tax-deductible. Questions to be asked concerning the use of convertible debentures include:

☐ **Does the candidate have any excess cash or sources of cash?** Such sources include assets that might be sold or operations that are not profitable or do not fit in with the acquiring company's long-term interests. Again, one such source might be the sale of previous acquisitions made by the candidate.

☐ **Are there assets that might be written up for tax purposes?** It should be remembered that this can be done only in a taxable transaction. Also, it will usually result in a reduction in reported earnings because of the higher depreciation charges.

☐ **In considering the amount of additional leverage available through the acquisition,** the acquired company's debt-to-equity ratio can be compared with the ratios of other companies in its industry.

☐ **Usually cash and debt financing will result in no dilution in earnings per share as a result of the merger, assuming that the interest on the debt used** to pay for the acquisition is not in excess of the acquired company's pretax earnings. However, if the purchase price is substantially above book value, the goodwill created may result in a charge against earnings. The reverse situation may also apply, resulting in "negative" goodwill and a credit to earnings.

☐ Another important consideration in all debt financing situations is the amount of debt coverage. How many times does the acquired company's pretax income cover fixed charges? While such charges may be met out of cash flow, this can result in a decrease in earnings per share after the merger.

Convertible Debentures

The future use of this type of security will to some extent be governed by the nature of the legislation that is finally passed regarding the treatment of interest paid on debentures issued for an acquisition. Some of the questions that should be asked are:

☐ What will be the effect of a convertible issue on reporting earnings per share? The Accounting Principles Board's latest Opinion requires that convertible debentures be regarded as common stock equivalents if at issuance the yield on market is less than 66-2/3 percent of the current prime interest rate.

☐ How will the issuance of convertible debentures affect future debt and equity financing?

☐ What provisions do the debentures have regarding the control of conversion into common stock? What are the call provisions?

☐ Given the interest rate and conversion terms, at what price will the debentures sell? Again, the service of an investment banker will aid in determining the terms of the debentures and in estimating the price range within which the security will sell.

☐ How many times do the acquired company's pretax earnings cover the interest charges? To what extent can usable funds be generated from cash flow?

SUMMARY

In this brief "overview" we have merely identified some of the acquisition financing methods currently in use. In addition, we have presented some of the key factors that must be analyzed. It is important to be aware of changes in reporting requirements, tax laws, and the other legal considerations that influence the financing of any business combination. Moreover, an attempt must be made to analyze the complex interrelationships of each of the financing instruments with one another and with the corporation's total financing program. Today's overemphasis on reporting requirements should not be permitted to obscure the basic financing considerations.

One of the most difficult problems is to get an estimate of the probable market price of the new security that will be issued. If the issuing company has issues of the same type outstanding, this aids in pricing. However, in many of these situations it will be necessary to get expert advice from investment bankers.

Again, the best transaction from a financing viewpoint may not be the best transaction in terms of tax, or even reporting, considerations. It is management's job to reconcile these sometimes conflicting objectives and perhaps in so doing develop a new financing approach.

Finally, it should be remembered that the financing decision comes *after* the tentative acquisition decision, which often should be made independently of the financing decision. The best transaction from a financing viewpoint may not be the best acquisition.

P/E Analysis in
Acquisition Strategy

DONALD J. SMALTER and RODERIC C. LANCEY

THE ACHIEVEMENTS of most successful growth companies have been based on a mixture of three types of strategies—internal programs for new products and market development, joint ventures, and acquisitions. Each of these routes provides top management with a means to implement over-all corporate objectives and goals.

Use of the mergers and acquisitions route has been increasing sharply during the past several years. Continued growth in its popularity is likely because it serves numerous corporate needs and growth motivations. An acquisition can strengthen a weakness; for instance, it can help to fill a raw material need or improve a vulnerable patent position. It can buy valuable time for a company. It can help management capitalize on the strengths of each partner and utilize the synergistic possibilities which may arise in terms of geographic and product line expansion. It can provide diversification opportunities. And it can enable a company to enter growth markets and reduce its dependence on existing activities for earnings growth.

One aspect of growth by acquisition which deserves particular attention is that of maintaining and improving the acquiring company's price/earnings ratio. The importance of this ratio in any acquisition strategy may not always be fully appreciated; yet the ratio has a decided impact on the

Donald J. Smalter is Corporate Director of Strategic Planning, International Minerals & Chemical Corporation, Chicago, Ill. Roderic C. Lancey is Corporate Planner for IMC.

range of purchasable companies. The relationship between the P/E ratio of the candidate and that of the prospective parent determines whether there is earnings dilution, and hence whether the survivor can afford to swap stock. Also, the stock market's valuation of the negotiating companies, as reflected in their P/E ratios, is by far the most important financial factor in the negotiation of agreeable exchange terms.

In this discussion we shall summarize the factors which most directly influence and control a company stock's P/E ratio. We shall attempt to develop a useful perspective on the ratio's controlling effect in stock-for-stock and stock-for-assets acquisition strategy. More specifically, these questions will be addressed:

☐ **What factors appear to control the level of the P/E ratio?**

☐ **How can a company raise its P/E ratio?**

☐ **How can an acquisition upgrade the company's per-share earnings results?**

☐ **How does a candidate company's P/E ratio affect the acquiring firm's acquisition strategy?**

☐ **Under what circumstances (if any) can both parties experience "magical gains"?**

A high P/E ratio brings a number of values to any company. It enables a more advantageous exchange of shares; that is, it enables "cheaper" acquisitions of other companies, a point to be developed later in this discussion. It also generates capital gains for shareholders and provides additional incentive for executive stock option compensation. It enhances the possible use of stock as a substitute for dividends, thereby preserving cash for internal expansion, and provides greater net proceeds to the company for any new equity offering.

Of course, good decision rules for selecting candidates for acquisition are not by themselves the answer to management's need. As we know well from the experience of our own company, International Minerals & Chemical Corporation, and other organizations, much work must also go into making contacts with the heads of other companies, negotiating prices, revising the postmerger organization structure, and related activities.

INFLUENCES ON P/E LEVEL

The range of P/E ratios for companies varies widely. Within the process industries, for example, the ratios range from a low in the vicinity of 8 to a high of over 40. Exhibit 1 shows average ratios during the period 1963–1965 for several components of the process industries.

Exhibit 1. Average Price/Earnings Ratios in Selected Process Industries

Source: Quarterly service of Value Line Investment Survey, Part III (New York, Arnold Bernhard & Co., Inc.).

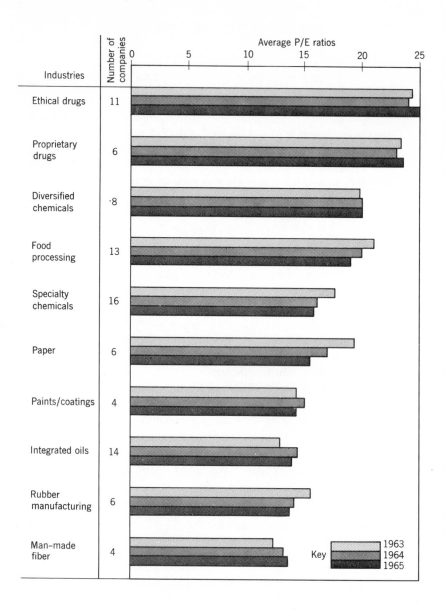

Generally a few companies in each category enjoy a P/E ratio considerably higher than the group average. To illustrate, Pennsalt, a specialty chemical manufacturer, consistently commanded a P/E ratio of at least 20 during the three-year period. Two points seem to stand out: first, the company maintained an aggressive R&D program, with emphasis on "glamor" chemicals; and second, it frequently introduced new chemical specialty products which apparently impressed investors.

In the diversified chemical category Du Pont enjoyed a ratio typically 20 to 25 percent above the group average. This highly diversified corporation has supported an innovative research program for years, and regularly introduces new products which seem to convey promises of great commercial potential, such as Corfam, its substitute for leather.

We have conducted an extensive study of the literature to learn more about the factors affecting the P/E ratio. No great agreement was found among investment analysts on how to rate the price of a stock. In fact, the consensus of experienced investment analysts seems to be that much of the rating process is based on psychological reactions to future prospects and on subjective judgments rather than on detailed, soundly conceived quantitative analysis. Only recently have there been any serious attempts to develop formulas for determining the future market value of a stock in a systematic, mathematical manner.

Controlling Factors

On the basis of our study we have selected six factors controlling P/E ratios. Ranked in order of importance, they are as follows:

1. The prospect of future per-share earnings growth is the obvious primary influence affecting the P/E ratio.

2. Investors want minimum fluctuation from the anticipated earnings trend line. In other words, lower risks are associated with stocks which appear to promise lower per-share earnings volatility.

3. Investors favor companies which promise earnings growth for the long term. They develop confidence, based on a company's historical performance, that the company's earnings growth will continue steadily for many years' duration.

4. Heavy emphasis on research and development is often a major component of a company's growth image. Investors are willing to pay high prices for Polaroid, Corning Glass, 3M, and IBM because they expect these firms to identify and successfully commercialize new products.

5. Frequent introduction of new products reinforces investors' confidence that R&D expenditures are productive. Thus, R&D results and

investors' expectations become closely associated, and help to sustain superior P/E ratios.

6. Companies which participate in recognized growth markets are apt to have bright futures. This point follows from the previous two, and means that companies which expend resources in growth markets will receive recognition from investors, provided earnings benefits appear achievable.

When judging the price they are willing to pay, many investors, especially the more speculative types looking for capital gains appreciation, tend to place relatively low marks on such well-known factors as these:

☐ A high rate of return on equity.
☐ A high rate of earnings retention or plowback.
☐ A high rate of dividend payout.
☐ A high rate of dividend yield.
☐ A low level of debt utilization in the capital structure.

The last point—de-emphasis of the level of debt utilization—appears significant. It can be shown that many companies with high P/E ratios possess long-term debt in excess of 30 percent of capital structure. This illustrates, perhaps, that such companies have generated numerous opportunities which warrant extension of their debt burden, with the benefits accruing to the stockholders through the effects of leveraging.

RAISING THE RATIO

From the preceding discussion we may conclude that management must continuously strive to produce a steady upward trend in per-share earnings over the long term. First of all, internally generated growth opportunities should be carefully considered. Projects should be appraised both for over-all profitability and for the incremental risks which would be incurred if additional debt financing were used to lever the anticipated profits for the common shareholder. Secondly, earnings growth can benefit directly from a deliberate acquisition strategy. A company can acquire other firms that (a) expand its market position in fields of high growth potential, (b) improve its technological capability and image, or (c) improve its per-share earnings because of a favorable trading position. Let us consider each of these three possibilities.

Picking Growth Prospects

In attempting to develop a rational approach for planning its growth, management should first examine growth opportunities and rates in the

Exhibit 2. Industry Growth Rate Projections Through 1980

Source: "Economists Paint a Bright Picture for 1980," *Chemical Engineering*, January 31, 1966, p. 34.

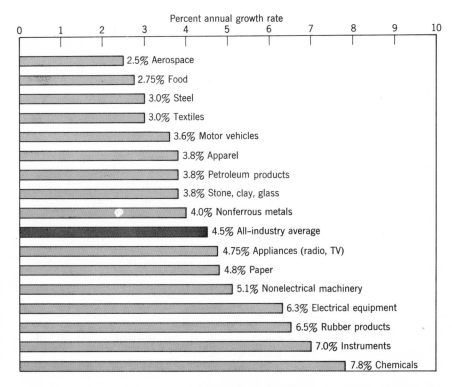

industries and/or business missions which it serves.[1] As illustrated in Exhibit 2, these rates can vary considerably, typically from 8 percent or 9 percent down to 2 percent per year. Spectacular growth in excess of 20 percent will be found in some of the newer, usually technically oriented and specialized markets until they begin to approach supply-and-demand equilibrium.

It is much more difficult to grow profitably in mature industries which demonstrate a decaying growth rate, or a rate below that of the gross national product. So it is desirable to identify those businesses which have good or even outstanding growth rate potentials. This objective

---

[1] For an exposition of corporate missions, see Donald J. Smalter and Rudy L. Ruggles, Jr., "Six Business Lessons from the Pentagon," *Harvard Business Review*, March-April 1966, pp. 65-68.

should dominate any searching process unless it is possible to pinpoint "bargain" candidates—sick or poorly performing companies that can be converted into healthy and contributing assets if marketing, merchandising, or other types of know-how are applied.

Buying of Technology

In considering the acquisition of companies with desired technological strengths, management should ask if the time is right for buying. In a business where technology is critical, there is a well-known time lag before it is possible to capitalize on scientific findings. For instance, over the years Textron has demonstrated awareness of this fact; it has acquired companies that already have expended substantial efforts in developing new technology. At the appropriate time, but not before, these companies were acquired, and additional financial resources were applied to capitalize on their know-how.

Naturally, it is preferable to acquire firms whose products are in early growth phases of the life cycle, rather than declining phases, and that possess exceptional potential for creating new products from their R&D programs. But simply to look at an industry segment and find that it is growing is not enough. Inspection must take place in depth, and analyses must be conducted which determine where the profits are to be made. In devising a growth strategy questions like these must be addressed:

☐ **Should horizontal moves be undertaken for the purpose of broadening the product line?**

☐ **What products, when combined with present products, could be sold profitably through common distribution channels?**

☐ **Should vertical integration be pursued?**

☐ **What percentage of the market will be a captive market in the future?**

☐ **What are the possibilities for technical innovation?**

☐ **Could any shortcuts in distribution channels be developed that would increase profits and bring a unique competitive advantage?**

☐ **Are there companies available which might fulfill these needs and desires?**

The answers to these questions do not come easily. They require inquisitive, perceptive, and time-consuming analysis.

Favorable Trading Position

In any acquisition involving the use of common stock or other securities exchangeable into common stock, it is essential that the acquired earnings be evaluated for their per-share contribution to the surviving company.

If the increase in the number of shares is proportionally greater than the increase in annual earnings, then dilution is incurred. However, the opposite can also occur. Whether or not dilution results depends on:

1. The ratio of the buying price to the earnings of the acquired company.

2. The value assigned to the securities to be exchanged by the surviving company.

This brings us to the next major question in our discussion—determining whether an acquisition will upgrade earnings per share in the merged organization and improve its P/E ratio.

IMPACT ON EARNINGS

Here we want to propose a way of analyzing anticipated earnings. For the sake of specificity, let us consider the hypothetical case outlined in Exhibit 3.

The management of a growing corporation, Company A, is considering the purchase of either of two smaller companies, B and C. Both B and C are believed to offer A some attractive opportunities to serve A's needs and growth objectives. Although B and C have the same sales, earnings, and shares outstanding (an extremely unlikely occurrence, in reality, but convenient for purposes of illustration), B has a considerably greater P/E ratio. This advantage substantially differentiates the bargaining positions of B and C in merger negotiations. As a result, B negotiates a selling price of 22.5 times earnings, well above A's multiplier of 18. A's shareholders would then incur some minor and immediate dilution in their per-share earnings if B were bought.

This would not be true, however, if Company C were bought. Here shareholders of Company A would benefit by obtaining an immediate boost in per-share earnings in the current year. In this case A would utilize its higher P/E ratio to escalate per-share earnings. (Looking at the problem from the standpoint of stockholders of B and C, per-share earnings for B would rise from $5.00 to $5.82, and per-share earnings for C would drop from $5.00 to $4.37.)

But these numerical comparisons do not provide the answer. It is axiomatic that A should carefully identify its motivations and needs in acquiring C instead of, or in addition to, B. Immediate per-share benefits may well prove illusory unless the composite company can exploit some available strengths and capabilities which will boost the acquired earnings over the longer term, at a rate at least equivalent to what A

Exhibit 3. Comparative Effect on Earnings of Two Prospective Acquisitions (purchase by exchange of stock)

FINANCIAL DATA PRIOR TO ACQUISITION

	Company A	Candidate B	Candidate C
Sales ($ millions)	$300	$100	$100
Earnings ($ millions)	$25	$10	$10
Shares (millions)	10	2	2
Earnings per share	$2.50	$5.00	$5.00
Stock price	$45	$100	$75
P/E multiple	18	20	15

ACQUISITION OF B BY A

Negotiated price is $225 million, or 22.5 times current estimated earnings. This is equivalent to a 12.5% premium over the current P/E ratio for B's stock. To make the purchase, therefore, A must issue 5 million shares of its common stock ($225 million divided by $45).

Earnings-per-share computations are as follows:
(a) *Company B* — $2.00 per share ($10 million earnings divided by 5 million shares).
(b) *Composite operations* — $2.33 per share (composite earnings of $25 million plus $10 million, or $35 million, divided by 10 million shares of A's stock outstanding plus 5 million shares issued to B).
(c) *Effect on shareholders of A* — 6.8% dilution ($2.50 minus $2.33, or $0.17, divided by $2.50).

ACQUISITION OF C BY A

Negotiated price is $150 million, or 15 times current estimated earnings. This is the same ratio as the current one on the market for C's stock. To make the purchase, therefore, A must issue 3.333 million shares of its common stock ($150 million divided by $45).

Earnings-per-share computations are as follows:
(a) *Company C* — $3.00 per share ($10 million divided by 3.333 million shares).
(b) *Composite operations* — $2.62 per share (composite earnings of $25 million plus $10 million, or $35 million, divided by 10 million shares of A's stock outstanding plus 3.333 million shares issued to C).
(c) *Effect on shareholders of A* — 4.8% gain ($2.62 minus $2.50, or $0.12, divided by $2.50).

expects to achieve without acquiring C. Otherwise, C would gradually exert a "sea anchor" effect on Company A's over-all earnings growth—that is, C would gradually increase future dilution.

Company A should also attempt to estimate how investors will react to an acquisition of B or C. Exhibit 4 shows composite stock prices which could result from a range of P/E multiples for each merger, as well as the values associated with the "extinguished" shares of B or C.

☐ If A acquires B, investors would have to upgrade A's multiplier to at least 19.3 to sustain its current $45 stock price; otherwise, the dilutional effect of acquiring B will immediately lower A's stock value, and B's original shareholders would not obtain the value originally anticipated.

☐ If A acquires C, the multiplier could relax to 17 without reducing A's current stock price, and any higher value would benefit both A's and C's shareholders.

These are only the immediate effects on A's existing shareholders. Of equal, if not greater, importance are the price effects over the longer term. Management should, therefore, focus major attention on the likely P/E multipliers which investors will apply to future composite earnings.

Testing for Dilution

The reader may already have noted in these straight common-for-common swap examples that there is a simple method to test for dilution: divide the acquiring company's stock value by the negotiated P/E multiple being applied to the acquired earnings. (For instance, if A acquires B, divide $45 by 22.5 to get $2; if A acquires C, divide $45 by 15 to get $3.) The quotient should equal or exceed the acquiring company's current per-share earnings; if it does not, immediate dilution will result, as illustrated in Exhibit 3.

In more complicated swap arrangements involving the use of securities convertible into common stock at some future date, the same technique

Exhibit 4. Range of Stock Prices Due to Merger of Company A with Company B or Company C

P/E ratio	Composite stock price of A and B	Value of extinguished B stock	Composite stock price of A and C	Value of extinguished C stock
15	—	—	$39.30	$65.50
16	—	—	41.87	69.87
17	—	—	44.50	74.25
18	$42.00	$104.75	47.25	78.62
19	44.25	110.62	49.75	83.00
20	46.62	116.37	—	—
21	49.00	122.25	—	—
22	51.25	128.00	—	—

can be used. Here the conversion price is divided by a multiplier based on the level of acquired earnings at the probable date of conversion. The quotient is then compared with per-share earnings anticipated at that future date without the proposed acquisition.

Strategic Considerations

Exhibit 3 was designed to illustrate how the P/E ratio relates to immediate dilution or additions to per-share earnings. However, these two simple examples fail to provide adequate perspective on how the P/E ratio can influence selection and implementation of an acquisition strategy. To do this, the amount of earnings being acquired must be considered simultaneously along with the negotiated P/E multiplier being applied to them, as illustrated in Exhibit 5. This diagram is constructed with Company A data (10 million shares, earnings of $25 million, a stock value of $45, and a P/E of 18). It measures per-share effects on Company A's current earnings ($2.50 per share) for any combination of negotiated P/E ratios over the range of 10 to 30 for a given amount of acquired earning power.

Exhibit 5.   Immediate Per-Share Effects of Prospective Acquisitions by Company A

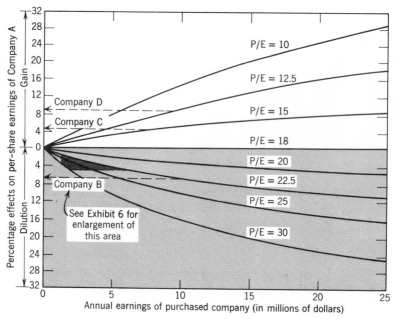

A similar diagram could be readily constructed for any company whose management desires a tool for quick, visual reading of the effects on earnings of prospective acquisitions.

Exhibit 5 obviously divides into two fields of interest, with an 18 multiplier representing the boundary line between dilution of and additions to per-share earnings. Consider the field of prospective acquisitions with earnings at negotiated P/E ratios below 18:

☐ Company C, which earns $10 million, would bring an immediate beneficial boost of 12 cents, or 4.8 percent, to Company A's per-share earnings. But perhaps another candidate—call it Company D—with the same approximate earning power and attributes for A's particular needs is available at a P/E of 12.5. The benefits to A would be over 9 percent, or double those of Company C.

☐ Alternatively, perhaps A should be considering a larger candidate with a somewhat lower P/E than 15, and reach for substantially greater benefits than C can offer. A candidate with $15 million in earnings and a P/E of 12.5 would generate an addition of about 32 cents (approximately 13 percent) to A's immediate per-share results.

Accounting for Growth

To refer back to the example previously described, acquisition of Company B by Company A would immediately reduce A's current per-share earnings by 17 cents, or nearly 7 percent (see Exhibit 3). Before proceeding to absorb this impact, A's management should consider the following kinds of question:

☐ Should there be a guideline or decision rule which sets a limit on dilution due to acquisitions?

☐ If so, should this statement apply uniformly to all candidates or should a range of limits be selected in recognition of the purpose or motive that may be served by selected types of candidates?

☐ Even after adjusting for anticipated synergisms and savings, will the acquired earnings grow fast enough to eliminate immediate per-share dilution over the next several years?

☐ Is it likely that some permanent drawbacks will result which are justifiable in terms of over-all corporate needs and objectives?

One area likely to be of special interest to growth-oriented companies is the acquisition of new technology. Company A, for example, may have inadequacies or even voids in its R&D skills, manufacturing tech-

Exhibit 6. Field of Interest in Searching for Acquisitions

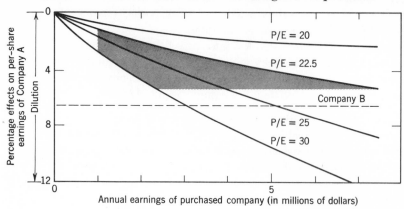

y-axis: Percentage effects on per-share earnings of Company A — Dilution (0, 4, 8, 12)

labels: P/E = 20, P/E = 22.5, Company B, P/E = 25, P/E = 30

x-axis: Annual earnings of purchased company (in millions of dollars) (0, 5)

nologies, or patent position in an attractive growth market. By identifying its technical needs A could set some specific acquisition decision rules for this area:

☐ **Up to 5 percent immediate dilution is acceptable even though there are no direct assurances that acquired earnings will grow as fast as A's projected rate.**

☐ **The acquired company's P/E ratio should exceed 22.5.**

The shaded area in Exhibit 6 blocks out the resulting "field of interest" for A's searching process. This delineation restricts A's candidate list to small companies—those with earnings ranging from $1 million to $7.5 million. (The lower limit of $1 million is selected arbitrarily for this discussion, since, in Company A's case, dilution resulting from buying a company with earnings below this level would be minor.) A prime motivation would be to exploit substantially greater P/E ratios of qualified candidates which have already obtained recognition of technical competence for investors. Note that a candidate earning slightly over $2 million would be acceptable, even with a negotiated P/E of 30! Company A would, therefore, deliberately search for technology sources whose P/E ratio would "rub off" onto A's over-all image to investors and either reduce or eliminate adverse stock-price effects.

Company B does not strictly satisfy these guidelines; it falls outside the shaded area. Perhaps B is attractive, however, because it could save A several years in building a position in a desirable growth market. If so, this means that A is looking to B primarily for direct contributions to A's earnings growth. This in turn raises a more serious issue: How fast must acquired earnings grow to wash out immediate dilution during the next several years? Exhibit 7 has been prepared to illustrate the answer to this problem.

The exhibit assumes that Company A is planning on a 10 percent per year growth in its per-share earnings for current operations. To learn how fast acquired earnings must grow to eliminate dilution completely within three or four years for a range of negotiated P/E ratios, run a line horizontally from the acquisition's P/E ratio to the time period curves; the growth rate figure directly beneath the point of intersection is the answer.

The results are somewhat unsettling, as Company B's earnings, including synergistic contributions and savings, would have to grow at 18 percent per year to eliminate dilution within three years, and 16 percent per year to wash out dilution in four years. A higher-priced candidate—say, Company E, priced at 25 times earnings—would demand acquired earnings growth in excess of 20 percent per year to eliminate dilution. Since these levels of earnings growth are so high, A's management is challenged to define (at least to itself) the reasons which would justify some permanent dilution in its per-share earnings.

Exhibit 7. Earnings Growth of Acquired Company Required to Eliminate Dilution

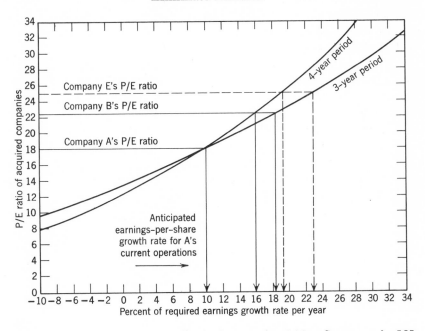

It is difficult to generalize on these issues, since each company encounters a unique set of circumstances, including its own anticipated rate of earnings growth, its P/E ratio, and the P/E ratio of desirable acquisition candidates. It seems clear, however, that management should deliberately define its acquisition decision rules and clearly perceive the per-share effects of each acquisition candidate. Preparation of charts similar to Exhibits 5 and 7 is particularly helpful in developing this perspective, and in formulating an over-all acquisition strategy.

CONCLUSION

Growth companies have been sharply increasing their use of acquisitions as a major component of their over-all corporate growth strategy. At the same time, they apparently recognize that an acquisition program can be meaningful and truly successful only if it is closely keyed to corporate motives, needs, and objectives, and contributes to the company's longer-term growth goals for its per-share earnings.

Per-share earnings are directly affected by any acquisition based on the exchange of common stock or securities convertible into common stock. When this is the case, management's acquisition strategy should be formulated to link earnings growth goals to the company's P/E ratio. This ratio, when compared with the most likely negotiated P/E ratio of qualified acquisition candidates, directly determines whether per-share earnings will be diluted or beneficially boosted, both immediately and during the longer-term future.

In this discussion we have suggested that acquisition strategy can be more clearly perceived and communicated if management defines the firm's fields of interest—that is, identifies preferred zones in a diagram like Exhibit 5, which correlates the amount of acquired earning power, the related P/E ratios, and the resulting per-share effects. Such a diagram forces management to "think through" the role being assigned to acquisitions, and to ascertain whether or not candidates which serve business needs and motives are also compatible with the company's basic financial goal—sustained growth in per-share earnings.

The Rising Cost of Mergers

RICHARD A. WINFIELD

"**H**OW MUCH IS MY COMPANY WORTH?**"** This has never been an easy question to answer, and it may have been even more difficult to answer in 1967 than it was in previous years. In 1966, in reporting on a similar survey of prices paid for companies during 1965, B. R. Wakefield and R. M. Sykes noted a tendency for companies to be sold at their quoted market price and for privately owned companies to be sold for a somewhat lower price than comparable publicly held companies.[1] In the two years since there has been a tendency for acquisitions to be made at higher prices in relationship to the stock market. It also appears that acquisitions in 1967 had less correlation with stock-market rises and more correlation with the price/earnings ratio of the acquiring company than was true in 1965. Nonetheless, there was clearly enough correlation between acquisition prices and stock-market prices in 1967 for a comparison of the two to yield some useful guidelines for acquisition pricing decisions.

[1] B. R. Wakefield and R. M. Sykes, "Valuing Companies for Sale or Acquisition: A Survey of Prices Paid in 200 Acquisitions in 1965," *The Arthur Young Journal*, Summer 1966. Reported in *Alert*, newsletter of the Research Institute of America, September 28, 1966, and in *Case & Comment*, November-December 1966.

Richard A. Winfield is a member of the New York audit staff of Arthur Young & Company. He gratefully acknowledges the assistance of Richard J. Morris and Martin Rothman, also of Arthur Young & Company, in compiling the information for this survey.

The 1965 survey was designed to answer the following questions:

☐ **What prices are being paid, in relation to earnings and net worth, for companies in various industries?**

☐ **How closely do these prices relate to the stock-market averages?**

The primary reason for conducting the 1965 survey was that little reliable information was available concerning the prices actually paid for acquisitions. As reported by the firm of W. T. Grimm & Company, there were a total of 2,125 mergers and acquisitions in 1965. In 1966, a year of tight money and a bear market, the number of transactions increased by 12 percent, to 2,377, and in 1967 the number of transactions increased by 25 percent, to 2,975. Because of the lack of reliable information about the prices paid in these transactions, we have reviewed the information available for acquisitions entered into during 1966 and 1967 with the same objectives as impelled the 1965 survey. In addition, we attempted to determine whether any significant trends were discernible.

NATURE OF THE SURVEY

We reviewed the information available on all mergers and acquisitions reported in the 1967 issues of *Mergers & Acquisitions* magazine's monthly newsletter. We also reviewed all listing applications filed with the New York and American Stock Exchanges for securities issued to acquire or merge with another company.

Only transactions with an agreement date in 1967 were included in our survey. In order for an acquisition to be included in the survey, the net income of the selling company for the most recent 12-month fiscal period had to be available. Whenever possible, we also tabulated the most current balance of stockholders' equity. (No adjustment was made to this equity for intangibles such as research and development or goodwill.) In most cases, the date of agreement was used to determine the value of the securities used in a transaction. In those cases where the date of agreement could not be determined, the date of announcement in the press was used.

The earnings figures used to determine the price/earnings ratios included in this survey in many cases are not the earnings figures used by the acquiring company. As mentioned above, we used the latest available 12-month results of operations—generally the latest audited figures included in a prospectus. The acquirer, of course, may have used more recent figures or adjusted figures.

One problem we encountered was determining the value of a new issue of convertible securities used to acquire a company. After comparing a limited sample of the market prices of convertible securities with the market prices of the common stock into which they are convertible, we concluded that the value of convertibles was, on the average, about 15 percent higher than the prices of the related common stocks. To price new issues of convertible securities, therefore, we "converted" the securities into common stock, priced the common stock, and then added a 15 percent premium to this price.

To test the validity of this assumption with respect to convertible securities that were traded publicly, we compared the value we arrived at with the range of prices at which the security was traded, subsequent to its issue, during 1967. With only a few exceptions we found the value we arrived at to be within the range of the traded prices during 1967.

The survey included only transactions involving the acquisition at one time of 80 percent or more of the outstanding common stock of a company.

If the selling company operated at a loss during the most recently reported 12-month period, the transaction was not included in the survey. Also excluded were approximately 190 transactions which involved possible additional payments of cash or securities contingent upon the future earnings of the acquired company.

Each acquired company included in the survey was classified by industry. The industry classifications used were generally those for which industry price/earnings ratios are published in Standard & Poor's *Industry Surveys*. One of the most difficult tasks in gathering the data for the survey was the classification of acquired companies by industry on the basis of the information available. There is no assurance that our classifications are completely consistent with Standard & Poor's. Also, certain industries are defined too broadly for their P/E ratios to be truly meaningful. Thus, for example, the markets served and the products manufactured by most of the companies classified as "metal fabricating" are so significantly different that one would expect a wide range of P/E ratios paid for companies so classified. We did in fact find that these companies varied from a high of 36.9 to a low of 6.6.

RESULTS OF THE SURVEY

Of the approximately 2,975 transactions that were agreed to in 1967, 468 met the criteria for inclusion in our survey. The total purchase price

Exhibit 1. Acquisition Price Survey—1967

Industry	Number of Acquisitions	Total of Prices Paid (000)	Earnings of Acquired Companies (000)	Acquisitions: Purchase-Price-to-Earnings Ratios	Net Assets of Acquired Companies (000)	Acquisitions: Purchase-Price-to-Net-Assets Ratios	Stock Market: Market-Price-to-Earnings Ratios High (1967) Low
Aerospace	6	$ 140,848	$ 4,982	28.3	$ 29,166[1]	4.6[1]	22.5–15.5
Air transport	5	85,578	4,677	18.3	20,362	4.2	18.5–12.1
Apparel manufacturers	7	129,029	9,030	14.3	49,139	2.6	17.0–13.6
Auto parts and accessories	8	1,045,331	70,411	14.8	389,796	2.7	15.0–11.2
Auto trucks and parts	4	17,552	1,939	9.1	7,973[1]	1.5[1]	17.0–11.5
Baking and milling	3	9,419	652	14.5	3,424	2.8	15.6– 7.3
Banking and finance	4	8,220	353	23.3	5,519	1.5	14.4– 9.0
Broadcasting	3	11,759	354	33.2	2,612	4.5	14.1–11.2
Building:							
cement companies	6	100,225	6,852	14.6	72,580	1.4	18.4–10.2
heating and plumbing	7	66,241	4,266	15.5	53,647	1.2	17.8– 7.2
Chemicals	28	489,053	28,869	16.9	236,271[1]	2.0[1]	18.4–15.1
Consulting:							
computer-oriented	5	47,579	1,753	27.1	6,524	7.3	
non-EDP	9	67,386	4,289	15.7	26,563	2.5	
Distributors and retailers (miscellaneous)	16	508,755	19,076	26.7	109,508	4.7	
Educational	7	16,959	875	19.4	2,361	3.8	
Electrical equipment	23	541,017	28,396	19.1	212,506	2.5	22.3–15.3
Electrical home appliances	5	106,376	5,726	18.6	73,341	1.5	20.3–14.9
Electronics	27	413,599	19,321	21.5	102,649[1]	3.8[1]	32.2–19.7
Film processing	4	5,623	220	25.6	1,470	3.8	
Foods, packaged	6	164,368	13,921	11.8	132,443	1.2	18.4–16.0
Home furnishings	5	101,930	7,645	13.3	63,526[1]	1.6[1]	17.2–10.8
Hotels and restaurants	5	191,458	8,068	23.7	43,914	4.4	

Machinery:						
construction and material handling	8	37,845	4,194	9.0	26,443	1.4	23.7–16.2
industrial	10	63,175	4,902	12.9	22,074¹	2.7¹	14.0– 9.5
machine tools	8	46,733	3,221	14.5	14,743	3.2	13.3– 6.5
specialty machinery	11	153,191	9,571	16.0	68,926¹	2.2¹	15.8–10.2
Medical and dental supplies and equipment	6	39,390	2,655	14.8	12,457	3.2	
Metal fabricating	33	618,956	41,272	15.0	232,818¹	2.5¹	17.4–11.5
Motion pictures	5	273,763	15,480	17.7	81,661	3.4	15.4–12.1
Office equipment	7	93,910	5,006	18.8	41,159¹	2.1¹	53.6–31.7
Oil:						
crude producers	3	13,524	886	15.3	5,789	2.3	19.8–16.3
oil-well suppliers	4	46,890	1,549	30.3	7,226¹	5.4¹	15.4– 9.6
Paper	11	342,689	21,401	16.0	161,843¹	2.1¹	16.2–13.3
Publishing	14	478,831	15,025	31.9	72,565	6.6	32.4–23.7
Radio and TV manufacturers	5	159,140	6,793	23.4	23,548	6.8	33.4–25.0
Retailing:						
department stores	4	32,758	2,417	13.6	16,256	2.0	17.5–12.7
food chains	3	135,076	8,742	15.5	97,806	1.4	13.8–11.7
Shoes and leather	4	12,589	1,030	12.2	12,641	1.0	15.7– 8.5
Sporting equipment	6	43,037	3,593	12.0	16,702¹	2.4¹	
Telephone utilities	30	569,347	17,405	32.7	163,640	3.5	17.1–13.9
Vending	14	197,132	5,840	33.8	38,412	5.1	
All others	86	3,248,895	190,492	17.1	1,575,505¹	2.0¹	
TOTALS	468	$10,886,770	$603,820	18.0	$4,340,385	2.5	18.2–15.3

[1] The net assets of one or more of the selling companies in this industry were not available. Before calculating the purchase-price-to-net-assets ratios the purchase price of these companies was excluded from the industry total.

[2] From Standard & Poor's Industry Surveys.

of these 468 transactions was close to $11 billion. We included several industry classifications, primarily in service-oriented fields, for which we had no stock-market P/E ratios for comparative purposes. The purchase-price-to-earnings ratio and purchase-price-to-net-assets ratio for each industry were calculated using the total dollar amount of the three quantities for each industry. Thus, these figures are weighted averages. The results, by industry, are shown in Exhibit 1.

It cannot be proved statistically that the 468 transactions included in this survey are a representative sample of the 2,975 transactions consummated in 1967. When interpreting the results of this survey, the many limitations of the data used should be considered. In our opinion, however, none of these limitations are of such significance that they would negate the conclusions expressed here.

Exhibit 2.   Distribution of Price/Earnings Ratios

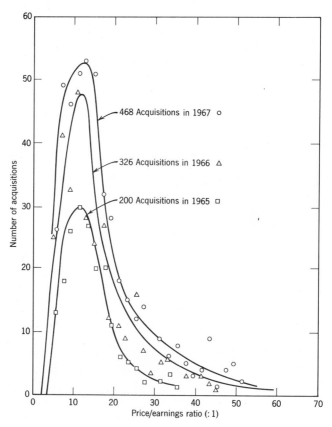

On the basis of the survey results it would appear that the average acquisition price paid for the earnings of companies within the same industry relates quite closely to the stock-market average for that industry. Of the 32 acquisition P/E ratios we were able to compare with the stock-market averages, only eight were significantly different from the market averages. The remaining 24 ratios that were compared with the industry averages support the conclusion of Wakefield and Sykes that "stock-market industry averages are a valid starting point in valuing companies for acquisition or sale."

The purpose of this survey was to compare prices paid with broad industry P/E ratios. Any individual company interested in determining a fair price for its earnings should determine the P/E ratios of those publicly held companies that are most similar to it in products manufactured and markets served.

Exhibit 2 is a distribution of the P/E ratios for the 468 transactions included in the survey. The majority of the ratios (33 percent) range from 7 to 17 times earnings. The distribution is skewed to the right, however, and as a result the average price paid for the earnings of the 468 companies is 18 times earnings. Also shown in Exhibit 2 are the distributions of P/E ratios for acquisitions during 1965 and 1966. These distributions are similar to the 1967 distribution, but they show a trend toward higher ratios. The average in 1965 was 15.8, and in 1966 it was 16.3.

The average purchase-price-to-net-worth ratio in the 1967 survey is 2.5, as compared with 2.4 for 1965 and 2.2 for 1966. As suggested in the report on the 1965 survey, this ratio serves the rather negative purpose of showing that prices paid in corporate acquisitions and mergers bear little relation to the book values of the companies under consideration. Another way of looking at this ratio is to consider that the 468 transactions included in the survey created $6.4 billion worth of problems for the accounting profession. This represents the difference between the prices paid and the book values acquired in the 468 transactions and highlights the significance of the current controversy over "purchase" versus "pooling" accounting for mergers and acquisitions.

COMPARISON OF 1965, 1966, 1967

There has been a significant change in the nature of the mergers and acquisitions market since 1965. Consider the comparison in Table 1 of the aggregate acquisition P/E ratios from our surveys with the highs and lows of Standard & Poor's 425 industrial averages for the three years.

TABLE 1

	No. of Acquisitions	Aggregate Ratio	Standard & Poor's Average
1965	200	15.8	17.8 – 15.6
1966	326	16.3	17.1 – 13.3
1967	468	18.0	18.2 – 15.3

In general the acquisition ratio averages were near the low of the range of stock-market P/E ratios for 1965. In the aggregate, the acquisition ratio averages have moved from the low side of the range of stock-market ratios to the high side.

Exhibit 3 is a comparison of purchase-price-to-earnings ratios for 1965, 1966, and 1967 for various industries included in our surveys of those years.

For each industry in the surveys, we compared the acquisition P/E ratios to the median of the stock-market high and low ratios for the year. For the year 1965 we found the great majority of acquisition P/E ratios to be below the median ratio for the industry. For 1966 we found the acquisition ratios to be approximately equally divided above and below the industry median. The comparison for 1967 shows the great majority of acquisition ratios to be higher than the median industry P/E ratio for the year.

Evidently the acquisitions market has moved from a discount below the stock market in 1965 to a premium above the stock market in 1967. To study this situation we selected at random several acquisitions included in our survey which resulted in the exchange of common stock. We compared the P/E ratio of the selling company on the agreement date to the P/E ratio based on the purchaser's shares exchanged in the transaction. The results of this comparison are given in Table 2.

TABLE 2

Buyer	Seller	Price/Earnings Ratio	
		Acquisition	Stock Market
Teledyne Inc.	Firth Sterling Inc.	26.3	18.9
Harris Intertype Corp.	Radiation Inc.	41.0	36.4
Scott Paper Company	S. D. Warren Co.	15.0	13.0
Litton Industries	Stouffer Foods	28.6	22.0
General Instrument Corp.	Jerrold Corp.	28.6	21.1
Itek Corp.	Applied Technology Inc.	73.7	47.4

Exhibit 3. Three-Year Comparison of Acquisition Purchase Price/Earnings Ratios By Industry

This exhibit includes only industries for which we determined purchase price/earnings ratios for at least two years.

Industry	1965 Price/Earnings Ratio	1966 Price/Earnings Ratio	1967 Price/Earnings Ratio
Aerospace		9.4	28.3
Apparel and textile manufacturing	12.4	11.0	14.3
Auto parts and accessories	11.9	12.8	14.8
Baking and milling		11.7	14.5
Banking and finance	10.8	23.1	23.3
Building products	15.1	10.8	15.0
Chemicals	22.2	17.2	16.9
Confectionary	14.4	18.7	
Containers	14.0	17.9	
Drugs	18.6	18.8	
Electrical equipment	15.0	17.6	19.1
Electronics	19.8	37.5	21.5
Foods, canned	12.8	7.9	
Foods, packaged	17.0	15.8	11.8
Home furnishings	18.4		13.3
Machinery, construction and material handling	15.6		9.0
Machinery, industrial	11.6	11.9	12.9
Machinery, machine tools		13.1	14.5
Machinery, specialty		10.5	16.0
Medical and dental supplies		19.9	14.8
Metal fabricating	12.1	9.5	15.0
Motion picture and broadcasting		21.3	18.0
Office equipment		19.6	18.8
Oil	23.5	14.3	24.8
Paper	19.2	17.2	16.0
Publishing		28.0	31.9
Retailing, department stores	15.7	10.7	13.6
Retailing, food chains	15.5		15.5
Retailing, miscellaneous wholesale and retail	14.0	11.3	26.7
Shoes and leather		10.6	12.2
Telephone		27.1	32.7
Vending		10.8	33.8

Thus it does in fact appear that the nature of the mergers and acquisitions market has been changing.

During 1966, and again in 1967, there was a significant increase in the use of convertible securities as consideration for companies being acquired or merged. In its simplest form, all other things being equal, the use of convertible preferred securities allowed the surviving entity to increase the apparent earnings available to common stockholders—and, as a result, its earnings per share—by changing the capital structure of the entity. This is the result if the dividend on the new securities exchanged for the common stock of the acquired company is less than the income of the acquired company and no consideration is given to the likelihood of the preferred shares being converted into common stock at some future date.

The potential dilution of earnings that could result from the existence of convertible securities led the Accounting Principles Board of the American Institute of Certified Public Accountants in its Opinion No. 9 to introduce the concept of "residual securities" in the calculation of earnings per share.

The Securities and Exchange Commission, in its Release No. 4910 of June 18, 1968, has taken a stronger position than the Accounting Principles Board. The release states:

"In general, *if at the time of issuance of a convertible security in an acquisition,* the terms are such as to result in immediate material dilution to pro forma earnings per share, assuming conversion, then that security should be considered a residual security whether or not a majority of its value may be derived from its conversion rights." [Emphasis supplied.]

In this light it seems likely that convertible securities will be a less popular acquisition currency in the immediate future.

CONTINGENT PAYMENT ARRANGEMENTS

As mentioned earlier, approximately 190 transactions were not included in the results of this survey because they involved payments based on the future earnings performance of the acquired entity. For an acquiring company which follows a policy of decentralized management, this type of transaction has several attractive features. The risk of overpaying for an acquisition is minimized because a portion of the payment is based on the actual future earnings of the acquired entity. If the reason for the payout agreement is to provide management with a tangible incentive to perform, the success of such an arrangement is contingent upon the management of the acquired entity retaining the authority to make decisions that will affect profits. This type of arrangement seems to work best when a minimum amount of synergistic effect is expected to be realized from the combination.

Because of the increasing interest in contingent payment arrangements, we reviewed the information available on the 1967 transactions to determine the major terms of the agreements. These terms create some interesting accounting problems which are beyond the scope of this article. Specifically, we determined, where the information was available:

☐ **The proportion of the total payment which is contingent.**
☐ **The period over which the contingent payments are to be determined.**
☐ **The number of determinations of the contingent payments.**
☐ **The basis of determination of the contingent payments.**

The number of agreements grouped by the percentage of the total consideration that was contingent on future earnings is presented in Exhibit 4. For example, 10 to 19.9 percent of the total consideration for 13 transactions was contingent on future earnings. The great majority of contingent payment percentages fall between 20 and 60 percent. The most common percentage of contingent payment to total payment is 50 percent, specified in 24 of 147 agreements.

In Exhibit 5, Table A shows the period over which the contingent payments are to be determined. The most common period of time was

Exhibit 4. Contingent Payment as a Percentage of Total Payment

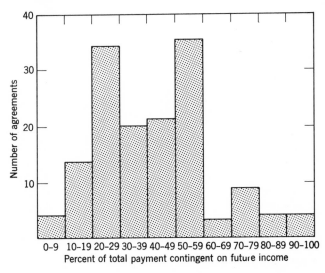

Percent of total payment contingent on future income

five years, with a significant number of agreements specifying two-, three-, and one-year periods. There were also two agreements that called for periods of 10 and 12 years, respectively.

The number of determinations of contingent payments is shown in Table B. The information available for a significant number of agreements specified only "from time to time," and we were unable to determine the exact number of determinations of payment. On the basis of the 107 agreements for which we could learn the number of determinations of payment, a single determination is by far the most common. Even after eliminating the 23 agreements which called for determination of the contingent payment over one year or less, there is still a significant number of agreements which call for only one determination of the contingent payment.

The basis for determining the contingent payment or payments is presented in Table C. A majority of the agreements specified pretax or after-tax earnings. The price of the buyer's stock at the time of the payment was specified as a contingency in addition to the earnings of the selling entity in 42 of 120 agreements.

Exhibit 5

TABLE A: PERIOD OVER WHICH CONTINGENT PAYMENT WAS DETERMINED

Period	No. of Agreements
1 – 11 months	3
1 year	20
13 – 23 months	4
2 years	27
25 – 35 months	1
3 years	27
37 – 47 months	4
4 years	9
49 – 59 months	4
5 years	35
61 – 71 months	0
6 years	9
73 – 83 months	1
7 years	3
10 years	1
12 years	1
	149

TABLE B: NUMBER OF DETERMINATIONS OF PAYMENT

Determinations	No. of Agreements
1	50
2	13
3	14
4	9
5	15
6	1
7	1
8	1
9	0
10	1
10+	2
	107

TABLE C: BASIS OF CONTINGENT PAYMENT

	Earnings	Earnings Above a Specified Level	Earnings and Price of Buyer's Stock	Earnings Above a Specified Level and Price of Buyer's Stock	Totals
Pretax	20	16	4	7	47
After-tax	6	14	5	12	37
Tax not mentioned	5	17	6	8	36
	31	47	15	27	120

As one might expect, the acquiring company was willing to share the earnings of the selling entity only above a specified level in a majority of the agreements.

As was pointed out in the report on the 1965 survey, any analysis such as that reported here will merely tell the potential buyer what he can expect to have to pay for a particular company. He will have to conduct a separate study to establish his own justification for the acquisition by determining *the value of the selling company to him.*

The Role of the Appraiser
in Mergers and Acquisitions

JOHN L. VAUGHAN, Jr.

THE ROLE OF THE APPRAISER in corporate acquisitions and mergers can be very simply stated. His only role in such transactions is to provide management with fully supportable estimates and opinions as to the fair market value of all assets involved in a corporate acquisition, merger, consolidation, or sale. The key words in this statement are "fair market value." Since the most frequent use of the appraiser's estimates and opinions is to provide a basis for the allocation of the purchase price, it is well to remember that Section 1.167(a)(5) of the Federal income tax regulations states that any such allocation or apportionment must be based upon the relative *fair market value* of each of the elements. All of the elements, including any intangibles, must be considered in relation to one another under this section of the regulations; and the appraisal procedures used must be those which are generally acceptable to taxing authorities.

While the role of the appraiser can be simply stated, the fulfillment of that role is considerably more complex. When we consider the diversity of the assets owned by many corporations, the ability of any single individual to provide expert opinions as to the value of all assets owned is questionable to say the least. Fortunately, the term "appraiser," as used in this discussion, is not intended to apply, in all cases, to a specific individual. There are appraisal firms today that are staffed with experts

John L. Vaughan, Jr. is Vice President of Marshall and Stevens Inc., Los Angeles.

in many fields. While it is true that the individual must coordinate the efforts of these various experts and be in a position to express an opinion as to the fair market value of the marketable entity or business, this conclusion is the result of staff analyses of many different elements, conducted by many different people.

Classification of assets for the purpose of allocation of purchase price, and the tax reasons for such allocation, are discussed elsewhere in this volume.* When one considers the many ways in which assets can be classified, and the different appraisal procedures required as a result, the complexity of the valuation task becomes apparent.

WHY USE AN APPRAISER?

Since the role of the appraiser is so difficult, why not use many appraisers, or why not rely on informed persons on the staffs of the corporations concerned?

It can certainly be logically argued that the engineering, accounting, and management personnel of a business have more specific knowledge of the actual cost (and possibly the value as well) of each of the component parts of the business than does the outside or independent appraiser. On the other hand, it cannot be denied that such personnel cannot, by definition, have a disinterested viewpoint in the matter. There is always the possibility that their opinions might be influenced by self-interest, and consequently they are simply not as acceptable to the taxing authorities as is the opinion of a disinterested appraiser retained for a specific job assignment. Certainly an experienced and prudent appraiser will consult with and obtain much of his technical information from company personnel, but his conclusions as to value must be his own, arrived at through his own independent analysis.

In today's economy, with the heavy tax burden most businesses must carry, it is no secret that a major consideration in many consolidations, mergers, and acquisitions is the potential tax advantages to be derived from such transactions. It is certain that all such transactions will be carefully scrutinized by the Internal Revenue Service to verify the fact that the positions taken by the corporate entities involved are in accordance with the regulations of the Service and the interpretations that the courts have made thereof. Unfortunately, there are no clearly defined rules, nor are there court decisions covering all the situations which arise.

* See "Tax Aspects of the Allocation of Purchase Price in a Corporate Acquisition," by William L. Gladstone, p. 172.

There is, in fact, a wide "grey area" in which different opinions as to the market value of a particular group of assets may occur. The best insurance that management can have against future tax penalties resulting from disallowed allocations and depreciation allowances is a well-prepared and carefully documented appraisal of all of the assets involved in such transfers of ownership made in conformity with current rules and interpretations of the Internal Revenue Service.

SIX WAYS THE APPRAISER CAN BE USED

For convenience in discussing the role of the appraiser, we may divide the areas in which his services are important into six different stages. In each of these stages the services of the appraiser can be used either in relation to that stage only or consecutively as negotiations continue. These six stages of development may be briefly summarized as follows:

1. At the time negotiations are begun, the knowledge of the appraiser may be used in providing estimates of the probable range of values which will be developed by an appraisal, and the probable allocation of such values to the depreciable and nondepreciable assets.

2. After tentative agreement has been reached as to over-all price, a tentative allocation of the total price can be made by the appraiser. Such a tentative allocation can serve as the basis for a management decision as to the type of acquisition or merger to be consummated (i.e., taxable or nontaxable).

3. When the total purchase price is finally established, an allocation of this price can be made on the basis of the appraiser's estimate of the market value of the various components.

4. When the allocation is made, the appraiser can make recommendations as to the remaining useful life of the component parts for depreciation purposes.

5. In many corporate acquisitions and mergers, the existing debentures (or, in some cases, long-term leases) require certification prior to accomplishment of the proposed action, and the appraiser is a logical choice to perform such certification.

6. In discussions and negotiations with taxing authorities, or in presenting expert testimony in the event litigation develops, the services of the appraiser can be most useful.

Now that we have defined the six stages of the appraiser's service, let us be more specific as to the role of the appraiser in each of these situations.

EARLY STAGES OF NEGOTIATIONS

The services of the qualified appraiser can be profitably utilized by either the buyer or the seller, or by both. Thus, for example, both parties to the discussion should know whether the book values of the fixed assets of the corporation being considered for acquisition are representative of the actual fair market value of such assets. In many instances, corporations have owned real estate for a number of years, and the book value of the land may be substantially less than the fair market value of the land. At the same time, the replacement cost of the building and structures may be substantially greater than the original cost, and the depreciated book cost may provide little or no measure of the actual value of these assets to the acquiring corporation. There are many circumstances under which the book value of machinery and equipment has little or no relation to its current fair market value. As an example, immediately after World War II and again immediately after the Korean hostilities, a large amount of surplus material was made available by the military services and other Government agencies. In some instances, this equipment was purchased by industry at a fraction of its actual worth. Today, in spite of the lapse of time subsequent to acquisition, some of this machinery and equipment might be worth substantially more than its original cost as reflected on the books of a company which bought it as war surplus.

A competent appraisal organization, by utilizing the specialists on its staff, can usually determine without an extensive survey a probable relationship between the book value and the fair market value of such assets. In addition, the appraiser, by using such guides as price/earnings ratios, net-worth estimates, yield rates, and other measures of value can provide estimates within a reasonable range of the value of the business.

In summary, the basic role of the appraiser in the preliminary negotiations leading to a contemplated acquisition or merger is primarily that of a consultant, advising management as to the probable range of values of the business and of the various types of assets acquired.

AFTER TENTATIVE AGREEMENT HAS BEEN REACHED

The next stage in which the appraiser can play an important part is after the two managements have reached a tentative agreement as to the consideration to be involved in the proposed acquisition or merger and the price has been agreed upon in principal. The tax aspects of the various types of acquisitions and mergers are discussed elsewhere in this volume. If management is to make well-informed decisions as to the type of acquisition or merger which will result in the most advantageous tax position, it is essential that it know the value of the component parts to be acquired. The fair market value of these component parts will provide the basis for depreciation.

As a specific example of the value of the appraiser's services in this area, the author recently fulfilled the role of an appraiser in an acquisition in which Corporation A had negotiated a satisfactory price to be paid for all of the assets of Corporation B. Corporation B was a family-owned corporation engaged in manufacturing mechanical devices, and it had a wholly owned subsidiary, Corporation C, which acted solely as its marketing agent. Our analysis of the assets owned by Corporation B clearly indicated that the value of the buildings, machinery and equipment, and patents owned were substantially in excess of book value. On the other hand, Corporation C had virtually no fixed assets, although it did have an impressive net income record. Corporation A concluded that the most favorable tax position would result if the fixed assets of Corporation B could be acquired for cash while the stock in Corporation C could be acquired through a tax-free exchange of stock in Corporation A. As a result of this decision, the acquisition was successfully completed. Corporation A ended up owning the fixed assets of Corporation B, acquired for cash. Consequently, a new cost basis for depreciation purposes was permissible. At the same time, Corporation C was acquired through a tax-free exchange of stock which provided no new depreciation base but did permit the acquisition of Corporation C by Corporation A without tax penalty to Corporation B, the seller. It is important to remember that the entire transaction was based on an independent appraisal of the fair market value of all assets acquired.

ALLOCATION OF PURCHASE PRICE

The role of the appraiser is particularly important in the allocation of the purchase price in a taxable transaction when the assets are set up on the books of the acquiring corporation as a new basis for depreciation purposes. In the specific case described above, the fair market value of the assets of Corporation B served as a basis for allocating the total purchase price to the component parts. In this instance the value of the buildings, machinery and equipment, etc. was substantially in excess of the former book value. In addition to these assets, Corporation B owned a number of patents which were not carried as assets on its books. A detailed analysis of these patents resulted in an appraisal which permitted an allocation of cost to these assets amortizable over the remaining economic life of the patents. Inasmuch as the price paid for the assets of Corporation B was based on the detailed appraisal and this price was determined prior to the completion of the transaction, a direct allocation was possible. In essence the appraisal becomes a bill of sale, reducing the risk of later changes by the Internal Revenue Service. In many other instances we have been asked to make an allocation of a total purchase price when the price had been agreed upon without a detailed appraisal of the underlying assets.

ESTIMATES OF REMAINING LIFE OF ASSETS

The role of the appraiser is of critical importance in providing management with an estimate of the remaining economic useful life of the components to which the purchase price has been allocated. In general, as previously mentioned, the allocations will segregate the total purchase price into land (which is, of course, nondepreciable), structures and improvements, and personal property in the form of machinery and equipment.

Until Revenue Ruling 66-111 was issued by the IRS in 1966, that portion of the purchase price allocated to structures was frequently further broken down into those structural components with long remaining lives and those components with short remaining lives. This procedure is still permitted in the case of new buildings, but where there has been a change of ownership of an existing building Revenue Ruling 66-111 prohibits the use of component depreciation on the structures.

Although it is beyond the scope of this discussion to go into the technicalities of such allocations, it is highly probable that subsequent decisions will show that, although depreciation cannot be taken on component parts of the structure as such, the relative effect of the component parts on the basic structure can be used as a means of establishing the composite life applicable to the building as a whole. Although the degree of acceptance of this theory is questionable, it is certain that, if it is to be accepted at all, it must be based on thorough engineering analysis of the structural components of the building. Furthermore, for any such allocation to be acceptable to the Internal Revenue Service, it must not only be based on physical and structural factors but also give consideration to all pertinent economic factors, including the remaining economic useful life of the structure or structures as a whole.

Insofar as the remaining useful life of individual items of machinery and equipment is concerned, estimates should be made by experts having competency in the eyes of the Internal Revenue Service. Such estimates of remaining life must give consideration not only to the physical and functional use of the component but also to the influence of changing economic conditions and the projected use of the plant facilities.

CERTIFICATION OF DEBENTURES AND LEASES

Although the foregoing areas of discussion are generally known and widely recognized, there is another area in which the role of the appraiser is less widely known. Even those who have had considerable experience with acquisitions and mergers are sometimes surprised to learn that many debentures, agreements, mortgages, and long-term leases contain provisions which can be a stumbling block to accomplishing the planned action. In particular, the standard form of debenture used by banks for years frequently contains a provision under Article VIII (Mergers, Consolidations, or Sales) which requires the appointment of a disinterested person to prepare certifications regarding the effect of the proposed merger, consolidation, or acquisition on the debenture holder.

Standard lease agreements providing for long-term leases of real estate frequently incorporate basically the same requirement for certification. In any consolidation, merger, or agreement involving the lessee the lease requires a certification from a disinterested person which states in substance that, in his judgment, such merger is not in its over-all effect against the interest of the lessor or the person whose interest is derived through the lessor.

The scope of the work involved in such certification frequently requires close cooperation between the accountant handling the merger or acquisition, the legal counsel for the corporation, and the appraiser making the certification. In such instances the role of the appraiser can be critical to the successful completion of the proposed merger.

PRESENTING EXPERT TESTIMONY

At the beginning of this discussion, it was stated that the role of the appraiser was solely to provide corporate management, the accountant, and legal counsel with factual knowledge relating to the fair market value of the assets involved in corporate acquisitions and mergers. It may be further stated that his role is not only to provide such information but to provide it in a form which will be acceptable to the taxing authorities. In the event of litigation—which, unfortunately, cannot always be avoided in connection with problems resulting from our tax laws—the appraiser must be qualified and prepared to testify as an expert on valuations.

IV

Tax Considerations

"The Commissioner of Internal Revenue is a partner in every business enterprise."

MODERN AMERICAN PROVERB

Tax Considerations in Buying or Selling a Corporate Business

ROBERT H. MONYEK and RICHARD L. KESSLER

WHEN A CORPORATE BUSINESS changes hands, income tax considerations present one of the most significant opportunities for both the buyer's and the seller's tax advisers to be of assistance to their clients. Through careful analysis of the many possible methods by which the combination can be effected, the tax adviser can determine which approach yields the most favorable tax consequences and, assuming this to be compatible with the relevant business considerations, recommend that that method be employed. As will be seen, until the form to be followed has been established, any agreement between the parties on the purchase price is meaningless, since a disadvantageous tax result might leave one or both parties in a worse position than would have resulted from a less satisfactory price in a more favorable type of transaction. Too often, business men reach tentative agreement on price without agreement on the form of the transaction. It is at this point that the tax adviser's task becomes especially difficult and important, as the tentative agreement on price must frequently yield to a price which is more appropriate in light of the income tax result of the form in which the transaction is eventually cast.

Unfortunately, those types of transaction more beneficial to the buyer's tax position are typically less beneficial to the seller's, and vice versa.

Robert H. Monyek, CPA, is a partner in the Chicago office of Arthur Young & Company. Richard L. Kessler, CPA, is a member of the tax staff in that office.

It is therefore foolhardy for either party to insist blindly upon the approach most attractive to him, with no consideration of its effect on the other party, since the tax advantage to one party may be exceeded by the second party's tax disadvantage, with the result that the combined taxes are greater than would have resulted from another form of transaction. Good planning requires that the tax advisers of both parties determine the method which will result in the optimum combined tax result, recommend this method to the principals, and assist them in reaching agreement on a price which will, after taxes, leave each party as close as possible to the position which makes the transaction acceptable.

It is our purpose here to describe the possible methods of carrying out a corporate combination, the relative tax advantages and disadvantages of each method to buyer and to seller, and the type of situation in which each method would most likely be more attractive than any other. We assume in every case that the purchaser wishes to conduct the business in corporate form, rather than as a partnership or sole proprietorship, as for many reasons (taxes generally included) this is usually the case. In describing the results of a particular type of transaction, we shall confine our comments to tax considerations. It should not be inferred, however, from the absence of nontax considerations from this discussion, that the authors believe they may safely be ignored. No plan which is not a sensible business transaction should ever be pursued merely for its supposed tax advantage. Since the scope of this discussion is limited to tax implications, and since great importance should be placed on other implications, the reader should also consider these nontax legal and business implications and evaluate them in connection with the desired tax result.[1]

Although each of the several different types of transactions discussed herein produces a somewhat different combination of tax effects on the buyer and seller, the precise tax considerations affected by the choice of the transactions are few. If the importance of each consideration is understood, the format producing the most desirable combined effect on all considerations can easily be determined by reviewing the various possible types of transactions discussed below.

From the seller's point of view, the tax considerations may include the following:

---

[1] For a checklist of nontax as well as tax considerations see *Buyer's and Seller's Points in Sale of Corporate Business: An Outline Checklist*, N.Y.U. 21st Inst. on Fed. Tax., 1065 (1963).

1. If stock is sold, will the resulting gain or loss be recognized for tax purposes?
2. If the transaction takes the form of a sale of corporate assets—
   (a) Will gain or loss be recognized?
   (b) Will any portion of the recognized gain be ordinary income instead of capital gain?
   (c) Will any portion of investment credit claimed in prior years result in an addition to the tax for the year of sale?
   (d) If the corporation is subsequently liquidated, will the liquidation result in recognized income or loss to the shareholders?
3. What is the cost basis of any property other than cash received?

The buyer will generally want to consider these questions:

1. If stock is purchased, will a subsequent liquidation of the corporation result in recognized income or loss to the shareholder (the buyer) or the corporation?
   (a) Will any portion of that gain be ordinary income?
   (b) Will any investment credit previously claimed be added to the tax for the year of liquidation?
2. What is the cost basis of assets acquired by purchase or upon liquidation of the purchased corporation?
3. What is the cost basis of the stock acquired?
4. Are net operating losses and other favorable tax characteristics of the seller corporation available to the buyer?

As previously indicated, there are many ways of buying and selling a corporate business, and the tax effect varies with each method. In the discussion which follows, we shall explain the tax implications of several different methods of business combinations, including cash purchases of assets or of stock and tax-free reorganizations. If the facts of a given situation are measured against the tax effect of each method, the method producing the most favorable tax result in the case at hand can readily be determined.

TAXABLE TRANSACTIONS

Shareholders Sell Their Stock

One of the simplest methods of selling a corporate business is for the shareholders to sell their stock to the purchasing corporation for cash.

The selling shareholders realize gain or loss[2] to the extent the amount realized exceeds their adjusted basis (normally cost),[3] although they may be able to defer the recognition of gain by electing to report the gain on the installment basis where proceeds in the year of sale do not exceed 30 percent of the selling price.[4]

Since the corporation remains in existence exactly as before, no corporate tax can be created by the transaction.

The buyer may favor acquisition of stock where there are favorable tax attributes (such as net operating loss carryovers) in the corporation being acquired, since these generally may be availed of by the buyer after the acquisition.[5] It may also be advantageous when the corporation has primarily high-basis, low-value assets, since the basis remains unchanged, thereby ordinarily allowing greater depreciation deductions than would be possible if assets were purchased. If the reverse is true, and the corporation has high-value, low-basis assets, an acquisition of stock would thus appear to be disadvantageous; however, as explained below, if the acquiring corporation obtains at least 80 percent of the stock of the selling corporation, it can generally establish a new basis for the assets, equal to their values, by meeting certain conditions of the Internal Revenue Code.[6]

Two-year liquidation. This new basis for the assets can be achieved by liquidating the acquired corporation pursuant to a plan of liquidation adopted within two years following the purchase[7] of 80 percent of the stock, by reason of an Internal Revenue Code provision.[8] The effect of this provision is to treat the purchase of stock followed by a liquidation almost as if the transaction had been a purchase of assets in the first instance. This is accomplished by allocating to the assets, in proportion to their fair market values, the price paid by the acquiring corporation for the stock,[9] adjusted for transactions between the date of acquisition

[2] Int. Rev. Code of 1954, §1001.
[3] Int. Rev. Code of 1954, §1012.
[4] Int. Rev. Code of 1954, §453(b).
[5] This is subject to the limitations of the Int. Rev. Code of 1954, §§ 269, 382, described herein.
[6] Liquidation under Int. Rev. Code of 1954, §332, with basis determined under Int. Rev. Code of 1954, §334(b)(2).
[7] Int. Rev. Code of 1954, §334(b)(3), defines "purchase," which is generally considered to be any acquisition from an unrelated party in a taxable transaction.
[8] *Supra,* note 6.
[9] Treas. Reg. §1.334-1(c)(4)(vi)(b)(1958).

and the date of liquidation.[10] In a case where the stock is purchased at a price in excess of the net basis of the corporation's assets, this will generally bring about greater depreciation deductions in future years than would have been allowable if the acquired corporation had remained in existence. Management must therefore ascertain whether the facts of the case at hand are such that it would be beneficial to liquidate in this manner. If the plan of liquidation is not adopted within the two-year period, or the applicable statutory provision is not satisfied in any other respect, the assets received in liquidation will have a basis equal to their basis to the acquired corporation,[11] so that no change in basis will result from the liquidation. Needless to say, if the buyer wishes to take advantage of the opportunity to establish a new basis, he must be meticulous in complying with the terms of the statutory provision.

A liquidation giving rise to a new tax basis for the assets creates no recognized gain or loss to the parent corporation upon receipt of the liquidating distributions.[12] The liquidated corporation, however, will generally incur a tax liability as a result of the liquidation, as follows:

1. To the extent that the assets distributed in liquidation consist of depreciable personal property, the amount by which their values exceed their tax bases (but limited to the depreciation claimed thereon after December 31, 1961) is ordinary income to the liquidated corporation.[13]

2. Depreciable real property distributed in liquidation may also result in ordinary income to the liquidated corporation where depreciation in excess of straight-line has been claimed, to the extent of a percentage of the amount by which the depreciation claimed thereon since December 31, 1963 exceeded the depreciation that would have been claimed under the straight-line method of computing depreciation.[14]

3. To the extent that the liquidated corporation had in prior years claimed the 7 percent investment tax credit on acquisitions of property which, at the date of liquidation, had been held for a shorter period of time than was estimated as the property's useful life for purposes of com-

---

[10] These adjustments are enumerated in Treas. Reg. §1.334-1(c)(4)(v)(1958) and provide that the stock must be increased by earnings and unsecured liabilities assumed by the parent and decreased by losses and distributions between the date the 80 percent ownership was acquired and the date of the last distribution in liquidation.

[11] Int. Rev. Code of 1954, §334(b)(1).

[12] Int. Rev. Code of 1954, §332(a).

[13] Int. Rev. Code of 1954, §1245, and Treas. Reg. §1.1245-1(c), Example (2) (1965).

[14] Int. Rev. Code of 1954, §1250, and Example in Proposed Treas. Reg. §1.1250-1(a)-(4), 31 Fed. Reg. 92 (1966).

puting the credit,[15] the excess credit thereby claimed in prior years is added to, and becomes part of, the liquidated corporation's tax for the year of liquidation.

A liquidation giving rise to a new tax basis for the assets received will not entitle the parent corporation to avail itself of the net operating loss carryovers and other favorable tax attributes of the liquidated corporation.[16]

Advantages of avoiding the two-year liquidation. If for any reason the Code provision by which the assets received in liquidation acquire a new tax basis is not satisfied, so that they retain the same basis as in the hands of the liquidated corporation, this disadvantage is at least partially offset by a more favorable outcome under some of the other tax considerations discussed above. The tax on the liquidated corporation from income arising out of the distribution of depreciable property is eliminated, as the Code provides for nonrecognition of this income in a liquidation on which the assets retain their bases.[17] Similarly, no investment credit claimed in prior years is added to the tax of the liquidated corporation if the assets retain their bases.[18] Finally, the parent corporation, after the liquidation, is entitled to take advantage of net operating loss carryovers and other favorable tax attributes of the liquidated corporation.[19]

In many instances it is better to arrange a liquidation purposely in such a manner that the assets will not take a new tax basis, as the tax benefit of the new basis may be less than the benefit of avoiding the

[15] Int. Rev. Code of 1954, §47.

[16] Int. Rev. Code of 1954, §381(a)(1).

[17] Where basis is determined under Int. Rev. Code of 1954, §334(b)(1), there is no depreciation recapture except for distributions to minority shareholders (Int. Rev. Code of 1954, §1245(b)(3) and §1250(d)(3)). However, depreciation deductions of the subsidiary must be taken into account by the parent upon subsequent disposition. (See Treas. Reg. §1.1245-2(c)(2) (1965) and Proposed Treas. Reg. §1.1250-3(c)(3), 31 Fed. Reg. 92 (1966).)

[18] There is no investment credit recapture according to Int. Rev. Code of 1954, §47(b)(2), since Int. Rev. Code of 1954, §381(a), applies where basis is determined under Int. Rev. Code of 1954, §334(b)(1). However, subsequent disposition of such property will result in recapture according to Int. Rev. Code of 1954, §381(c)(23).

[19] Int. Rev. Code of 1954, §381(a), does not exclude from the carryover provisions the general rule of Int. Rev. Code of 1954, §334(b)(1), in the liquidation of a subsidiary under Int. Rev. Code of 1954, §332. Int. Rev. Code of 1954, §382(a), disallows net operating losses in certain acquisitions when the acquired corporation's business does not remain substantially unchanged.

additional tax on the liquidated corporation and causing the carryovers and other attributes to become available to the acquiring corporation. The tax adviser must carefully consider which procedure, all factors considered, produces the best over-all tax result, and recommend to management that this plan be followed.

Corporation Sells Its Assets

As an alternative to the sale of stock, the corporation could sell the corporate assets. The buyer may want to purchase assets when the seller's basis for the assets is lower than the price to be paid in order to obtain a higher basis, or where it is desirable to avoid taking over the seller's unfavorable tax attributes such as substantial accumulated earnings or an undesirable depreciation method. The sale of assets would be advantageous to the seller when the asset sale would create a net operating loss carryback to prior profitable years, thereby permitting seller to recover a portion of the taxes paid in prior years, or when it is desirable to keep the corporation in existence permanently so that the only tax paid will be the corporate tax on its gain, instead of the shareholder's tax on his presumably larger gain.

If the purchaser acquires the assets for cash or for any other property in a taxable transaction, the basis of the assets is their cost.[20] No loss carryovers or other tax attributes of the selling corporation become available to the purchaser.

The tax effect on the selling corporation and its shareholders is dependent upon whether the corporation is liquidated, and the precise timing of any such liquidation. The different possibilities are discussed and explained below.

Twelve-month liquidation. If the corporation adopts a plan of liquidation prior to the sale of assets and does in fact liquidate within twelve months after the adoption of the plan, the corporation (with one major exception, as indicated below)[21] recognizes no gains and losses from transactions during the twelve-month period.[22] The only tax paid is thus that imposed on the shareholders' gain on liquidation. The net effect to the shareholders is approximately the same as if they had sold

---

[20] Int. Rev. Code of 1954, §1012.
[21] Int. Rev. Code of 1954, §§1245, and 1250. See also Int. Rev. Code of 1954, §47.
[22] Int. Rev. Code of 1954, §337. But see Int. Rev. Code of 1954, §337(b), where gain will be recognized on nonbulk sales of inventory and certain dispositions of installment obligations.

to the purchaser their stock in the corporation.[23] The only significant differences from the result of selling stock are that the corporation recognizes gain (notwithstanding the twelve-month liquidation provision) to the extent attributable to depreciation on personal property after 1961[24] and (subject to exceptions) to depreciation in excess of straight-line on buildings after 1963,[25] and that the corporation's tax for the year of sale is increased by the investment credit claimed in prior years which has become excessive by reason of the short period of time for which the property which generated the credit was in fact held.[26] On a sale of stock, this tax would not have become due. However, if after a purchase of stock the purchaser had later liquidated the corporation in a transaction so arranged that the assets took a new basis, the tax generated by prior depreciation and investment credit claimed by the corporation would then be paid, in that case by the purchaser.[27] To this extent the buyer benefits by buying assets instead of stock, and this difference in tax incidence must be kept in mind when negotiating the price and the form of the transaction.

The twelve-month liquidation provision is not elective, and although it has the advantage of not recognizing gain, it also has the disadvantage of denying the recognition of losses. If there are substantial losses from the sale, the liquidation could be delayed until after the twelve months have elapsed.

Even if the buyer pays for the assets over a period of years, the installment method of reporting gain[28] will not be available if the corporation is liquidated, as the taxable incident to the stockholder is the corporate liquidation, not the sale. If an installment sale is contemplated, it is therefore often best to sell stock instead of assets.

Deferring liquidation. If a sale of assets results in a substantial loss, so great that a portion of it remains available as a carryover to future years, it is generally best not to liquidate the corporation until after the

---

[23] Where the corporation sells its assets and then liquidates under Int. Rev. Code of 1954, §337, amounts distributed to the shareholders will be treated as full payment in exchange for the stock under Int. Rev. Code of 1954, §331(a)(1), and the stockholders will be required to pay a capital gains tax on the excess, if any, of the cash plus fair market value of the liquidating distribution (Treas. Reg. §1.1001-1(a)(1957)) over the basis of their stock.

[24] Int. Rev. Code of 1954, §1245.

[25] Int. Rev. Code of 1954, §1250.

[26] Int. Rev. Code of 1954, §47.

[27] Int. Rev. Code of 1954, §§1245(a)(1), 1250(a)(1), and 47(a)(1).

[28] Int. Rev. Code of 1954, §453.

loss carryover has all been applied against the income of future years or has expired.[29] If, however, the corporation is closely held and derives at least 60 percent of its income from investments (as distinguished from the active conduct of a business), it will have the status of a "personal holding company"[30] and be subject to a penalty tax of 70 percent, increased by any applicable surcharge,[31] on any income which it does not distribute as a dividend. In such an instance it is generally just as well to liquidate in the year following the sale, as under the personal holding company provisions loss carryovers are allowable only in the year immediately following the loss year.[32]

There is often a different reason for maintaining the corporate existence after it has sold its assets. The obvious reason is that if the corporation is kept in existence permanently, the shareholders will never pay tax on the amount by which the value of the corporation exceeds the basis of their stock. A liquidation would cause the shareholders to pay tax on their resulting gain, while the continued existence of the corporation may postpone permanently the payment of this tax.[33] Even though the continuing corporation may be a personal holding company, its existence will ordinarily not create an annual income tax liability for a tax on current income significantly greater than that which would be paid if the corporation had been liquidated. The corporation generally pays only a nominal tax[34] and the shareholders pay tax on their entire investment income, just as they would if the corporation had previously been liquidated and the shareholders had received the investment income directly as own-

[29] Int. Rev. Code of 1954, §172, provides for a three-year carryback or a five-year carryback of a net operating loss.
[30] See Int. Rev. Code of 1954, §§541–547. Generally, the corporation will be a personal holding company if five or fewer individuals own more than 50 percent in value of the outstanding stock and at least 60 percent of its adjusted ordinary gross income (capital gains excluded) is from dividends, interest, royalties, annuities, and rents. Special rules for inclusion of rents and royalties are provided in Int. Rev. Code of 1954, §543(a)(2)–543(a)(4).
[31] Int. Rev. Code of 1954, §51(b).
[32] Int. Rev. Code of 1954, §545(b)(4).
[33] Under the present law, Int. Rev. Code of 1954, §1014 provides that the basis of property received from a decedent will generally be the fair market value of the property at the decedent's death. A shareholder's stock may thus be redeemed at no tax cost after his death.
[34] As long as the corporation's investments are confined to stocks, its tax rate cannot exceed 7.2 percent (increased by any applicable surcharge under Int. Rev. Code of 1954, §51) because of the dividend-received deduction provided by Int. Rev. Code of 1954, §243.

ers of the income-producing property. No personal holding company tax will ever be paid as long as the corporation distributes its entire income as dividends each year,[35] and the tax adviser must be sure that his client pays sufficient dividends each year to accomplish this.

NONTAXABLE TRANSACTIONS

If the transfer of a corporation's business to another corporation takes the form of a tax-free reorganization,[36] the seller will obviously benefit from the nonrecognition of any gain resulting from the transfer.[37] If instead the transfer generates a loss, the reorganization approach has a disadvantage to the seller in that this loss will similarly not be recognized for tax purposes. As explained below, the seller in a reorganization transaction will be paid in stock of the acquiring corporation rather than in cash, and the tax cost basis of the stock will generally be the same as that of the assets or stock transferred,[38] so that upon a later disposition of the stock of the acquiring corporation the gain not now recognized will become taxable. Before a conclusion is reached that a reorganization is the best plan in a given situation, consideration must be given to the possibility that the gain deferred because the transaction qualified as a reorganization may become taxable at a later date, thereby nullifying what may have been one of the important reasons for choosing the reorganization approach initially. If this appears likely, it may be better to have a cash purchase instead of a reorganization, if the other effects of a reorganization, as discussed below, are less desirable than the outcome of a cash purchase. Since the acquiring corporation would in no event have taxable income from the acquisition,[39] the tax-free nature of the reorganization is of no direct interest to it.

Those consequences of a tax-free reorganization which are relevant from the buyer's point of view are that any assets (stock or other property) acquired in a reorganization retain the tax basis which they had in the hands of the prior owner,[40] and net operating losses and other favorable tax attributes generated by the transferor corporation are available.[41]

---

[35] Int. Rev. Code of 1954, §541.
[36] Int. Rev. Code of 1954, §368(a)(1).
[37] Int. Rev. Code of 1954, §354.
[38] Int. Rev. Code of 1954, §362.
[39] Int. Rev. Code of 1954, §1032.
[40] *Supra,* note 38.
[41] Int. Rev. Code of 1954, §381.

These effects, both of which differ from the result in a cash purchase, may cause the purchaser to be greatly benefited or harmed by the choice of a reorganization approach.

In order to qualify as a reorganization a transaction must be motivated by a legitimate business purpose[42] and must result in a continuity of interest to the selling corporation's shareholders.[43] These reorganizations, including the tax significance[44] and the advantages and disadvantages of each, will be the subject of the following discussion.

Stock for Stock

One of the methods of acquiring a business tax-free is to acquire 80 percent or more control[45] of the stock of the seller, solely in exchange for the acquiring corporation's voting stock. This method will be referred to hereinafter as a "stock-for-stock reorganization" and is sometimes referred to as a "B" reorganization.[46] The stock-for-stock reorganization permits the acquired corporation to continue taking advantage of its own loss carryovers and other favorable tax attributes. Since the acquired corporation remains in existence, no corporate tax is generated, whether from prior depreciation or investment credit or any other cause.

In a stock-for-stock reorganization the buyer does not have to acquire the 80 percent or more control at one time and may even have previously owned some stock acquired in a taxable transaction. In order for the

---

[42] Treas. Reg. §1.368-2(g) (1955).

[43] Ibid. See also Comm'r v. Segall, 114 F.2d 706 (6th Cir. 1940), reversing 38 B.T.A. 43 (1938), cert. denied 313 U.S. 562 (1940); Roebling v. Comm'r., 143 F.2d 810 (3d Cir. 1944), affirming 2 CCH Tax Ct. Mem. 392 (1943), cert. denied 323 U.S. 773 (1944).

[44] The operating provisions applicable to reorganizations are as follows: (1) Int. Rev. Code of 1954, §354, providing for nonrecognition of gain or loss on the exchange of stock or securities between parties to a reorganization as defined in Int. Rev. Code of 1954, §368(b); (2) Int. Rev. Code of 1954, §361, providing for nonrecognition of gain or loss to corporation upon the exchange of property for stock or securities pursuant to a reorganization; (3) Int. Rev. Code of 1954, §§356 and 357, providing for the treatment of "boot" and liabilities in reorganization exchanges; (4) Int. Rev. Code of 1954, §§358 and 362(b), providing for carryover of basis in reorganization exchanges; and (5) Int. Rev. Code of 1954, §381, providing for certain carryover attributes subject to the net operating loss carryover limitation of Int. Rev. Code of 1954, §382(b).

[45] "Control" is defined in Int. Rev. Code of 1954, §368(c), as ownership of stock possessing at least 80 percent of the total combined voting power of all classes of voting stock and the ownership of at least 80 percent of the total number of shares of each class of outstanding nonvoting stock. See Rev. Rul. 59-259, 1959-2 Cum. Bull. 115.

[46] Int. Rev. Code of 1954, §368(a)(1)(B).

transfer presently under consideration to be tax-free, it must be an exchange solely for the buyer's voting stock.[47] The term "solely for voting stock" means that the use of any additional consideration prevents the entire transaction from qualifying as a reorganization.[48] A contingent right to receive only additional voting stock satisfies the "solely for voting stock" requirement where the number of shares to be issued is determined by a formula.[49]

In a stock-for-stock reorganization, the acquiring corporation's basis for the stock acquired would be the seller's basis,[50] and the holding period will include the holding period of the seller.[51] The seller's basis for the stock of the acquiring corporation is the basis of its stock given in exchange,[52] and the holding period will include the holding period of the old stock.[53]

Stock for Assets

The other methods of acquiring a business tax-free both involve a corporation's acquisition of the assets of another corporation in exchange for its own stock. The requirements of and differences between the two methods of accomplishing this are discussed below. Since there are many similarities between the results of the two plans, and therefore between the types of situations in which each will be attractive, it is appropriate to consider first what they have in common.

Any tax-free asset-for-stock transaction entitles the acquiring corporation to take advantage of any loss carryovers or other favorable tax at-

---

[47] Treas. Reg. §1.368-2(c) (1955). However, where part of the stock is acquired for cash and soon thereafter controlling stock is acquired in an attempt to qualify as a "B" reorganization, the step transaction theory may be applied to treat the two acquisitions as one, and the second acquisition would be taxable, as the transaction was not solely for stock. See Rev. Rul. 59-259, *supra* note 45.

[48] *Turnbow v. Comm'r.,* 368 U.S. 337 (1962), *affirming* 286 F.2d 669 (9th Cir. 1961), *reversing* 32 T.C. 646 (1959). But see *Mills v. Comm'r.,* 331 F.2d 321 (5th Cir. 1964) *rev'g.* 39 T.C. 393 (1962).

[49] This formula may be based on the future market price of the acquiring corporation (Rev. Rul. 67-90, 1967-1 Cum. Bull. 79) or on future income (Rev. Rul. 66-112, 1966-1 Cum. Bull. 68). Rev. Proc. 67-13, 1967-1 Cum. Bull. 590, indicates six specific requirements for securing a ruling where a contingent payout will be used in connection with a stock-for-stock reorganization.

[50] Int. Rev. Code of 1954, §362(b).

[51] Int. Rev. Code of 1954, §1223(1) and §1223(2).

[52] Int. Rev. Code of 1954, §358(a).

[53] Int. Rev. Code of 1954, §1223(1), if such stock was a capital asset in their hands.

tributes of the transferor corporation.[54] The transfer of assets is completely tax-free to the transferor corporation (except to the extent that part of the consideration is not stock or securities eligible for tax-free treatment under the particular section)[55] even to the extent of gain resulting from prior depreciation,[56] and no tax results from the transfer of property on which investment credit has previously been claimed.[57] The tax basis to the transferee corporation of the assets received is the same as their basis to the transferor corporation,[58] and the basis of stock received from the acquiring corporation is the same as the basis of the property surrendered in exchange therefor.[59]

Merger or consolidation. One method of accomplishing a tax-free stock-for-asset reorganization is the statutory merger or consolidation (sometimes referred to as an "A" reorganization)[60] consummated pursuant to the corporation laws of the United States, a state or territory, or the District of Columbia.

This approach permits more flexibility than the stock-for-stock reorganization in the choice of the type of securities to be transferred in exchange for the assets. Under the statutory merger or consolidation plan, nonvoting common stock, preferred stock, or other securities of the acquiring corporation may be transferred, without causing the transaction to lose its tax-free status. If cash or other property is transferred in

[54] Int. Rev. Code of 1954, §381(c), enumerates the items which are carried over and Treas. Reg. §1.381(a)-1(a) to §1.381(a)-1(b) make such provisions applicable to an "A" and "C" reorganization as defined in Int. Rev. Code of 1954, §368(a)(1).

[55] Int. Rev. Code of 1954, §356.

[56] Gain on depreciation recapture will be recognized, but only to the extent that gain would otherwise be recognized (to the extent of "boot" under Int. Rev. Code of 1954, §356) on the transfer of such assets. (Int. Rev. Code of 1954, §1245(b)(3), and §1250(d)(3); Treas. Reg. §1.1245-4(c) (1955) and Proposed Treas. Reg. §1.1250-3 (c), 31 Fed. Reg. 92 (1966).) Depreciation deductions of the seller on the property transferred which exceeded the depreciation recapture recognized on the transfer of such assets must be taken into account by the buyer upon subsequent disposition according to Treas. Reg. §1.1245-2(c)(2)(1965) and Proposed Treas. Reg. §1.1250-3 (c)(3), 31 Fed. Reg. 92 (1966).

[57] Int. Rev. Code of 1954, §47(b)(2).

[58] *Supra,* note 38.

[59] Int. Rev. Code of 1954, §358(a). The basis of the property acquired is the same as the basis of the property exchanged reduced by any "boot" under Int. Rev. Code of 1954, §356, and increased by any gain recognized. "Boot" has a basis of fair market value under Int. Rev. Code of 1954, §358(a)(2).

[60] Int. Rev. Code of 1954, §368(a)(1)(A).

addition to stock and securities of the acquiring corporation, the transaction will be taxable only to the extent of the cash or other property,[61] rather than in its entirety as under the stock-for-stock reorganization.[62]

A merger of two or more corporations takes place when one of the corporations retains its corporate existence and absorbs the other or others, which thereby lose their corporate existence. A consolidation is a combination of two or more corporations by the formation of a new corporation into which the old corporations are dissolved. In either case, stock of the continuing corporation is issued to the former shareholders of the absorbed corporations.

In addition to meeting the requirements of the applicable state statute, the transaction must perpetuate the taxpayer's original investment (referred to as continuity of interest)[63] and be motivated by a legitimate business purpose.[64] A transfer for cash, promissory notes, and debentures may constitute a statutory merger or consolidation for purposes of state law, but if it fails to preserve the investor's proprietary interest in the enterprise it does not qualify as a reorganization.[65] The same is true if common stock forming part of the consideration has a value representing only a small fraction of the total consideration paid.[66]

A statutory merger or consolidation need not meet the "solely for voting stock" requirement of the stock-for-stock reorganization, and the acquiring corporation may therefore issue stock or securities other than its common stock in exchange for the properties of the merged corporations.[67] Furthermore, a nonvoting common or preferred stock may be utilized and the exchange can qualify as a merger or consolidation even if money or other property changes hands. The money or property (and securities in some circumstances) will constitute "boot"[68] taxable to the recipients, but will not result in disqualifying the transaction in its entirety, as can occur when money, property, or securities are used in a stock-for-stock

---

[61] Int. Rev. Code of 1954, §356.

[62] *Supra,* note 48.

[63] *Morgan Manufacturing Co.,* 124 F.2d 602 (4th Cir. 1942), *affirming* 44 B.T.A. 691 (1941).

[64] Treas. Reg. §1.368-2(g) (1955).

[65] *Supra,* note 43.

[66] *Southwest Natural Gas Co. v. Comm'r.,* 189 F.2d 332 (5th Cir. 1951), *affirming* 14 T.C. 81 (1950), *cert. denied* 342 U.S. 860 (1951), where the stock represented less than 1 percent of total consideration received by the old shareholders.

[67] See *National Gypsum Co. v. Comm'r.,* 1 CCH Tax Ct. Mem. 349 (1942), Rev. Rul. 54-396, 1954-2 Cum. Bull. 147.

[68] Int. Rev. Code of 1954, §354(a)(1) and §356.

reorganization. This allows the seller's common voting-stock equity to be converted into a nonvoting or preferred stock equity, or into a combination of both voting and nonvoting not possible under other reorganization provisions.

The basis of the stock or securities received as a result of a statutory merger or consolidation is the same as the basis of the stock or securities surrendered, increased by the amount of any gain recognized on the transaction and decreased by the amount of any cash received.[69]

Stock-for-assets reorganization. The second nontaxable method of acquiring assets for stock is what is sometimes referred to as a "C" reorganization.[70] The tax effect of this transaction is virtually identical to that of the merger or consolidation, except that here the consideration must (with limited exceptions) consist solely of voting stock.

This type of reorganization occurs when one corporation acquires substantially all the properties of another corporation, solely in exchange for all or a part of its voting stock.[71] In determining whether the exchange meets the requirement of "solely for voting stock," the assumption by the acquiring corporation of liabilities of the transferor corporation will be disregarded.[72] If substantially all the property is acquired, and at least 80 percent of the fair market value of all the property is acquired solely for voting stock, the remainder of this property may be acquired for cash or other property without completely disqualifying the transaction as a reorganization.[73] However, gain will be recognized by the transferor to the extent of the cash or other property.[74]

The term "substantially all" is not precisely defined in the Internal Revenue Code or the related regulations and, as a result, is subject to judicial interpretation. In determining what constitutes "substantially all," the Internal Revenue Service will consider the amount and the nature of the properties retained by the transferor and the purpose of the retention, rather than any particular percentage of the properties held.[75]

---

[69] Int. Rev. Code of 1954, §§358(a) and 362.
[70] Int. Rev. Code of 1954, §368(a)(1)(C).
[71] *Ibid.*
[72] Treas. Reg. §1.368-2(d)(1) (1955).
[73] Int. Rev. Code of 1954, §368(a)(2)(B)(iii).
[74] *Supra,* note 61.
[75] Rev. Rul. 57-518, 1957-2 Cum. Bull. 253: Only 70 percent of the assets was sufficient where 3 percent of its inventory and enough cash, accounts receivable, and notes receivable were retained to pay its outstanding liabilities before liquidating.

Generally, however, even though no particular percentage is controlling, it would appear that 90 percent or more of the assets would be considered "substantially all"[76] but that less than 80 percent may not be considered substantially all.[77] In order to obtain an advance ruling from the Internal Revenue Service that the transaction qualifies as a "C" reorganization, it must be shown that there will be a transfer of at least 90 percent of the fair market value of the net assets, and at least 70 percent of the fair market value of the gross assets held by the corporation immediately before the transfer.[78]

After a corporation has transferred substantially all of its assets to another in exchange for voting stock, the transferor is left with virtually no property other than the stock of the transferee. Keeping this corporation in existence as an investment company would generally serve no useful purpose, and since it can be liquidated in a transaction creating no gain or loss to the shareholders or the corporation,[79] the customary practice is to liquidate it shortly after the exchange of stock for property. After this liquidation, the shareholders of the liquidated corporation own the stock acquired in exchange for the property of the corporation. The end effect is thus identical with that which would have resulted from a merger, in which the corporation's existence would have terminated simultaneously with the transfer of assets.

Limitations of carryovers and attributes. In several instances described above, reference has been made to the availability in the future of loss carryovers and other favorable tax attributes gathered by the acquired corporation in prior years. In certain instances, the Code restricts the availability of these attributes.[80] Prior to adopting any plan of acquisition, consideration should be given to these possible limitations.

The most definite limitation applies in every instance in which after a reorganization taking the form of a transfer of assets (an "A" or "C"

---

[76] *Britt v. Comm'r.*, 114 F.2d 10 (4th Cir. 1940), *affirming* 40 B.T.A. 790 (92%), *Cortland Specialty Co. v. Comm'r.*, 60 F.2d 937 (2nd Cir. 1932), *affirming* 22 B.T.A. 808 (1931), *cert. denied* 288 U.S. 599 (1932) (91½%); *American Foundation Co. v. United States*, 120 F.2d 807 (9th Cir. 1941) (92.6%), *Nelson v. United States*, 69 F. Supp. 336 (Ct. Cl. 1947), *cert. denied* 331 U.S. 846 1947) (91.6% and 95.7%).
[77] *Pillar Rock Packing Co. v. Comm'r.*, 90 F.2d 949 (9th Cir. 1937) (66%); I.T. 2373, VI-2 Cum. Bull. 19 (68% or 75%), but see Rev. Rul. 57-518, *supra* note 75 (70%).
[78] Rev. Proc. 66-34, 1966-2, Cum. Bull. 1232, *amplified by* Rev. Proc. 67-13, 1967-1, Cum Bull. 590.
[79] Int. Rev. Code of 1954, §354.
[80] The limitation or reduction of the net operating loss carryover is computed under Int. Rev. Code of 1954, §382(b)(2).

reorganization) the shareholders of the corporation which generated a loss carryover from prior years own less than 20 percent of the acquiring corporation.[81] In such a situation, the loss allowable in future years is reduced by 5 percent for every percentage point by which the ownership of the acquiring corporation is less than 20 percent.

Another provision of the Code, very general in its application, provides that whenever an acquisition was for the principal purpose of securing a tax benefit which would not otherwise have been available, the tax benefit will be disallowed.[82]

CONCLUSION

The tax adviser of a party to a proposed transfer of a corporate business should review the plans discussed above and determine which of them are feasible from a business point of view, ignoring taxes. The tax effects of each feasible plan on buyer and seller should then be determined, and each party's position under each plan should be compared with his position under each other plan. The plan which provides the best combined result for buyer and seller should then ordinarily be recommended, even though a different plan might be better for either the buyer or the seller individually.

In setting the purchase price, consideration should be given to how much tax advantage each party has given up by agreeing to the plan recommended instead of the plan that is best for him. If this tax cost differential is kept in mind, the parties will be reaching their agreement on price on an informed basis, and will not later be surprised to learn of a hidden tax which, if recognized earlier, would have caused one party to refuse to accept the transaction.

[81] Int. Rev. Code of 1954, §382(b)(1).
[82] Int. Rev. Code of 1954, §269.

Tax Aspects of the Allocation
of Purchase Price
in a Corporate Acquisition

WILLIAM L. GLADSTONE

WHEN A CORPORATE EXECUTIVE is negotiating for a purchase of another company, it is no longer sufficient for him to consider only the business and economic aspects of his prospective purchase. He must also be cognizant of the tax and accounting aspects of the purchase, since these considerations may make the difference between a successful acquisition and a poor one. This approach does not take away from the business executive the responsibility for making the best business deal he can; it merely supports the likelihood that he will, in fact, make the best deal. Obviously, business considerations must be paramount and should not become obscured by tax and accounting technicalities. Although careful attention to tax and accounting considerations can make a good deal better, it can seldom make a bad deal good.

THE ACCOUNTANT'S ROLE

With the business executive established as the key man in an acquisition, let us briefly consider the role of the accountant who is his adviser on tax and financial matters.

William L. Gladstone, CPA, is a partner in the New York office of Arthur Young & Company.

One of the reasons many business men have, in the past, failed to prepare themselves adequately for certain financial technicalities of an acquisition is that, too often, they have felt there was no one they could talk to about their problems. This was caused by two factors which are not so prevalent today: first, a real shortage of competently trained tax personnel; and, second, a lack of sophistication on the part of the business executive which caused him to ignore the assistance that *was* available. Partly this was because the business executive looked upon the tax adviser as a technician and not as a technician–business man; and in this connection he often had a valid point. Even today, many tax advisers are not sufficiently aware of the nature of the business about which they are giving advice, and history has proved that the best tax advice comes from advisers who are business-oriented.

In my experience the finest tax ideas come more from applying a solid knowledge of the tax rules to a business situation which the adviser understands than from trying to fit a business situation into a complicated tax plan devised before the business situation arose. Accordingly, the accountant–financial adviser must understand the business and speak the business's language before attempting to advise on tax and accounting matters. Then he must be prepared to explain his position in language which the business man will understand (we have to learn his language but he, the client, cannot be forced to learn ours). If the business man doesn't understand his adviser—and this is possible even if the adviser knows his technical subject well—he won't listen to his advice. Although the business man may admire the fact that his adviser can quote sections of the Internal Revenue Code without stopping for breath, he will write him off as a technical oddity and go on without the benefit of his advice.

THE ALLOCATION PROBLEM

The major objective in the allocation of the purchase price of a business is to spread the cost realistically over the assets purchased, so that financial position will be fairly stated and, upon realization of the assets purchased, income will be reflected in a reasonable manner. Within this broad general objective there is room for considerable maneuverability and exercise of judgment. Application of the rules on allocation is not rigid, since proper allocation depends on the particular facts of each situation. However, there are some basic guidelines which should be followed, and these will be set forth later.

We used to consider the allocation problem as mainly that of the buyer. Where he made a lump-sum asset acquisition he viewed his allocation problem (from a tax viewpoint) vis-à-vis the anticipated position of the Internal Revenue Service. The seller could generally find a way of reporting his proceeds as a capital gain and, with certain exceptions, did not particularly care how the buyer allocated the purchase price. Since 1963 all this has changed dramatically because of certain amendments to the Internal Revenue Code. The seller now has a much greater stake in the form and allocation aspects of a transaction with the advent of depreciation recapture rules on sales of both real and personal property, investment tax credit recapture, and IRS administrative rules relating to the recovery of previously expensed items through a sale. Today the mere form of a business arrangement can shift the tax incidence to one of the parties and change the financial complexion of the transaction.

In view of the fact that tax considerations can be determinative in a negotiation, the buyer and the seller must each consider separately whether his own over-all business interests will best be served by an open and candid discussion of tax aspects or, alternatively, whether each should try to seek an advantage by taking a beneficial tax approach which might operate to the detriment of the other party (but which might succeed if the other party is not as well advised). The resolution of this question has to be on a case-by-case basis, since it encompasses many considerations, including the business relationship of the parties after the transaction. (Everything else being equal, a buyer who could obtain a tax advantage by couching the contract in a certain way to the detriment of the seller might well have a different point of view, depending on whether after the transaction he will have no further business with the seller or whether the seller will thereafter become part of management and/or be a shareholder of the surviving entity.) While I personally think that it generally is better to have all the tax aspects laid out clearly to both sides, I can conceive of situations where this would not be appropriate. In the last analysis, this must be the decision of the principals. However, it would be imprudent to assume that the opposition is not as well advised as you are.

Communication Between the Dealmakers

The issue of communication between the "dealmakers" could be the subject of a chapter in itself. Suffice it here to say that very often the principals shake hands on a "deal" for $1 million and ask their financial men to "work out the details." Then the financial men have to determine if the $1 million was for stock, or assets, or assets subject to liabilities, or a variation on one of these themes. This is where the jockeying for advantage may come into play and cause ill feeling and possibly break up an otherwise mutually beneficial business arrangement.

There must be a determination of what the essence of the deal is before an attempt is made to suggest an allocation procedure. If there had been communication between the dealmakers and their tax advisers before the handshake agreement, there would be a better chance for ultimate consummation of the transaction. Since this may be a utopian thought, I suggest that there at least be better communication between the dealmaker and his tax adviser *after* the handshake.

Most often the buyer will agree on a purchase price based on factors which have no definite relationship to the value of the specific assets acquired. Of course, the underlying asset value is deemed to be there, but it has not been quantified. It becomes the tax adviser's duty to make such allocation of the whole to the parts. The technical aspects of this will be discussed below, but one illustration of a practical experience may help to emphasize the importance of fact finding *before* the technical tax rules are applied.

An Approach to Fact Finding

In seeking to determine the nature and amount of assets acquired, you must develop an approach. Review of the balance sheet and discussions with the seller are not always fully enlightening, for the seller may well overlook assets which, because of his method of accounting, are not considered to be assets. An experience demonstrating this point occurred in the acquisition of a company which made styled ladies' garments. The purchase price was considerably in excess of the book value of the assets, and the buyer was very much concerned that there would be a goodwill element in the purchase which would make the acquisition unattractive. (See later discussion for the tax effect of goodwill.) Discussions with the seller produced information on a few items of which the buyer, not having previously been in this particular business, was unaware. There were such things as supplies inventory and wrapping materials which accounted for a significant dollar amount, but these items had been expensed under the accounting practice of the sellers. This was not enough to produce the absorption of the purchase price, and some further probing was required. The seller was asked to describe what happened from the time he purchased his raw materials until they left the plant in the form of finished goods. In a rambling way, the seller described how he ordered the goods, how they were shipped to his plant, how they were stored and then taken from storage to be put into the manufacturing process.

The goods were rolled onto a cutting table, the patterns of the particular style placed over the material, and the material cut; the goods were then further processed, the various parts sewn together, and the finished garments packed and shipped. This was a very interesting description (somewhat abbreviated) because the seller mentioned one key fact which to this point had been overlooked by the "allocators." You couldn't come up with the finished product unless you cut it in the shape which was then the style; and this, of course, required the use of the proper patterns. To the seller, patterns were not a balance sheet asset, since the costs of developing them had been previously written off in the form of paper, salaries, etc. However, without these patterns no buyer could produce the varied styles which were one of the keys to the success of the business. These patterns had value—in fact, more than enough value, on an appraised basis, to absorb the purchase price. The very simple procedure of going through each step of the manufacturing process brought out this fact. The result may seem obvious in retrospect, but it was not obvious to a number of sophisticated people at the time.

Limits of This Discussion

The following discussion does not consider tax-free reorganizations, since that is an entirely separate subject; nor will there be any commentary on the accounting concept of "poolings of interests." Tax-free reorganizations and poolings most often involve the same concepts. However, all tax-free reorganizations are not poolings and all poolings are not tax-free reorganizations. Allocation-of-purchase-price problems generally arise in taxable transactions, which are accounted for as a "purchase" in most instances. The taxable transaction which is accounted for as a purchase is the transaction being discussed here. The accounting for a purchase for financial reporting purposes and for tax purposes should generally follow the same principles—an allocation based on the fair market value of the assets acquired. There are, however, certain differences caused by the practicalities of a given situation which will be covered.

CONFLICTING OBJECTIVES

One significant problem which is ever present in a purchase of assets is the possible conflict between tax objectives and accounting (financial reporting) objectives. While real economic earnings may be increased by effective tax planning, in certain instances the most favorable tax approach will have a negative effect on reported earnings. This is a problem which should be faced early in the consideration of a potential acquisition. The short-run objectives of management should be weighed carefully with the ultimate benefits to be derived from the acquisition so that short-run thinking is viewed in perspective.

As a general introduction to the technical considerations of allocation of purchase price, we must consider the basic objectives of the seller and the buyer. Generally, the seller seeks long-term capital gain, without any recapture of depreciation or investment credit being charged to him. The buyer seeks to allocate the purchase price to deductible, depreciable, or amortizable assets, and hopes to avoid an allocation to goodwill or other nondepreciable assets.

The greatest obstacles to the seller's achievement of capital gain are Internal Revenue Code Sections 1245, 1250, and 47, and certain revenue rulings concerning the tax effect of a sale of items which were previously expensed. Section 1245 provides, generally, that where there is a sale of personal property which is of a character subject to the allowance for depreciation or amortization, the gain from such sale (or other disposition) to the extent of depreciation or amortization claimed after December 31, 1961, will be treated as ordinary income. (This is referred to as "depreciation recapture.") Section 1250 provides, generally, that gain on the sale of real property on which accelerated depreciation has been taken, may, with certain significant exceptions, be treated as ordinary income to the extent of depreciation in excess of straight-line depreciation claimed after December 31, 1963 (also referred to as depreciation recapture). Section 47 requires a repayment of investment credit claimed for assets sold or otherwise disposed of before the close of the useful life which was taken into account in originally computing the credit. The revenue rulings deal primarily with recovery of amounts previously expensed for small tools and supplies and the treatment of a reserve for bad debts for which a tax benefit has been previously claimed where accounts receivable are sold or otherwise disposed of.

The simplest and most effective type of transaction from the seller's viewpoint is a sale of stock (assuming, of course, that the assets being sold represent the entire company and are not part of a division of a larger company). The sale of stock has certain business advantages and from a tax viewpoint avoids for the seller the recapture problems in connection with depreciation and investment credit. Except for special situations involving collapsible corporations or foreign corporations, the seller should achieve capital gain treatment on the sale of stock.

The benefits to the seller are conversely detriments to the buyer, since the sale of stock shifts the tax problems to the buyer. These problems can be avoided if the buyer retains the corporate structure and operates the acquired company. However, allocation-of-purchase-price problems result because the purchase price is generally in an amount greater than the tax basis of the assets and the buyer wants to obtain a tax benefit from his "excess cost" by allocating it to the assets and "stepping up" their basis. If the buyer purchases stock, he can still achieve his objective, but to accomplish it he has to liquidate the acquired company under certain prescribed rules. Thus, from a tax viewpoint the buyer will attempt to purchase assets (usually subject to liabilities), since this will shift the tax detriments to the seller.

A purchase of stock followed by a liquidation to obtain a "stepped-up" basis leaves the buyer with the tax problem. The rules of Sections 1245, 1250, and 47 (and, in the view of the Revenue Service, the rules with respect to recovery of previously expensed items) will apply to the buyer, since the tax detriments fall on the liquidating corporation as if it had sold its assets and the liquidating corporation is now wholly owned by the buyer. In the purchase-of-assets-subject-to-liabilities situation the detriments fall on the seller, since the selling corporation bears all the recapture problems.

ALLOCATION TO SPECIFIC ASSETS

Not only does the form of the transaction (i.e., stock or assets) cause a significant tax difference, but the ultimate allocation of the purchase price to specific assets can modify this difference within the framework of the Code and rulings. For example, recognizing the recapture problems, the seller may still agree to sell assets subject to liabilities but will try to modify his tax burden by having the buyer make an allocation which, if sustained, will produce a minimum of depreciation recapture. This can be done most simply by a weighting of the allocation toward land or other assets not subject to recapture rules. Of course, this all must be done on a basis of reason and cannot be arbitrary.

So that the magnitude of the problem can be viewed in perspective I have listed below items to which allocation may be made. The list is obviously not all-inclusive, since in every fact situation there may be an asset or group of assets which is encountered once in a lifetime. Some of the assets are obvious; others are so unique as to have limited application: cash, land, buildings, machinery, equipment, furniture, fixtures, patents, trademarks, leaseholds, securities and investments, contracts for purchase or sale or employment or service, accounts receivable and installments receivable, goodwill, customer lists, trade names, copyrights, formulas, patents, drawings, secret processes, patterns, inventories, supplies, covenants not to compete, prepaid and deferred items, paintings and sculpture, samples, spare parts, insurance expirations, etc.

It is impracticable to discuss each item here, so I will refer only to certain items which seem to be the basis of most problems which arise in the allocation of purchase price. Some, being more basic, will be treated rather quickly.

Real Estate, Machinery, and Equipment

With respect to *real estate,* the question usually revolves around the allocation between buildings and land. Gain on the sale of land is generally treated as capital gain, while gain on the sale of buildings may result in some recapture of depreciation under Section 1250. The buyer naturally wants the allocation weighted in favor of the depreciable buildings.

In the *machinery and equipment* category, the recapture rules of Section 1245 come into play. The purchaser, from a tax viewpoint, will achieve eventual tax benefit if he can sustain an allocation to this category; the benefit will be derived sooner if the allocation is weighted in favor of short-lived assets. This may not necessarily conflict with the seller's desires. In fact, from a negotiating viewpoint, the buyer who can support a significant allocation to machinery and equipment may be able to satisfy a seller within the framework of Section 1245. Once the post-1961 depreciation is recaptured, any gain in excess of this is still treated as capital gain under Section 1231 of the Code. Thus, for example, if the seller had two units of machinery and equipment, each with a potential $200,000 depreciation recapture, the seller would benefit if all the excess cost (assume it to be $400,000) were allocated to one of the units of assets, rather than one-half to each. In the former case there would be $200,000 ordinary income and $200,000 capital gain; in the latter case the $400,000 of gain would all be ordinary income. A detailed review of the machinery and equipment category may well indicate appreciation in assets which were fully depreciated for tax purposes at December 31, 1961. Allocation of purchase price to these assets should produce capital gain.

These examples seek to illustrate the tax differences. Of course, in practice the allocation cannot be arbitrary.

Inventory

The subject of inventory, including finished goods, work in process, and raw materials, poses one of the most interesting and complex tax problems. The allocation to inventory should be, as it is in the case of other assets, on a fair-market-value basis. What is the "fair market value" of inventory? Should the seller care what amount the buyer allocates to inventory?

Fair market value is obviously not necessarily the amount at which the inventory is carried on the books of the seller. Generally, the seller is carrying the inventory at cost or at the lower of cost or market. There is no definition in the Code or regulations as to how to compute fair market value for inventory when allocating purchase price. Decided cases on this point are sparse, althrough there is a district court case[1] touching on this issue which involved the complete liquidation of a corporation by the individual shareholders. The question presented was how the shareholders should value the inventory received by them along with other assets in the liquidation. The shareholders contributed the inventory and other property to a partnership immediately after the liquidation. Therefore it was in the shareholders' best tax interests to put a high value on the inventory and pay tax at capital gain rates, and thus have the newly formed partnership obtain a tax basis for the inventory in an amount equal to the high value thus reported.

On sale of the inventory by the partnership the effect is to charge high-basis inventory as part of cost of sales, thus reducing the partnership's ordinary income to be taxed to the shareholders who are now the partners. The Internal Revenue Service took the position that replacement cost should be the value of the inventory. (This is a unique twist, since the IRS usually would argue for the highest possible value in a liquidation; but in this instance such a position was more beneficial to the taxpayer.) The taxpayer argued that retail sales price, less dealers' discounts, less estimated selling expenses produces the correct fair market value of the inventory. The Court agreed with the taxpayer.

In my opinion the taxpayer had a reasonable position and the case was properly decided. Interestingly enough, the Revenue Service did not appeal the case and, since it was a district court case, did not indicate acquiescence or non-acquiescence. While the case concerned a liquidation, the same theory of fair market value should apply to valuation of inventory in a purchase-of-assets situation. Of course, this method is not

[1] *Berg,* 167 F. Supp. 756 (D.C. Wisc., 1958).

the only approach, and each situation must be decided on the basis of the particular facts involved.

Should the seller care how much of the purchase price the buyer allocates to inventory? The answer is "Yes," even in the case of a sale of stock or in a Section 337 liquidation situation, and the reasons are clear. If the seller had been overly conservative in valuing its inventory, the higher valuation placed upon the inventory by the buyer might well call the attention of the Revenue Service to this fact. While I have indicated that the purchaser should probably have a higher valuation, since he can use fair market value while the seller uses the lower of cost or market, a substantial difference might indicate to the Revenue Service an area of possible controversy. This might result in tax deficiencies to the seller for earlier tax years not barred by the statute of limitations and, in unusual situations, might also prompt the Revenue Service to consider negligence penalties and possibly fraud penalties.

Inventory is one of these areas where, for accounting purposes, it is common for the buyer to allocate an amount equal to the inventory carried on the books of the seller. The earnings of a company may not be clearly reflected if purchased inventory is accounted for on a realizable-value basis. The turnover of the purchased inventory will produce no gain or loss, and thus, for the period required to turn over this inventory, there will be no profit from operations. In the appropriate circumstances, it is proper to have a different allocation to inventory for tax purposes than for financial reporting purposes. Perforce this must alter other elements of the allocation, and the tax benefits to be derived may be outweighed by the bookkeeping involved. Any difference, of course, will show up clearly on the tax return as a reconciliation between book income and taxable income, and the taxpayer must be prepared to have his allocation challenged. (It will be challenged in all probability in any event.)

Supplies and Small Tools

Supplies and small tools often cause tax problems. It is not uncommon for a buyer to follow a policy of expensing these items as purchased. On acquisition of another company, it often occurs that similar items, which have also been expensed by the seller, are acquired and have considerable value to the buyer. The buyer wants to allocate part of his purchase price to these items. What happens when a year's supply of items in this category is $20,000 but the buyer acquires $100,000 fair market value of such items from the seller and wishes to allocate this amount to them? This causes tax problems for the seller and tax and accounting problems for the buyer.

If the seller is selling assets and thereafter liquidating, he will seek the tax relief afforded by Section 337, which says in essence that gain on the sale or exchange of property within a twelve-month period after the adoption of a plan of liquidation will not be taxed at the corporate level. The Revenue Service has taken the position in a revenue ruling[2] that the disposition of small tools and supplies inventory is not a "sale or exchange" within the meaning of Section 337, and holds that the selling corporation is recovering an item which it previously expensed and therefore should treat the proceeds as ordinary income. I believe this ruling is wrong, but revenue agents must follow it. In a very recent case[3] the Tax Court, in rejecting the reasoning of the revenue ruling, stated: "The conclusions reached are not supported by the authorities cited therein, are clearly contrary to the provisions of Section 337(a), and, in our opinion, are not a valid interpretation of the statute."

In one Tax Court case,[4] the Court upheld the expensing of supplies inventory. In this case, the Revenue Service did not argue under the revenue ruling cited above, but, since the year in issue was the first and only year of the company's existence and it had not established a history of expensing supplies as a method of accounting, the Revenue Service merely sought to set up supplies on hand as a closing inventory. The Court held that the taxpayer's method of expensing the supplies was reasonable.

The buyer must determine whether he should follow his regular method of accounting for supplies and small tools and thus expense them in the year of purchase where this has been his past practice. While expensing a purchase gives the buyer a tax advantage in the year of acquisition, I question whether the buyer has any choice, since treating these items otherwise might be considered by the Revenue Service as a change in method of accounting. Perhaps, in a given situation, the buyer might distinguish the acquired supplies and small tools from his present items in this category and then set up an inventory of the purchased items.

Where amounts in excess of one year's supply are acquired, the financial statements may not clearly reflect income if these amounts are charged to income in the year of purchase. It may be reasonable, for accounting purposes, to amortize these costs over an estimated period of years, contra to preferred tax treatment. This, unfortunately, will show

[2] Rev. Rul. 61-214, 1961-2 CB 60.
[3] D. B. *Anders,* 48 TC 815 (Appealed 10th Circuit).
[4] *Smith Leasing Co., Inc.,* 43 TC 37 (1964), acq. 1965-2 CB 6.

clearly in the reconciliation on the tax return and puts the burden on the taxpayer to justify the expensing of these items in one year. By raising the question on the purchaser's return, it also leads the Revenue Service back to the seller, who may be required to report a portion of the proceeds as ordinary income, as described earlier in this chapter. In view of this possibility, both buyer and seller should focus on this point before closing the transaction where the effect can be material.

"Reserve" for Bad Debts

Where the seller uses the "reserve" method for bad debts, the Revenue Service and the courts have taken the position that a sale of all accounts receivable negates the need for the "reserve" and it should be taken into income in the year of sale.[5] The Revenue Service also feels that income from a bad-debt reserve arises on the liquidation of a subsidiary where there is a basis allocation under Section 334(b)(2).[6] The Tax Court has agreed with this latter position.[7] While the reserve must be included in income of the liquidated subsidiary, a very recent case[8] holds that inclusion of the reserve in income gives rise to additional tax basis to the buyer under a technical interpretation of the regulations applicable to a Section 334(b)(2) liquidation. The buyer may also be able to sustain an addition to its own bad-debt reserve. Although application of the recovery-of-reserve rule to a Section 351 incorporation of a sole proprietorship was denied by a court of appeals decision reversing the Tax Court,[9] the Tax Court has reiterated its position in a recent decision.[10]

Contracts and Licenses

One of the most intriguing problems in allocating purchase price arises where the seller has contracts which give him some economic advantage or benefit. The simplest type would be a favorable lease on certain premises. The buyer would like to allocate to such lease, and the seller could treat the gain as a capital gain. For example, if the seller had a ten-year lease requiring an annual rental of $50,000 and there is a five-year remaining life to the lease, and if the buyer, seeking a five-year lease for similar premises, would be required to pay rent of $70,000

[5] Rev. Rul. 57-482, 1957-2 CB 49; *West Seattle National Bank*, 288 F. 2nd 47 (9th Cir., 1961).
[6] Rev. Rul. 65-258, 1965-2 CB 94.
[7] *Argus, Inc. Transferee*, 45 TC 63.
[8] *First National State Bank of New Jersey*, 51 TC No. 41.
[9] *Estate of Heinz Schmidt*, 355 F.2d 111 (9th Cir., 1966).
[10] *M. Schuster*, 50 TC 111, No. 12.

per year, then it is clear that the buyer has purchased a valuable lease. The measure of this value on the facts as given is $20,000 per year for five years, or $100,000. This sum should be discounted by a present-value calculation, and an allocation of a portion of the purchase price should be made to the lease agreement.

A more controversial situation arises when the purchaser acquires a going business and attempts to allocate the purchase price to the component parts which make the business go, and the Revenue Service takes the position that what the purchaser acquired was not individual assets but, in effect, goodwill in the form of a going business. This has arisen in cases where the business calls for rendering a service or delivering a product under contract for a fixed term of years, and often the contract contains a renewal option or, if no option is contained, then historically the contract has been renewed. In such instances the buyer tries to allocate the purchase price to specific contracts and write off the cost over the life of the contracts. The Revenue Service takes the position that the contracts are indivisible from the goodwill of the business, and that they *are,* in fact, the goodwill of the business, and says that the asset purchased is a right which does not have a determinable useful life. This term, "determinable useful life," is the key to the whole problem of allocation of purchase price, because if an asset *has* a determinable useful life, its cost should be written off over that life. This applies to goodwill as well; the only reason goodwill cannot be deducted for tax purposes (except on abandonment or liquidation) is that a determinable useful life cannot be ascertained.

There are many instances where there is great merit to a taxpayer's position of allocating to contracts. Unfortunately, the Revenue Service has taken a rigid position against taxpayers in this area and, more unfortunately still, the courts have, with relatively few exceptions, upheld the Service's position. In fact, the trend of the cases seems clearly to treat acquired contracts and licenses as assets which do not have a determinable useful life and therefore may not be amortized.

The classic case is where the taxpayer acquired a group of customer contracts under which taxpayer was to render a service in return for agreed compensation.[11] These contracts were originally for five years, with renewal clauses which were often exercised. The purchase price was allocated specifically to these contracts in the agreement between buyer and seller, and it was shown that the amount so allocated was arrived at by estimating the expected income from each contract. Nevertheless,

[11] *Thrifticheck Service Corporation,* 287 F.2d 1 (2nd Cir., 1961).

the Court said that the taxpayer was acquiring a bundle of rights in the nature of a going business and would not allow amortization inasmuch as the type of asset acquired precludes a reasonable determination for a period of amortization. The only ray of hope was the parting comment by the Second Circuit Court of Appeals: "Whether, under appropriate methods of allocation or accounting, a deduction might be taken upon cessation of relations with one or more of the [customers] in question, we do not decide." Although holding that the taxpayer was not entitled to amortization, the Court intimated that there may be an abandonment loss on a contract-by-contract basis where there is no renewal at the end of the contract term. However, this is purely dictum and cannot be relied upon.

In a very recent Tax Court case[12] a taxpayer who had acquired customer lists for a home pickup and delivery laundry and dry-cleaning business claimed a deduction for a portion of the cost each time it lost a customer who was on a list. The majority of the Court allowed the taxpayer to depreciate 75 percent of its cost over a five-year period, thus treating the lists as indivisible assets. Three judges said they thought the taxpayer's method was reasonable.

Two recent cases involving a purchase of television broadcasting stations and their FCC licenses to operate the TV channel for a period of three years plus renewals are most interesting, although disappointing. Both the Fourth Circuit[13] and the Fifth Circuit[14] Courts of Appeals held that, although the license is for a limited period, such license is generally renewed and therefore must be considered to be of indefinite life. A 1963 Tennessee District Court Case[15] on the same subject put the problem in perspective when the Court, allowing amortization of the TV license, said that the Federal Communications Commission and the Revenue Service should attempt to be consistent. While the Revenue Service argued that the renewal provisions of the TV licenses indicate that they have an unlimited life, the Court pointed out that the FCC limits the license to a three-year period and retains the right to take it away. This is a major weapon of enforcement by the FCC. The case was not appealed, but the Revenue Service has announced that it would not follow the case.[16] However, in none of these TV license cases was the tax-

---

[12] *Manhattan Company of Virginia*, 50 TC No. 11. (Appeals to 4th Circuit and D.C. Circuit dismissed.)
[13] *Richmond Television Corporation*, 354 F.2d 410 (4th Cir., 1965).
[14] *KWTX Broadcasting Company, Inc.* 272 F.2d 406 (5th Cir., 1959).
[15] *WDEF Broadcasting Company*, 215 F. Supp. 818 (D.C. Tenn., 1963).
[16] Rev. Rul. 64-124, 1964-1 CB (Part I) 105.

payer able to produce statistics which would clearly indicate the estimated life of the license plus its renewals.

In a similar area, that of television-network affiliation contracts, the Seventh Circuit,[17] reversing the Tax Court, held that an affiliation contract of a local station with the CBS television network did not have a useful life determinable with reasonable accuracy. The Appeals Court held this way despite convincing statistical evidence (enough to convince the Tax Court) that CBS changed affiliates over the years and that the life expectancy of the affiliation contract could be determined statistically. The taxpayer in this case seemed to me to have persuasive arguments. This decision indicates the strong trend against allowing amortization where a right is acquired which is inherent in the continuation of a business where such right does not have a known determinable useful life. However, a very recent Court of Claims case, which discussed this subject in great detail, allowed a deduction upon termination of television-network affiliation contracts.[18]

Patents, Trademarks, and Formulas

Patents are intangible assets which have more promise of sustaining an allocation of purchase price. If the patents have been developed by the seller and the costs charged off as research and development expenses, the allocable proceeds should be treated as capital gain and there should be no recapture-of-depreciation problem. The buyer acquires an amortizable asset which can be written off over the remaining life of the patent. (Patents have a legal life of 17 years.) The problem of allocation in this area arises in the difficulty of distinguishing patent rights from an established market and sales organization, which the Revenue Service holds is in the nature of goodwill. Demonstrated earning power of the patents, based on past performance, gives a solid basis on which to compute a fair market value.

With such nondepreciable property as trademarks and formulas, the purchaser who allocates to these items can have no tax benefits from depreciation or amortization (although loss may be claimed on sale or abandonment). One company has sought to solve this problem by selling its trademarks, formulas, and goodwill to its employees' pension plan. The company will pay the pension plan an agreed royalty over a period of years which will assure the pension plan the recovery of its investment.

[17] *Indiana Broadcasting Corporation,* 350 F.2d 580 (7th Cir., 1965), Cert. Den. . . . U.S. . . . (January 31, 1966).
[18] *Meredith Broadcasting Company,* Ct. Cl. No. 30-59 (December 31, 1968).

The company will deduct the royalties as expenses in the year incurred, and in this way will have the business benefits of the trademarks and formulas, yet still obtain a tax deduction. A danger in this area would be a royalty or licensing agreement under which the seller-licensee could be considered not to have made a sale in the first place and the transaction treated as merely a financing arrangement—as is the case today with certain leases of machinery and buildings.

Goodwill

Goodwill, an intangible asset which does not have a determinable useful life, is the type of asset which buyers seek to avoid when allocating purchase price. As previously mentioned, this asset is not depreciable, although upon abandonment of a business or product line to which the goodwill relates the taxpayer may obtain an ordinary loss in the year of abandonment. The seller will be able to treat the sale of goodwill for an amount in excess of tax basis as capital gain, and a loss on sale will probably be a capital loss.[19]

The classic questions in the goodwill area are: Should the taxpayer follow the theoretical rules and set up a fair market value for every asset, including goodwill (if any), and thereafter allocate the purchase price to all the assets in the ratio which the value of each bears to the total fair market value of all the assets? Or should an allocation be made first to tangible assets and specific intangibles such as patents and, if anything is unallocated, the balance be indicated as goodwill? This latter approach, known as the "subtraction," "gap," or "residual" method, is the one which is used most frequently in practice. It has some support in the cases. The Revenue Service, on the other hand, does not ordinarily approve of this method. The chief of the Engineering Appraisal Branch of the Internal Revenue Service, in an article published in *The Journal of Accountancy*,[20] indicates quite clearly the attitude of the Service against the use of the subtraction theory. However, in the last analysis it comes down to a question of fact, and thereafter taxpayers must select a reasonable approach which can be defended. Just because there is excess cost not allocable to any specific asset does not mean there is goodwill per se. If assets of a company with a history of losses are acquired, the Revenue Service might be hard pressed to show goodwill where the buyer can make a reasonable allocation to other assets or can show that he may have overpaid for certain assets.

[19] Rev. Rul. 55-79, 1955-1 C.B. 370.
[20] Karl Ruhe, "The IRS Position on Allocation of Intangibles in Business Acquisitions," *The Journal of Accountancy*, September 1965, p. 50.

Goodwill for accounting purposes poses a number of problems, as discussed elsewhere in this volume and in the American Institute of CPAs' Accounting Research Study No. 10, *Accounting for Goodwill*. Suffice it here to note that many otherwise attractive acquisitions have been aborted by goodwill problems.

SUPPORTING THE ALLOCATION

After a reasonable allocation is made, the successful defense of the allocation becomes a question of proof. In certain instances it is to the advantage of both buyer and seller to have the allocation agreed to in the contract. Such agreement will not preclude the Revenue Service's challenging the allocation, but the cases hold that, where a reasonable allocation is made by parties who have adverse tax interests, the Revenue Service needs strong evidence to overcome the allocation. However, it has its disadvantages to the buyer from a very practical point of view. It often happens that, after operating an acquired business, the buyer realizes that assets exist which he did not consider in his original allocation. If he has prevented himself from making an allocation to these assets by his contract with the seller, he will not be able to take tax advantage of his newly discovered assets. Also, hindsight is a great thing, and a binding agreement on allocation in the contract will make the buyer's position less flexible.

The question of who should value the assets invariably arises. Should it be done by company personnel or by an outside appraisal company? Should it be done partly by each? In my experience, even though company personnel may be amply qualified to appraise specific assets, the report of an independent outside appraiser carries more weight with the Revenue Service. As to which assets should be appraised, it is generally preferable to have all assets appraised by the outside company if it is within its competence to do so. I believe that costs incurred in obtaining the appraisal are deductible if they are expenses in connection with determining tax liability. The taxpayer cannot determine such liability until he knows the basis of his assets and the depreciation thereon. In practice, the appraisal expenses are often allocated to the assets as a cost of their acquisition.

The subject of allocation of purchase price is immense, and I have just touched upon it very lightly here. Most of my comments have been directed toward the problems of corporate buyers and sellers. Also, it has been assumed that there has been excess cost, while in many acquisitions there is a "bargain purchase." The problems encountered in this latter situation are different in many respects. (For example, where inventory is purchased at a discount, an election to use the LIFO method will "lock in" the discount, and, assuming continuing purchases of similar items, the tax consequences on disposition of the inventory are minimized.)

It should be apparent that the form of the transaction and the method of allocation can have a significant effect on the over-all desirability of an acquisition. Cooperation between the dealmaker and the accountant who is his adviser on tax and financial matters is essential.

Business Combinations and the Qualified Retirement Plan

ERNEST O. WOOD

USINESS COMBINATIONS affect the tax treatment of qualified retirement plans. The plans of each of the participating parties may be modified, terminated, or combined. New plans may be activated. Each such step may have an effect upon the tax posture of the participating parties and their employees. Tax planning before the business combination may ensure favorable tax posture after the transaction.

As used in this discussion, "business combination" is a generic term which includes such tax-free acquisition patterns as a merger or consolidation (Section 368(a)(1)(A)), an exchange of stock for stock (Section 368(a)(1)(B)) and an exchange of stock for assets (Section 368(a)(1)(C)). It also includes the taxable acquisition of assets or stock for cash or other property.

The term "qualified retirement plan" refers to the employee pension, profit-sharing, and stock bonus plans which are given special tax treatment under Sections 401 to 404 of the Internal Revenue Code as to qualification, taxability, and contributions.

THE MERGERMAKER'S OVERVIEW

The designer of the business combination, the mergermaker, at times alone and forsaken, at times besieged with ideas from all manner of men, never-

---

Ernest O. Wood, CPA, is a partner in the Pittsburgh office of Arthur Young & Company.

theless and ultimately must treasure up his bright design. He must travel on the ridges with dry feet. His eyes must adjust to the overview. He will have burdenbearers to walk and observe the sloughs of specifics and details. Sufficient to him that his ears are open to the cries of warning from below.

The role of the mergermaker is to take the various elements of the present and rework them into something which, hopefully, will be more acceptable in the future. While his prime responsibility is to present the face of the future, a further responsibility exists to do as little damage as possible to present bystanders in the conversion processes.

So it is particularly with employee retirement plans. In the beginning there are two groups of employees. Each group was acquired, employee by employee, at a competitive price set in the marketplace and fashioned into a talent pool which operates under a compensatory package which is absolutely unique. No two compensation programs are alike. Presumably each group is considered to be an asset of the present business that must be preserved.

The Raw Materials

As the mergermaker looks at the business with which he must work, he might be fairly dazzled by the splendor of the variegated forms and methods of qualified plans in existence: Pension and profit-sharing plans. Annuity and stock bonus plans. Industry and salaried-only plans. Contributory and noncontributory. Overfunding and underfunding. Trusteed and insured. Investments at cost and at fair market value. Vested and nonvested. The list goes on. Each plan, each method, each feature an integral part of a whole. Each part, each whole to be investigated and understood before the formation of the business combination design.

Conversion Changes

A careful reading and detailed analysis of the retirement programs of all parties to the business combination prior to the execution of any acquisition agreement is imperative in order to make intelligent decisions on how to convert the present raw material into a suitable retirement program for the future. The steps to the future are these:

1. Understand the present retirement benefits.

2. Determine the future retirement benefits goal.

3. Examine the ways and means of converting the present into the future.

At the outset basic choices might be looked at, such as these:

☐ **Should all plans be discarded and a new plan adopted?**

☐ **Should the acquiring corporation's plan be extended to the transferor's employees, or should the reverse action be adopted?**

☐ **Should all plans be continued in the same or amended form?**

A choice made, whether one above or some other, generally requires the application of conversion changes which cause or affect:

Terminations	Vesting
Coverage	Funding
Benefits	Deductions
Discrimination	

An incomplete list, to be sure. The important point, nevertheless, is that when hands are laid upon a qualified plan, when changes are made, the tax life of the plan responds. For example, this chain of events might take place:

☐ **Employee coverage is changed.**

☐ **Discrimination results.**

☐ **The plan forfeits its qualification.**

☐ **Termination is required.**

☐ **Benefits are distributed.**

☐ **The employee is forced into an unfortunate tax posture.**

All for the want of care in planning.

Preacquisition investigation and planning—the phrases may be reworked, reworded, and repeated, but not forgotten—must be within the overview of the mergermaker.

Acquisition Price and the Qualified Plan

The employee retirement responsibilities involved in a business combination may be a can of worms to be tossed on the scale which weighs the purchase price. But on which side? Perhaps it cannot be done by the can. Perhaps an allocation must be made, worm by worm, because each worm is singular. Four to look for are these:

1. What is the amount of the unfunded past service costs?

2. Will a new retirement program increase the transferor's unfunded liabilities?

3. Are the assets in the transferor's retirement fund undervalued or overvalued? Is there overfunding in the plan?

4. Does the transferor have unused contribution carryovers? (See discussion under "Employer deductions.")

The last item tends to increase the purchase price if the carryovers can be deducted by the acquiring corporation.

It may be found that the assets in the transferor's retirement fund are overvalued, thus increasing the unfunded past service costs assumed by the purchaser. The assets may be undervalued to an extent that unfunded past service costs are reduced or eliminated entirely. The condition may be so extreme that the plan is overfunded and future normal costs are reduced.

If the answer to the second item is in the affirmative, should the purchase price be adjusted or is this a cost chargeable against future operations? A question for the mergermaker.

The amount of the unfunded past service cost should also be considered. If substantial in amount and if assumed by the acquiring corporation, a reduction in purchase price is indicated. The situation is to be handled gingerly, however, because Section 381(c)(16) provides, with respect to certain tax-free reorganizations, that if the acquiring corporation assumes an obligation of the transferor corporation which gives rise to a liability, and such liability, if paid by the transferor, would have been deductible, the acquiring corporation shall deduct such item when paid as if it were the transferor, but *no deduction will be allowed if the purchase price is reduced because of the obligation.* The application of Section 381(c)(16) must be carefully determined.

EMPLOYEE TAXATION

The termination of a qualified plan requires a distribution of benefits to the employee beneficiaries. (A principle but not a postulate. See Rev. Rul. 67–213 where the interests in a transferor's terminated pension plan are transferred to the transferee's stock bonus plan without taxation to the employees.) Depending upon the terms of the plan, the distribution may take the form of a lump-sum distribution or some type of annuity payment. Generally speaking, an annuity payment is taxed as ordinary income and a lump-sum distribution is taxed as a capital gain.

The business combination may result in a termination of a qualified plan of one or more of the participating parties. The termination may be by design or it may be by misdesign. The termination may occur as an integral part of the business combination or as a subsequent and perhaps unforeseen event.

From a tax viewpoint, the problem is the lump-sum distribution arising from the termination of a plan which is caused, directly or indirectly, by a business combination. The question is: Will the lump-sum distribution be taxed to the employee as capital gain or as ordinary income?

Capital Gain Taxation

Section 402(a)(2) provides that an employee shall treat a lump-sum distribution from an exempt employees' trust as a long-term capital gain provided certain conditions are met:

1. The distribution must be a total disbursement of all funds standing to the credit of the employee's account. Much consideration has been given to what constitutes a total distribution. (Regs. 1.402(a)–1(a)(6)(ii).) Definitions on this point have developed to an extent that it presents no problem in the case of well-cared-for plans.

2. The distribution must be paid within one taxable year of the recipient. The distribution does not have to be in the same year that the employee severs his employment.

3. It must be paid on account of the employee's death or other separation from the service of the employer.

Section 403(a)(2), relating to the taxation of employee annuities, contains a similar capital gain provision.

A business combination may result in a terminated qualified plan. A terminated plan may cause a total distribution to be paid to an employee. The final link in this chain of events is the taxation of the distribution to the employee. That final link is forged by reference to the phrase "separation from the service of the employer." If separation occurs, the distribution is taxed as a capital gain. If there is no separation, the distribution is taxed as ordinary income under Section 72.

The framers of the business combination must understand the relationship between separation and taxation if they have a desire to control the tax fortunes of the employee.

Separation from Service

Unfortunately, but not unusually, tax consequences flow from a tax phrase which is defined neither in the Code nor in the regulations. Any definition of the key phrase must come from court cases and Revenue Service rulings. Despite the bramblebush nature of such source definitions, certain benchmarks are visible.

1. Look to the severance of the employer/employee relationship. Generally, the employment tax regulations are a guide to when a severance occurs.

2. Do not look to the termination of the plan. The termination may cause the distribution of benefits, but it does not determine its taxability.

3. Do not look to a mere change in stock ownership; it does not produce a seed from which capital gain will sprout.

Separation may occur in two ways in a business combination. First, an employee may be completely severed from his employer. He quits or is discharged or he retires. He is out and away. The separation-from-service definition is not an issue insofar as a lump-sum distribution is concerned.

The second type is the troublesome one. Picture the employee standing behind the counter nonchalantly selling fish hooks to the same old customers while around him, unnoticed, swirl the machinations of acquisition, merger, reorganization, liquidation, etc. In the midst of demonstrating a No. 3 snelled hook, the business changes hands. He continues his demonstration. Has the employee changed employers?

Illustrations—Cases

U.S. v. Johnson, CA–5, 1964. Lee purchased the stock of Waterman. Waterman terminated its qualified plan and made a distribution. Subsequently, Lee merged downstream into Waterman, which continued in business. Capital gain income was denied to Waterman's employees. The distribution was on account of the termination of the plan, and such termination did not sever the employment relationship between Waterman and its employees. Neither the change in stock ownership nor the subsequent merger severed the relationship. Waterman employees still worked for Waterman.

Jack E. Schlegel, 46 TC 706 (1966). Worthington purchased the stock of Annin. At a later date Annin was liquidated into Worthington. Worthington took over Annin's employees, one of whom was Schlegel. Worthington also took over Annin's profit-sharing plan, but soon terminated it. Schlegel was denied capital gain treatment because the lump-sum distribution was made to him on account of the termination of the plan. At the time of termination it was Worthington's plan. Schlegel was Worthington's employee before and after the termination.

Robert E. Beaulieu, TCM 1965–303. P purchased the stock of S. S terminated its qualified plan and distributed. S was later liquidated into

P. The distributions were taxed as ordinary income to the recipients because they remained in the employ of S after the termination of the plan. There was no separation from service.

These three cases are set forth to illustrate the benchmarks. The cases are by no means unusual. These benchmarks appear time and again as cases, favorable and unfavorable to the taxpayer, are reported. (Among others: *Funkhouser,* 44 TC 178 (1965); *Peebles,* CA–5, 1964; *Glinske,* 17 TC 562 (1951); *Buckley,* 29 TC 455 (1957); *Rieben,* 32 TC 1205 (1959); *Martin,* 26 TC 100 (1956); *Miller,* 22 TC 293 (1955); *Fry,* 19 TC 461 (1952); *McGowan,* CA–7, 1960.)

Illustrations—Rulings

The Revenue Service has attempted to clarify the separation-from-service issue through a series of revenue rulings. The rulings relate largely to business transfers—that is, business combinations, as that term is used in this discussion—and transfers of businesses by liquidation. It will be noted that these rulings further illustrate the benchmarks set forth above.

1. *Sale of a division.* The assets of a division are sold for cash. The qualified plan covering the seller's employees is continued by the seller but a total distribution is made to the employees who are taken over by the purchaser. There is a separation from service. After the sale the divisional employees work for a different employer. *Benchmark:* Look to the severance of the employer/employee relationship. (Rev. Rul. 58–97.)

2. *Sale of a subsidiary.* One qualified plan serves the employees of both a parent company and a subsidiary. The subsidiary's stock is sold to other interests. The qualified plan is discontinued as to the subsidiary's employees. A total distribution is made to the employees of the subsidiary. There is no separation from service. *Benchmark:* Do not look to a mere change in stock ownership. (Rev. Rul. 58–99.) In this situation the employment relationship does not change. The employees work for the same employer before and after the change in ownership. The distribution was caused by the partial termination of the plan (as to the subsidiary's employees) which was caused by the change in ownership.

3. *Sale of assets.* In preparation for liquidation, a corporation sells all of its assets for cash. The qualified plan is terminated and all employees receive a total distribution. There is a separation from service even as to those employees who go over to the purchaser incident to the sale of assets. *Benchmark:* Look to the severance of the employer/employee relationship. (Rev. Rul. 58–96.)

4. *Tax-free acquisition of assets.* P Corporation exchanges its voting stock for all the assets of M Corporation, which assets are then transferred to S Corporation, a subsidiary of P Corporation. The reorganization is tax-free under Section 368(a)(1)(C). The qualified plan of M Corporation is terminated as part of the reorganization. The employees of M Corporation become employees of S Corporation. A separation from service occurs. *Benchmark:* Look to the severance of the employer/employee relationship. (Rev. Rul. 58–94.)

5. *Merger of businesses.* In this ruling two corporations enact two tax-free transactions under one plan of reorganization. First, there is an exchange of stock so that S becomes a subsidiary of P. Second, the subsidiary is merged into the parent. The qualified plan of the subsidiary is terminated as part of the second transaction—the merger. A total distribution is made at this point. A separation from service takes place and the subsidiary's employees are in a position to claim capital gain treatment. *Benchmark:* Look to the severance of the employer/employee relationship. (Rev. Rul. 58–383.)

This last type of transaction is in reality an exchange of stock for assets. One step, not two. (See Rev. Rul. 67–274.) If two steps had been involved—that is, two separate reorganizations—the consequences might have been different. The first would have been a Section 368(a)(1)(B) transfer of ownership (no separation) and the second would have been a Section 332 liquidation (separation possible, but read immediately below).

Certain Technical Separations

A lump-sum distribution plus a separation from service equals a capital gain. But not always. There are circumstances under which a separation occurs in a technical sense but nothing of real substance takes place insofar as the employee is concerned. An example of this might be the liquidation of a long-time subsidiary under the tax-free provisions of Section 332 and the continued operation of the business of the subsidiary as a division of the parent. A technical separation has occurred. The employee has left one employer and joined another—although he might not have been fully aware of it. The offspring of the coupling of such a technical separation with a total distribution from a qualified plan will be hard put to find legitimacy as a capital gain in the eyes of the Revenue Service.

The legislative history of Section 402(a)(2) indicates that a reorganization or liquidation must bring about a "substantial change" in the make-up of the employees if capital gain status is desired for the distribution. (Rev. Rul. 58–94.)

As used in the tax law, as opposed to the theater, the word "make-up," when used in connection with Section 402, refers to the people who are employed and what their positions are and how many there are. Let me illustrate: If X acquires Y and then liquidates Y into X without disturbing the jobs of any Y people, there is no change in the make-up of the employees. If, however, X acquires Z and discharges all of its sales personnel, there is a substantial change in the make-up of the employees.

The term "substantial change" will be defined with difficulty in many instances, but ordinarily a distribution incident to the tax-free liquidation of a controlled subsidiary will be taxed as ordinary income even though a separation from service takes place.

Substance over form, however. The liquidation of a controlled subsidiary may be more than a mere technical separation.

Example: P Corporation wishes to acquire the operating assets of S Corporation and continue the business of S as a division of P. P purchases the stock of S for cash. P liquidates S. Incident to the plan of liquidation, the qualified plan of S is terminated and a total distribution is made. A separation from service exists. (Rev. Rul. 58–95.)

The form of this two-step transaction would appear to preclude a real separation from service. The first step, the acquisition of stock for cash, was a mere change in stock ownership. (Rev. Rul. 58–99.) The second step, the liquidation of a wholly owned subsidiary, generally does not result in the necessary substantial change in the make-up of employees. (Rev. Rul. 58–94.)

In substance, however, this transaction was a one-step acquisition by P of the assets of S. (Section 334(b)(2).) In reality, and regardless of the form of the transaction, a separation from service occurs. (Rev. Rul. 58–96.)

At the present time considerable uncertainty exists in the capital gains area. In *Victor S. Gittens,* 49 T.C. No. 419, January 25, 1968, the Court held that no separation from service existed in a "C"-type reorganization because there was no substantial change in the make-up of the employees. Not only is the validity of Rev. Rul. 58–94 placed in jeopardy by *Gittens,* but also the separation-from-service benchmark.

In a majority of business combinations there is no substantial change in the make-up of employees as understood in *Gittens.* An extension of the *Gittens* holding may eliminate capital gain possibilities from substantially all business combinations. Alternatively, separation from service may have to be decided on a case-by-case basis, with no benchmarks to guide the taxpayer.

Tax Planning

It is said that he who does not remember the past is condemned to relive it. Judging by the continual conflict over the definition of the phrase "separation from service," taxpayers do indeed relive the past.

In retrospect it would appear that preacquisition investigation and planning coupled with an understanding of the three benchmarks could have produced capital gain situations in *Johnson, Schlegel,* and *Beaulieu.*

In *Johnson,* Lee bought Waterman, Waterman terminated its plan, Lee merged downstream into Waterman. If Waterman had merged upstream into Lee and if the Waterman plan had been terminated as a part of the merger, Johnson would have been in a capital gain position. His severance of employment with Waterman would have related to receipt of the distribution. The termination of the plan would have been related only as a part of the mechanics. The change in stock ownership would have been an unrelated factor.

In *Schlegel* the subsidiary was liquidated and the parent took over its qualified plan, only to terminate it at a later date. In *Beaulieu,* the subsidiary's plan was terminated and then the subsidiary was liquidated into the parent. In each instance the employee was forced to the sands of termination from which to claim the capital gain advantage. In each instance, if the plan had been terminated as a part of the liquidation transaction, the employee could have stood on the solid ground of separation from the service of his employer.

Rearranging the events in *Johnson, Schlegel,* and *Beaulieu* by the pleasant application of hindsight in order to reach a satisfactory tax result is done only to further validate the benchmarks. Hindsight here ignores the reality that tax considerations must at times give way to conflicting nontax considerations in business combinations. Perhaps it was so in *Johnson, Schlegel,* and *Beaulieu.*

There are times when the tax adviser, feet well in the slough of technical matters, shouts warnings to the mergermaker on the ridge only to be told to keep his counsel. The microcosm of tax specifics must not veil the macrocosm as revealed by the overview. When this happens the tax planner must examine other ways and means to avoid or soften the sharp edges of ordinary income taxation. The following might be considered:

1. The lump-sum distribution is postponed until the day of real separation from service (retirement, death, resignation, etc.) To accomplish this

end the plan will be "frozen." The plan will be adopted by the successor company so that the employee will receive the payout as a result of separation from the employment of the successor company. The exempt trust will remain in existence to hold the assets of the plan. No further contributions will be made under the plan. This approach may lend itself to planning for a combination of capital gain and ordinary income for retirement: The terminated plan of the earlier business will pay out in a lump-sum distribution, taxable at capital gains, to provide immediately available funds for travel, purchase of a retirement home, investment, etc. The operating plan of the successor employer will pay out in installments to provide low-tax-bracket income during the retirement years.

2. The trust assets are converted into annuities which will begin to pay out only upon the occurrence of a future event such as retirement. The annuities can be distributed to the employee without incurring a tax. This method will permit the termination of the exempt trust. It does not produce capital gain taxation but it does permit low-bracket taxation in the retirement years, an alternative which may be more advantageous.

3. The distribution of benefits of the terminated plan is made in installments designed to level out taxable income. The provisions for "income averaging" may assist in this approach.

Essential to tax planning of the sort mentioned above is a thorough analysis of the qualified plan itself. The plan must be flexible enough to contain the shape of the tax idea. If it is not, it must be properly amended. The need for change is developed in the preacquisition investigation.

Planning Out the Capital Gain

I'm mad about mustard—
Even on custard.

Tax advisers are mad about capital gain situations and shoot their energies toward their creation. But mustard really doesn't go with custard, and capital gains are not for every man.

In some cases a lump-sum distribution from a qualified retirement plan to an employee, even though taxed at capital gains rates, is less desirable than distributions taxed as ordinary income. The net-of-tax amount retained by the employee from the total benefit paid is the important thing. The amount retained depends upon the tax bracket at which the benefit will be taxed. The mergermaker must remember that in this decision area he is dealing with high-bracket and low-bracket taxpayers as well as the many who fill the in-between brackets.

Ideally the qualified plan will be structured so that all recipients may be served the mustard as they like it—some as capital gains, some as an annuity, and some to their advantage under the "income averaging" provisions of Sections 1301 to 1305.

It requires a sophisticated plan, a patient planner, and a careful technician.

Guidelines

If there be a dogma which attaches itself to the qualified retirement plan, then this is it: The plan must be created and maintained for the exclusive benefit of the employee. (Sec. 401(a).) The care and feeding of this bit of dogma absorbs the time and talent of innumerable specialists, technicians, planners, blunderers, visionaries, and other irreplaceable members of the compensation team. If heresy is committed against this dogma, the heretics, if apprehended, will be pounded into the ground up to their earlobes by the Revenue Service. It is a dogma to believe.

The guidelines are clearly written. The qualified retirement plan will be created and maintained with the best interests of the employees in mind. But all the laws, regulations, rulings, and procedures, pound on pound, cannot compel the designer of the business combination to consider the problems of the qualified plan as an integral part of the whole transaction. However, if he lives by the dogma and possesses a middling amount of perspicacity, he will see that the spirit of the thing extends beyond the formalized procedures which protect the interests of the employees during the operating life of the plan. He will realize that he has a responsibility to guard the interests of the employees as to their tax posture in the event a distribution is necessitated by a business combination. With such a responsibility he will no more thrust on the employees an avoidable tragic tax burden because of his ineptness than he would permit shareholders to be damaged through his actions.

It is competent mergermanship to do the following:

☐ **Understand the tax impact of a total distribution and a separation from service.**

☐ **Plan for a total distribution, or any distribution, if one is necessary so that the employees attain the best tax posture.**

☐ **Assure the employee tax posture through expert opinions and, where possible, an advance ruling from the Internal Revenue Service.**

EMPLOYER DEDUCTION

Qualified retirement plans are a creation of the tax statute. It should follow that the cost of providing the benefits of a qualified plan is a tax-deductible expense. And so it is—within limitations, some of which are carefully prescribed by law, some of which are by administrative fiat. One series of limitations concerns itself with the timing of the tax deduction. In substance, these limitations place a maximum upon the amount of tax deduction which may be claimed in any one taxable year regardless of the amount of retirement cost actually funded during that year. (Sec. 404(a).) As a consequence of the limitations, certain "contribution carryovers" come into existence. If the retirement plan is funded in an amount which is greater than the maximum tax deduction for that year, the excess contribution becomes a contribution carryover to the future and may be deducted in a future tax year, provided it can be fitted within the limitations which apply to that future year.

Contribution carryovers are an asset of the business. While they are not the type of asset which normally appears on the books of the business, nevertheless they represent a deferred tax benefit which, if properly nurtured, may turn into cash through a reduction in Federal income tax liabilities.

The mergermaker should have a knowledge (perhaps indirectly through his technical advisers) of how the contribution carryover arises and what pressures it is subjected to in the atmosphere of business combinations. If a contribution carryover exists, it should at least be recognized and, if possible, given a chance to convert into a real asset of the survivor of the business combination. While it may be exchanged in negotiation for other benefits it should not be thrown away through neglect.

The tax aspects of the employer deduction problem are considered from the following angles:

1. The birthplace of the contribution carryover.
2. The transferee.
3. The transferor.

The Birthplace of the Contribution Carryover

In the case of a qualified pension plan, the tax deduction for contributions for any taxable year is initially limited to an amount not in excess of 5 percent of the compensation otherwise paid or accrued to all employees who are participants under the plan. (Sec. 404(a)(1)(A).) The 5 percent figure may be reduced by the Internal Revenue Service if it is found to be more than is required to fund the benefits under the plan. It may be found also that the 5 percent limitation is insufficient to fund the cost of past and current service credits when such credits are distributed as a level amount or level percentage of compensation over the remaining service of each employee under the plan. In such a case the required amount in excess of 5 percent of compensation is also deductible. (Sec.

404(a)(1)(B).) As a third choice, the employer may claim a deduction based upon the normal cost of the plan plus 10 percent of its past service cost.

In the case of a profit-sharing plan or a stock bonus plan, the deduction for contributions is limited to an amount equal to 15 percent of the compensation otherwise paid or accrued during the taxable year to the employees covered by the plan. (Sec. 404(a)(3).) If an employer has at least one employee who is covered under a pension plan and is also covered under a profit-sharing or a stock bonus plan, there is a special limitation on contributions. (Sec. 404(a)(7).) In any taxable year the total allowable deduction for contributions under all plans cannot exceed 25 percent of the total compensation to all participants under all plans.

Regardless of the limitation adopted for the taxable year, if the employer makes a contribution which is in excess of the applicable limitation for such year, the excess of the amount paid over the limitation may be carried forward to a later year. And that is the birthplace of the contribution carryover.

Making use of the unused carryover is usually not a difficult task for the employer under normal operating conditions. It is treated as a contribution in the later year. The later year, of course, has its own limitations, but the employer reduces the actual contribution under the plan to an amount below the limitation so that the combined actual contribution and the phantom contribution from the past can be fitted within the limitation of the later year. If it does not fit, it moves forward to a succeeding year. In the case of a business combination in a later year, new rules are infused and some of the old rules get a bit sticky for both the transferor and the transferee.

Transferee in General

For purposes of demonstrating the problems of the acquiring corporation in a business combination, the assumption is made that the transferee corporation is possessed of an unused contribution carryover. The unused carryover is the "asset" that the acquiring corporation craves. Whether it will pass over to the acquiring corporation will depend upon the shape of the combination transaction and the decision of that corporation to continue or to terminate the transferor's qualified plan.

Sanctioned Transactions

Under Section 381 of the Internal Revenue Code, an acquiring corporation steps into the shoes of the transferor corporation insofar as the deductibility of a contribution carryover is concerned, provided the business combination is a "sanctioned transaction." This is the same section that covers the tax attributes (operating losses, accounting methods, earnings and profits, etc.) which pass from one corporation to another in tax-free corporate reorganizations. The contribution carryover applicable to qualified retirement plans is considered to be a tax attribute for purposes of this section. The types of transactions which are sanctified are as follows:

1. The liquidation under Section 332 of a controlled subsidiary into its parent. No sanctification, however, is bestowed upon a Section 332 liquidation where the basis of the assets are determined by Section 334(b)(2). The latter section of the statute is designed to cover a situation where, instead of purchasing assets for cash, a corporation purchases stock in a corporation and then liquidates the corporation. The substance of the transaction is a cash purchase of assets. When the corporation is liquidated, the cost of the stock is apportioned to the assets. A Section 334(b)(2) liquidation is a different breed of cat. It is treated as a taxable liquidation, rather than a tax-free Section 332 liquidation, for purposes of Section 381.

2. A tax-free merger or consolidation under Section 368(a)(1)(A).

3. A tax-free exchange of stock for assets under Section 368(a)(1)(C).

4. Certain other tax-free reorganizations which are not relevant to this discussion.

The Section 368(a)(1)(B) method of acquisition—that is, the exchange of stock for stock—is not a "sanctioned" transaction. The reason for this is that the transaction merely creates a parent/subsidiary relationship. The corporate walls remain intact. The retirement plans within the walls are undisturbed. The reorganization does not create tax attributes. The "B"-type acquisition, however, is often followed by the liquidation of the subsidiary into its new-found parent. If that happens, the liquidation will qualify as a Section 332 liquidation, a sanctioned transaction. The tax attribute arises at the point of the Section 332 liquidation.

Another Section 368(a)(1)(B) by-pass exists. If the exchange of stock for stock and the subsequent liquidation of the subsidiary into the parent are separate steps in one business combination plan, the two steps will be ignored and a single step substituted. The legal niceties of the stock for stock plus liquidation will be brushed aside. The whole affair will be considered an exchange of stock for assets under Section 368(a)(1)(C), a sanctioned transaction. Substance triumphs over form! (Rev. Rul. 67–274.)

If the acquisition transaction is "sanctioned," excess contribution carry-overs under a pension, profit-sharing, or stock bonus plan are eligible for passage into the acquiring corporation. The acquiring corporation is considered to be the transferor corporation for all purposes of deduction contributions under a qualified retirement plan. (Regs. 1.381(c)(11).)

Deduction-Continued Plan

It is said that the Internal Revenue Code is lacking in literary quality—its plot is not sustained — but is unsurpassed as a mystery. So certainly it is with the tax attribute provisions. To attempt a simple restatement is to spread welcoming arms to disaster—but there are those who try:

1. If the excess contribution of the transferor becomes available to the transferee, it may be deducted by the latter. If the transferor's plan is continued, the acquiring corporation may absorb the contribution carryover within the normal rules of limitation applicable to the plan. If, however, the plan is terminated, special limitations are applicable. These special rules are discussed below as a part of the problems of the transferor. (See "Continued corporation," below.)

2. The continuation of the transferor's plan may be accomplished in one of three ways:

a. It may be continued as a separate plan.
b. It may be consolidated with another qualified plan.
c. It may be replaced with a comparable plan.

3. A pension plan and an annuity plan are "comparable." Neither is comparable to a profit-sharing plan or a stock bonus plan, but a profit-sharing plan and a stock bonus plan are comparable.

4. Unused contribution credits may be carried over and used by the acquiring corporation. The term "unused contribution credit" has not been used heretofore. It is not a deduction as such, but it might be considered as a passport to a future deduction. It arises only in the case of a profit-sharing plan or a stock bonus plan when an employer contributes less than the 15 percent of compensation limitation in any taxable year. The excess of the limitation over the amount actually funded becomes a credit carryover to the future, thus permitting the employer in a later year to contribute more than the 15 percent limitation of the later year. The unusued contribution credit is considered to be a "phantom" asset, but certainly not of the status of the unused contribution deduction. It may pass from the transferor to the transferee corporation under Section 381 if the latter corporation continues the former's plans as a separate plan, consolidates it with another qualified plan, or replaces it with a comparable plan; however, such plan must be qualified in the year the excess credit is used.

In summary, it would appear that the acquiring corporation may make use of the carryover benefits if the transferor's plan is properly handled and if the vehicle used to transport the benefit from the transferor to the acquiring corporation is sanctioned by Section 381.

Nonsanctioned Transactions

Not all acquisitions follow the sanctioned routes of Section 381. The purchase of assets for cash in a taxable transaction, for example, does not qualify under Section 381 and yet this is a well-traveled acquisition trail. In the event the unused carryover benefit is not a tax attribute under Section 381, the surviving corporation cannot use it. If it is to be used at all, the transferor corporation must find a way to do it.

Transferor in General

The transferor corporation has a myriad of problems of its own—similar and dissimilar to those of its partner in merger. Its problems must also be considered by the mergermaker for a satisfactory result for the business combination. The transferor with an unused contribution deduction must look for a way to convert the phantom asset into a real asset. As a guide to understanding the hazards of this adventure, three areas are examined:

1. Sanctioned transactions.
2. Continued corporation.
3. Liquidated corporation.

Sanctioned Transactions

The sanctioned transactions of Section 381 provide the avenue to the elimination of the unused contribution deduction (and the unused contribution credit) from the transferor's area of influence. The deferred tax benefit passes over to the acquiring corporation and out of control of the transferor.

Continued Corporation

A business combination may be structured as an acquisition of the assets of a business for cash (a taxable transaction), with the transferor corporation remaining in existence. New business assets are purchased and a new business enterprise undertaken. Alternatively, the corporation converts the cash into investments of some sort and remains in existence for the benefit of its shareholders as an investment holding company. In any event, the employees of the former business, presumably, travel with the assets from the transferor to the acquiring corporation.

The acquiring corporation may have taken over the transferor's qualified retirement plan at the time it received its purchased employees. It may have not accepted the plan; the transferor corporation may have terminated it when its employees left to go with the acquiring corporation.

Regardless of the actual mechanics, the transferor corporation now has an unused contribution deduction, a terminated qualified plan, and a burning desire to deduct a prior year's unused contribution in a taxable year after the sale of its business assets.

One problem has been put to rest. The transferor may deduct the unused contribution carryover in a taxable year subsequent to the termination of the plan. (Regs. 1.404(a)–7(b).)

With the end of that question, which indeed haunted the past, a new one arises: *How* does the transferor deduct the unused contribution carryover in a year after the termination of the plan?

The pattern for deducting the pension plan's unused deduction is found at Regs. 1.404(a)–6 and 7. If the amount is deducted in a year in which the pension trust or annuity plan is not qualified, or which ends after the trust or plan has terminated, the 5 percent of compensation limitation and the "level amount" limitation are not applicable. And rightly so, because there are no employee-participants upon which to base a computation. The excess contribution is allowable only to the extent of the limitation based upon past service credits—that is, 10 percent of past service or supplementary costs as of the date the past service or supplementary costs are provided under the plan.

It would appear that the transferor merely has to retain its patience and work out the unused contribution deduction at the 10 percent rate. *But,* the corporation may extinguish its existence before the full amount is recovered, in which case the unrecovered amount will be lost.

The pattern for a profit-sharing or stock bonus plan is a fright. (Regs. 1.404(a)–9(b)(2).) The unused contribution deduction may be deducted in a year subsequent to the termination of the plan, but only to the extent of 15 percent of the compensation otherwise paid or accrued to the employee-participants during the year the deduction is claimed. And where are the employee-participants? They are now being paid by the acquiring corporation. A sad state of affairs! The transferor has funded the retirement plan in advance. The advance-funded benefits accrue to the participants who, indeed, will be taxed upon them at some point in time. But the employer, he who provided the benefits, is deprived of a tax deduction because of a formula which comes out to zero. The answer may be right for the operating business which terminates its plan, but it offers no help to a transferor corporation.

It might be noted that the door to the courthouse may be ajar on this issue. The regulations say the limitation is based upon compensation paid to the employees "by the employer"—that is, the transferor corporation. The Code says it is based upon compensation paid to the employees. The phrase "by the employer" is not in the Code. Did the Code intend the limitation to be computed with reference to the compensation paid by the acquiring corporation?

These special rules of limitation are applicable also to the carryover deduction of a terminated plan in the hands of the acquiring corporation, but they are not there as troublesome. The acquiring corporation has the employees.

Liquidated Corporation

It has been noted that the unrecovered contribution deduction will be lost if the transferor corporation is liquidated. This point should not be lightly considered by the mergermaker because it is quite likely to happen.

Section 337 of the Code contains a most important relief provision which is often availed of in a taxable acquisition that follows the cash-for-assets pattern. The transferor corporation and its shareholders avoid double taxation on their side of the transaction. In general it works like this: The corporation adopts a plan of liquidation and within twelve months thereafter completes its liquidation. During the twelve-month period, the corporation sells its assets. The gain on the sale of the assets is not taxed to the corporation. The shareholders, of course, are taxed in the usual manner on any gain arising from the liquidation. No tax on the corporate level; tax at the shareholder level. Without Section 337, tax falls at both levels. A liquidation carried out under Section 337 requires propitious timing if the unused contribution carryover is to be recovered. Total recovery must be accomplished within the twelve-month period—an unlikely event. Section 337 usually sounds the death knell for the carryover.

CONCLUSION

Qualified retirement plans live only at the breast of the tax law. Each plan is uniquely created and administered for a particular group of employees. The very process of molding a business combination exerts pressures on the plan which affect its tax life. The pressures must be understood. The effect must be controlled. Perhaps these are tasks for the technician. Certainly they are the responsibility of the mergermaker.

V

Personnel Considerations

"The biggest trouble with industry is
that it is full of human beings."

JOHN L. MC CAFFREY, "What Corporation Presidents
Think About at Night," *Fortune,* September 1953

Mergers and People

THOMAS J. RIGGS, Jr.

A GREAT AMOUNT of industrial skill and energy these days is being dedicated successfully to the elimination of the human factor: principally in the data-processing of control information and in the automation of manufacturing processes. We should, however, give management teams and individual managers equal time. In some experienced managements, the human element and the communications factor are important items in a merger checklist; however, in most instances the people who have to integrate the merger on both sides find themselves low on the merger checklist after such items as profitability, cash, growth products, and markets. This is in spite of the fact that people are still the most important requirement and product of any business.

Since most problems concerning people arise *after* a merger, we shall concentrate in this discussion on postmerger difficulties. In regard to salaried management, standard operating procedures and corporate checklists for acquisition operations overemphasize the financial benefits to be derived and de-emphasize the matter of people. Any experienced manager knows the vital importance of the "thinking" side of the business —but, paradoxically, a large number of acquiring companies totally ignore it. When operating management stumbles into the problem of personality readjustment, everyone wonders what went wrong.

This situation highlights, among other things, the principal problem of management: communication. In more direct terms, this means the mo-

Thomas J. Riggs, Jr., is Group Vice President–Operations of Textron Inc., Providence, R.I.

tivation of people. In my opinion it is imperative that the operating management of the acquiring company be given the opportunity to consider the existing human engineering problems before being made responsible for them. In order to accept such responsibility, it must know at least the strengths and weaknesses of the people involved.

An acquisition made on a purely financial basis without consideration of the management capabilities and personalities is bound to give rise to integration problems. Take, for instance, the firm which bought a competitor's product line because of its market desirability. Sales and manufacturing groups subsequently refused to integrate this new line completely into their operations because they were not consulted on the original acquisition transaction. Reluctance to cooperate persisted because it was regarded as an inferior product line of a former competitor. However, another product line purchased later was smoothly integrated, even though a far more complicated engineering design change was required than in the previous case. This time the operating managers were consulted in advance.

ENVIRONMENTAL INFLUENCES

Of course, the importance of personal attitudes is more basic than we have been able to show. The vitality of people in business is dependent on the people themselves and their environment. Environmental influences can be grouped as follows: (a) the community, (b) the industry, (c) the principal personality, and (d) management in depth.

The Community Environment

Community influence is felt greatly by a small but profitable key industry in a small town where neither town nor industry has changed materially for many years. Such a stable atmosphere develops a relaxed and constant attitude among the inhabitants. People generally resist change because they are afraid of it; they tend to oppose new business practices if they have gotten along well without them. In short, provincial managements in provincial communities are basically reluctant to adopt ideas presented by the home office. It is easy to say that this attitude can be overcome by education and efficient communication, but it has been my experience that such remedies can be time-consuming, expensive, and occasionally nonproductive.

The Industry Influence

"Yesmanship" is an example of an attitude created by industry in autocratic organizations. It is as prevalent in small, one-man businesses as it is in large, well-organized corporations. In a small business, it is a result of one man making the decisions. There is no definite delegation of responsibilities, and there are no tests of ability to assume responsibility and make decisions. In most instances, in fact, the subordinate is asked for his opinion without being given adequate facts. Such a practice can only lead to yesmanship. In larger firms, this attitude is often caused by overorganization and results in the creation of a large number of specialists unable to see the over-all picture. Such persons are forced to generalize on decisions that involve more than one aspect of the business.

In all businesses, large and small, a security complex has become a factor contributing to yesmanship. This trend was engendered largely by the seller's market which prevailed from 1940 through the early 1950s and is still extant in some places. There has been a seller's market in people as well as in products, and some individuals have been promoted beyond their depth because management requirements have exceeded personnel availability.

Another manifestation of this weakness is the attempt by competing persons in the lower echelons to stand out. These efforts should be judged fairly, but they should not be allowed to disorganize the group's spirit of unity.

There is an additional manifestation which becomes noticeable in the postmerger period, particularly where a larger company has taken over a small company. Hemmed in by continually increasing competitiveness in a buyer's market and by the inability to finance operations internally in a tight money market, the small company sometimes accepts merger as a means of securing increased capital and credit. In the postmerger period, such an organization may develop a relaxed attitude in areas of expense control and proceed to dust off all R&D and merchandising programs that have been curtailed in the past and expand them overnight.

The Principal Personality

Habit is strong, but add to habit the fact that a strong personality—whether he heads a one-man business or is a key employee—has gotten where he is on the strength of his individuality, and you have defined another attitude problem that normally materializes only after the merger. Such men are usually party to the merger negotiations, and they naturally put their best foot forward to put the deal across. Only in the postmerger testing and probing does the true nature of each personality emerge. The problem is usually as large or as small as the difference between the practices of the merging organizations. If the difference is large and the personality fixed, readjustment can be slow and tedious.

Management in Depth

The difference between success and failure of any two managements, given the identical financial and operating circumstances, lies primarily in the relative performance of people in depth: the executives, the staffs, the supervisors, and the production workers. The successes and the problems with people are universal and very intangible. However, if objective attention were given to understanding more fully the management personnel we all work with, we would encounter or create fewer emotional problems and be able to release more productive effort. If one were to characterize managers, they would probably fall into three categories: (a) the Originators, (b) the Developers, and (c) the Finishers.

The Originator is the vital, self-starting type who challenges traditional practices with innovations. His principal liability is that he is continually starting such innovations and—without further thought of follow-up, development, and control—moving on to the next innovation. This has a tendency to create a management atmosphere where personnel are constantly reacting to new ideas without being able to assimilate existing ideas.

The Developer is the type who aggressively refines other people's ideas, implements their usage, and maximizes the result. The principal task he has is to recognize that the source of his ideas is not original and therefore will be limited by the depth and breadth of his exposure and his continued inquisitiveness.

The Finisher is the type who has been educated to an idea and performs well within the limits of his education. He is the static individual who does no more and no less than what he is told or has been exposed to. His principal liability is self-evident.

In management in depth all three categories are necessary. The liability lies in the improper evaluation and utilization of the types. These types have often been erroneously assigned or have inherited responsible management positions where their capabilities are grossly mismatched with the responsibilities involved. No one of us would select a Finisher to be the president of a growth company, but most of us know at least one such president. We would probably not hire a Developer if we were organizing the research department to work on a new product for which there was no known prior art. Nor would we deliberately assign an Originator to a job as a payroll clerk. Nevertheless, all of these mistakes have actually been made.

In many managements depth and balance in management types and aptitudes serve to disguise and defer such problems. However, if a recession or a competitive condition forces a drastic reduction in overhead expenses, attention is focused on some of these mismatches. The resulting failures are mutually tragic. The individual feels that he has been doing a good job for years and is now being forced out by economic considerations alone. Management made the original mistake in evaluation and selection; it must now either compromise the job, reassign the individual, or fire him.

These personnel problems have developed in independent companies as well as under merger conditions. The challenge is for alert managements to recognize the problem and to analyze their people. In some instances, where the emotions and traditional associations are deep, outside counsel is more effective and wise.

PREMERGER EVALUATION

It is impossible for any individual or group to foresee all of the postmerger personnel problems, nor would it be possible to compile a checklist of actions by which one may prevent them. It is possible, however, to minimize these problems by preparing for them through systematic research.

In the premerger phase of investigation there are obviously no universal standards for the human considerations involved in an acquisition beyond the principle of fair and equitable recognition and treatment throughout an organization. At best, any checklist can only form the basis of a program of integration and specify and evaluate the priority and scope of the human aspect. It is with this intent that the following program of premerger evaluation is proposed.

Organization

An evaluation of an organization can be completely informal or rigidly stylized. Since the integration requirements vary with the practices of the acquiring organization, the evaluation must be made from the standpoint of the organization's present effectiveness and the desirability of change. The refinement of organizational functions and the utilization of organizational elements are usually good measures of a company's efficiency. The "irreplaceable" value of key individuals can be offset by organizational depth. There is also usually less friction—visible and invisible—in a well-organized company.

Over-all company attitude can be tested by personal review of the organization's depth. Such investigations are preferably made by the various departments of the acquiring organization—that is, sales by sales, engineering by engineering, and finance by finance. This approach is more desirable both for the purpose of evaluation and for a later exchange of points of view. It also offers the possibility of more exact coverage and evaluation.

Remuneration

The acquired firm's salary program must be analyzed to discover where it is at variance with the acquiring company's system. The executive assistant or personnel manager should gather, evaluate, and report this information. The investigation should cover all fringe benefits accruing to the salaried employee, such as incentive bonuses, profit-sharing plans, retirement and pension plans, and stock options. When a firm acquires a company outside its industrial grouping or geographic location, it must study not only the efficiency of the plans in effect but the original and current reasons for them. If, for example, a company in the missiles field requires critical know-how, certain plans may have been formulated to attract and retain highly skilled technical personnel. In some instances, the salaries and fringe benefits of the company under investigation may reveal either high or low turnover—and the latter may exist only because of extreme loyalty to a principal personality. The liability of this situation should be measured from the standpoint of both company attitude and productivity.

Communications

In the final analysis, the communication system is probably the most important medium for smooth integration in a merger. Through effective communications, the acquiring firm can foster a feeling of mutual confidence and eliminate some otherwise inevitable friction. The acquiring company should secure samples of all internal reporting and analysis systems and evaluate them for their timeliness, effectiveness, and adequacy. Those that are mandatory should be considered first, then those that are desirable. Subsequent refinements of this reporting should be planned, and deadlines for priority improvements after the merger should be set. This gives the entire staff of the acquiring company an objective toward which it can work. Customarily, the acquiring company will want such reporting systems to parallel its own. During the initial phase, however, the amount of such reporting may vary, depending on the differences between the two companies.

Industrial Relations

Employee relations and the intangible asset of morale must also be inventoried. If two companies in the same industry and with the same products are merging and are fortunate enough to have the same union, the question is merely one of studying the past practices and experience of the acquired company and planning a gradual resolution of any small differences that may exist. If, however, the company to be acquired is in another industry or in a different geographic location, differences in attitude, productivity, and pay rates may be wide.

When small companies are acquired, there is often no union involved. In this instance, the acquiring company may expect an attempt at organization by its own union once the acquisition has been consummated. If the acquiring company is organized by one union and the company being acquired is organized by another, there will probably be few changes beyond an attempt to normalize pay rates—and fringe benefits.

An acquiring company under a central bargaining contract has still another problem when the absorbed company has a different union. In the case of a merger, however, there should be no jurisdictional disputes today; the no-raiding pact entered into by the AFL-CIO unions prevents an attempt by one union to obtain full control of other divisions of a company represented by other unions. This, of course, does not extend to "independent" unions or company-sponsored employees' associations.

Each question regarding unions must be considered in relation to the industry, the product, the average length of seniority, and local conditions. The industrial relations department should make full reports in cooperation with the cost accounting department, so that management can take full advantage of its position in striving to obtain fair rates and fringe benefits. Thus the company can remain competitive in its particular industry. Work pace, absenteeism, turnover, expansion possibilities, proportion of male help to female help, and other pertinent personnel data are absolutely necessary.

We cannot overemphasize the need for long-range personnel planning, collection of pertinent labor data, full and complete study of local customs, accurate interpretation by the legal department of the "management rights" clause, and examination of the absorbed company's contract. Only in this way can an acquiring company anticipate the demands of the union and be prepared to negotiate effectively.

CONCLUSION

There should be as much investigation, evaluation, planning, and development of personal relationships as possible during the premerger period. This should be done by the acquiring management, assisted by outside specialists where necessary. In all instances—except where immediate action is obviously necessary and acceptable—changes should be gradual, well planned, and carefully studied on a continuing basis to insure acceptance and effectiveness. When feasible, the newly acquired management should be given equal voice in approving proposed changes, so that its own sense of recognition and responsibility can remain stable.

The final watchword in merger procedure is objective patience. Patience induces confidence, calmness, and respect, and it permits a thorough integration of people. The limits of patience must be governed by the many objective factors involved in final management decisions.

Mergers and Fringe Benefits

JOHN L. HAWN

FRINGE BENEFITS, as they are commonly called, represent an ever-increasing element of the cost of goods sold. These benefits, ranging in cost between 25 and 35 percent of payroll, may be one of the controlling factors—and, in some cases, the most important factor—in determining the desirability of a merger.

To estimate these costs in the early stages of merger negotiations is not always an easy task. There may be a definite reluctance on the part of one party or the other to probe deeply into the personnel policies and practices of the company under consideration, but the full facts regarding fringe costs should very definitely be one of the major items for premerger negotiation. Merger-minded management cannot afford to be bashful. All the benefit cards must be on the table; and one must be especially wary of that notorious "ace up the sleeve"—pension past service liabilities.

ESTIMATING BENEFIT COSTS

In approaching the subject of the cost of fringe benefits experience suggests that one of the best methods of comparison is to express the net cost of the benefit as a percentage of payroll. This method makes it possible to estimate the cost to the parent company of adopting a particular benefit and, conversely, to estimate the cost of adding a given benefit

John L. Hawn is Director of Personnel Policy and Practices, Central Personnel Department, Monsanto Company, St. Louis, Mo.

or practice of the parent company to the benefit structure of the organization that is being merged. These costs may be reasonably estimated if all the facts are known. If all the facts are not known and the urge to merge is great, a possible solution is the establishment of an escrow fund that can be used to cover unknown or hidden liabilities.

It is reasonable to assume that we know in a general way what practices the company under consideration follows regarding the major fringe benefits such as pensions, profit sharing, group insurance, sick leave, vacations, and so forth. A review of union contracts and the booklets that are distributed to employees describing these plans will be helpful in determining whether all the major items are being considered.

MAJOR COST FACTORS

I have mentioned that the matter of fringe benefits should be a subject for premerger negotiations. It may be helpful to review some of the key questions that may be asked to pinpoint the cost of these benefits. In my opinion, these questions fall under four major areas:

1. *Pensions.*
   a. What is the normal cost?
   b. What is the past service cost?
   c. What is the method and rate of funding?
   d. What is the unfunded past service liability, if any?
   e. If the plan is a contributory one, what percentage of the cost is paid by the employee?
2. *Group insurance.*
   a. Is the plan on a contributory basis? If so, are the dividends from the insurance company retained or distributed in whole or in part to the employees?
   b. What has been the experience of the plan during the past two or three years? (We ask this question to determine whether the rate structure is sound or if it will be necessary to increase the rates in the very near future.)
   c. What does it cost the company to do business with the insurance carrier? (This cost is sometimes referred to as the "retention rate," and means the total premiums paid for the contract year, minus: claims paid and in the process of being paid, taxes, amounts transferred to reserves, and the amount of the dividend. This resulting figure, expressed as a percentage of the total premium paid, is a significant one when considering the cost of a group insurance program.)

3. *Savings or stock plans.*
   a. What is the cost of the company's participation?
   b. What percentage of the employees take part in the plans?
   c. Is there any outstanding obligation on the part of the company to deliver stocks or bonds at a future date?
4. *Sick-leave and vacation plans, service award plans, etc.*
   a. What is the average age of employees?
   b. The average pay?
   c. The average length of service?

With the answers to these four series of questions, one should be in a fairly good position to make an estimate of the cost of harmonizing the benefit plans. (Of the four areas, pensions, of course, are usually the largest single cost item. The difficult area of profit-sharing plans, conspicuous by its absence from the list above, will be discussed separately.)

I shall not attempt here a detailed review of the steps that are involved in estimating these costs for each particular type of benefit. It can fairly be stated, however, that with this information a person who is well versed in the fundamentals of pricing fringe benefits can come up with a reasonable estimate of these costs, which should then be reduced to a percentage-of-payroll figure and summarized. This method lends itself to a ready cost comparison of the two sets of policies. Such a cost analysis is basic to the merger decision and will determine to some extent whether the acquired company will be operated as a wholly owned independent subsidiary or made a part of the parent organization at once.

ACHIEVING UNIFORMITY OF BENEFIT PROGRAMS

A study of the mergers that have occurred during the past four or five years shows an interesting trend in the field of employee benefits. A few years ago, many of the acquisitions took the form of adding a smaller company as a wholly owned subsidiary and operating it as a separate organization, with little (if any) effort being made to bring about uniformity of benefit plans. Recently we have seen a trend toward the type of consolidation of companies where the objective has been to obtain uniformity of benefit structures at the earliest possible date. In my opinion, this is a sound trend because, in most cases, a higher level of benefit can be purchased by both the employer's dollar and the employee's contribution if the benefit plans are of a uniform or nearly uniform nature. Also, recent mergers have resulted in the transfer of top personnel to the parent company. This and the high cost of fringe benefits have been and are compelling reasons for harmonizing fringe benefits as soon as possible.

The growth of conglomerate companies in the past several years has reversed to a certain extent the trend toward company-wide uniformity of benefit plans. It is sound business practice to allow subsidiary corporations to maintain their own benefit programs and not be burdened with the overhead cost of the parent corporation's plan. In some situations, however, the desire for uniformity at an early date has resulted in a definite deterioration of employee morale. In one case, for example, the form letter from management informing the employees of the changes resulting from the merger emphasized that the company would now pay all of the premiums for the employees' group insurance. It pointed out that, from a cost standpoint, the employer was paying more money than he did under the old contributory plan. In changing the plan, however, the employer reduced the *amount* of group life insurance. Unfortunately, no provision was made for the employees to continue to carry the coverage they previously had under their former contributory plan. Since the employees were not terminating their employment, there was no conversion privilege to enable them to apply for personal insurance without a medical examination. The result, of course, was poor employee morale. This might have been avoided by negotiating with the insurance carrier a provision to allow conversion of part or all of the insurance coverage that was being lost by the employees. I mention this only as an example of the danger of rushing into a situation without first analyzing thoroughly the effects of the change on the employees.

In cases in which the benefit programs of the parent company are more liberal, there is no problem of achieving uniformity. In fact, where you can demonstrate that the employee is receiving more for less, or even more for more, the achievement of uniformity is not difficult. (One should not overlook, however, the effect of the additional cost on the profitability of the acquired company.)

REVISING BENEFIT STRUCTURES

There is no "best" pattern to follow in harmonizing two employee benefit structures. The facts in each case will govern the action that should be taken. I believe that we can, however, develop a set of guideposts or criteria that will be helpful in deciding the best route to follow in attempting to harmonize the two different structures. To this end, I believe that any revision in the benefit structure must:

1. Keep the acquired organization competitive, both as to cost of goods sold and in the labor market.

2. Maintain the level of benefits enjoyed by the acquired personnel (if consistent with point 1 above).

3. Provide the optimum benefit for the maximum number of employees.

4. Provide the highest return for the dollars spent.

5. Maintain the proper balance between hourly and salaried employees.

6. Anticipate future trends.

7. Permit simple explanation to the employees.

8. Permit efficient administration.

PROBLEM AREAS

What are some of the problems that are faced when we try to apply these criteria to a specific case? The first major factor, in this regard, is the impact of the different management philosophies of the merged organizations: Almost insurmountable problems result when the management of one company has maintained that benefit plans should be contributory and the management of another has followed the noncontributory principle. A second major source of problems is a difference in the philosophies and aims of the two union groups. It is generally recognized today that most unions are driving for (and getting) noncontributory plans in such fields as insurance and pensions. Experience, however, indicates a wide range in the degree to which this drive is pushed. Note, for instance, the fact that some union groups have agreed to a contributory comprehensive type of hospitalization and surgical plan incorporating a deductible amount, while, on the other hand, some unions demand (and get) a noncontributory plan that picks up the first dollar of hospital expense.

The third major problem area is the important question of individual adjustment. In today's society, the individual finds recognition in, and identifies himself with, a group. When the group is changed or enlarged, the individual, to some extent, loses his sense of identification. This is the reason why it is so necessary to re-establish the new group as an integral part of the larger organization and to make every effort to establish in it the corporate character of the parent company. Only when this is done will the individual be able to identify himself fully with the new organization and to find personal satisfaction and recognition in it.

PRINCIPLES OF SUCCESSFUL INTEGRATION

Regardless of the size of the company that is acquired, it is possible to enumerate a few fundamental principles to follow in solving these problems. Although these principles are in no way startling or new ideas, they are, in the long run, most important.

1. *Know your people.* It cannot be done by long-distance phone calls (although these are somewhat better than letters). Go out and visit the new people; get to know them and to understand their problems. This may play havoc with your travel budget, but will prove to be worth it. These people that we want to bring into the parent organization have a number of doubts and fears in their minds; whether these are real or imaginary, they are still *present* and have a very definite influence on the success or failure of integrating benefit programs. In this respect, it helps a lot if you have been on the "short end" of a merger yourself. In an effort to determine the attitudes of the new people, some companies have used an informal type of employee survey. Personally, I feel that direct contact is much more helpful.

2. *Take your time.* This is more difficult. I have mentioned the pressures that tend to force uniformity at an early date. But, in spite of this, a very persuasive argument can be made in favor of making a gradual, smooth transition. The people who are new to the company will soon learn of those benefits that are more liberal. Let them develop an appetite for these things. It will make it much easier for them to swallow some of the adverse factors when the plans are integrated.

3. *Train and sell.* We feel that the best results are obtained when the personnel staff and others from the acquired company are completely trained and indoctrinated in the new benefit programs. We think the best results are obtained when they go out and sell these plans to their own people. The importance of getting as many people as possible into the act by holding informational group meetings, making use of visual aids, cannot be overemphasized.

We have stressed the importance of knowing the cost of fringe benefits, developed some criteria for harmonizing the program, pointed out some problem areas, and suggested certain fundamentals to be followed. At this point, the natural question is: How do we know if we have done a good job? By what measures can we determine whether we have accomplished our objectives?

This is a difficult question to answer. It is involved with the controversial matter of how to determine the return from an investment a company makes in its employee benefit programs. I am well aware that I do not have the complete answer. I suggest, however, that one useful indicator is the degree of participation in voluntary contributory pension and group insurance plans, the acceptance of service award programs, and the like. The introduction of an entirely new type of plan a year or so after a merger can also serve as a good measuring instrument.

INTEGRATING PROFIT-SHARING PLANS

Earlier I mentioned that we would consider the problems resulting from the merger of two companies, one of which had a profit-sharing plan as well as a pension plan, the other only a pension plan. Let us examine briefly a situation where Company A, which has merged into the XYZ Corporation, has a full-refund profit-sharing plan and a life annuity plan (through an insurance carrier). The XYZ Corporation has a liberal retirement program. How can these plans be harmonized? In most cases, the profit-sharing plan tends to supplement or augment a pension plan. Thus, in this situation, one solution might be to determine the combined value of the profit-sharing and pension plans in terms of life annuity. This can then be compared with the life annuity values built up under the XYZ Corporation's retirement program. This type of analysis, by converting the plans to a common base, should lead to the determination of an equitable adjustment. It might develop, for example, that the profit-sharing plan plus pension plan is *more* than equivalent to the annuity values under the parent company's plan; or, conversely, it might turn out that, to harmonize the plans, it will be necessary to institute a certain amount of past service benefit for the old employees of the XYZ Corporation.

Don't Forget the Union

ARTHUR JACOBS

A COMPANY MANAGEMENT moves into the final stages of a merger. At the last minute, when everything is ready to go, the union gets wind of what's up. It requests negotiations, demanding fulfillment or protection of its contract. Result: the merger deal is stymied and the company is faced with a long and expensive Labor Board action.

This is a situation that has been occurring with increasing frequency and is likely to be even more serious in the years ahead. More often than suspected, sales or mergers have been accompanied by labor litigation because purchasers or sellers, or both, neglected to recognize that a union's interest in the proceedings is vital indeed. Court rulings and National Labor Relations Board decisions spell out rights and responsibilities of unions and employers when a company is about to reshuffle or dispose of some or all of its properties. It is ignorance of this important subject that often produces expensive delays for management officials.

Ignorance of legal precedents is only one failing of management in this area. Others are indifference or insensitivity to employees' concerns. Nothing can start the grapevine humming louder than excited rumors about a company's sale or decentralization or other basic shift. Nothing is equal to the demoralizing blow suffered by an employee when he hears from some unlikely source (in the cafeteria or restroom, perhaps) that the company may soon no longer need his services. While management may be doing everything it can to protect his job, the very fact that its merger negotiations have been conducted almost *sub rosa* is enough to produce an

---

Arthur Jacobs is a freelance journalist specializing in the field of labor relations.

employee reaction first of fear and then of anger. Such a performance on the part of management is even more explosive if it fails to alert the union spokesmen in a plant where the status of a union bargaining unit is well established.

So the first advisable step involving labor that should be taken before a merger or acquisition (or any other form of drastic corporate change involving contracting-out of work, moving a plant, or actually closing down) is to keep the employees informed as to what impends. Usually this can best be done through union representatives. Management would do well to keep the union advised as far in advance of actual completion of the deal as possible.

The second step is to be knowledgeable about rulings and regulations of the Federal courts, the NLRB, and arbitrators which have a bearing on special labor situations that almost inevitably arise when a merger takes place. Such issues as job security, seniority, wages, contracts, and union recognition loom large in the total picture. Later in this article, we will review some of the more important precedents incorporated in various administrative and judicial rulings which companies can use as guidelines in determining their own courses of action.

TWO SIDES TO THE UNION/MANAGEMENT COIN

Surprisingly enough, unions don't always fear merger actions. They did at one time, when union ideology equated merger with monopoly. In the period in which their bargaining power was weak they were helpless to stem the tide of merger. Even today there is little a union can do to head off a merger; however, the union is in a position to impede the merger and to cause potentially expensive delays.

In the 1930s a new philosophy of labor/management relations developed. Because of massive unemployment, Congress laid down a rule prohibiting the railroads from laying off employees because of consolidations or mergers.

This was a controversial rule. And it did not last long. The much-disputed "job-freeze" was ended in 1936. Four years later Congress voted Interstate Commerce Commission regulations requiring "just and reasonable" protection for employees affected by rail mergers. It is a regulation that is still on the books.

Over a quarter of a century later, the issue is still being wrangled over by railroads and union. In 1965, for example, 18 rail unions reached agreement with the Pennsylvania and New York Central railroads for protection of union members' security and other rights in the event the two giants should merge, as ultimately they did. The unions established well in advance of the final merger agreement the principles that jobs must be offered by the merged system to all employees presently covered by union agreements; that there would be no future pay cuts as a result of the merger; and that layoffs in the future would be limited.

Despite the ICC's "just and reasonable" regulation, employment on the railroads today is less than half of what it was thirty years ago. To what extent this is attributable to merger actions is debatable. It may well be that if the mergers had not taken place, the industry might be even sicker than it now is, and employment even lower. The historical fact remains, however, that many thousands of jobs disappeared in the railroad industry over the past thirty years as a direct result of mergers.

Until recently, employers have not been concerned with collective bargaining rights when planning a merger or acquisition. However, the same kinds of job rights that have developed on the railroads are now emerging in other nonregulated industries. These rights are reflected in developing decisions of the NLRB, in courts, and in arbitration judgments. There is no existing codification of these rulings, but they make very clear that yesterday's absolute privilege of business owners to merge or acquire or contract out without reference to their employees' interests is rapidly dissolving. It is a fair statement that employers ignore at their own peril union rights involved in merger actions.

Obviously unions do not have the final word. They cannot halt or even modify merger or similar moves taken for legitimate economic reasons. But in most cases they must be notified in advance, and management must negotiate on resulting conditions of employment. This developing new pattern of give-and-take between labor and management involved in merger discussions was stated by the Supreme Court a few years ago in the following terms:

"The objectives of national labor policy, reflected in established principles of Federal law, require that the rightful prerogatives of owners independently to rearrange their business and even eliminate themselves as employers be balanced by some protection to employees from a sudden change in the employment relationships."

What the Court is saying is that there are two sides to the union/management coin where merger actions are concerned. One is that management can acquire, sell, or transfer its property as it sees fit. The other is that union and employee contractual rights to security, seniority, and other privileges cannot be ignored.

HOW UNIONS REACT

How will unions react to news of a merger? Like everyone else, they are motivated by economic self-interest. Their reaction to the reality of an impending corporate reshuffling can be pretty well judged in advance, depending on how they are affected.

If there is a threat of loss of bargaining power for union members as a result of a merger or acquisition, the union will set up roadblocks—at least temporarily—if it can. But if the merger promises more jobs, more members, maybe higher pay, then you can guess where the union support will be.

Sometimes there are situations where two unions take opposing stances on a major proposal, both of them for logical reasons.

Thus, when American Telephone and Telegraph Company received suggestions from the Federal Communications Commission that its teletypewriter exchange facilities be turned over to Western Union, it found an ally in the Communications Workers of America, the union which represents thousands of phone workers.

Said the Communications Workers: Any such move would "cut competition, kill jobs, and corrupt free enterprise." Its president, Joseph A. Beirne, put it more bluntly when he argued: "The FCC proposal to divest AT&T of its TWX services and turn these facilities over to Western Union would destroy thousands of jobs now performed by men and women represented by CWA."

But the unions representing Western Union employees found in this instance that black was really white, and they spoke out in favor of the transfer of TWX facilities to Western Union. Such a consolidation, after all, could only add to the ranks of their members.

SOME QUESTIONS AND ANSWERS

Against this backdrop of history and union interest, one can find a fairly good guide for company behavior in merger actions affecting unions. What follows is a listing of some of the more common situations, stated as questions and answers, compiled from documented precedents established by the courts, the NLRB, and arbitration rulings.*

* Editors' note: Needless to say, any discussion such as this, based on decisions and rulings current at the time of writing, is likely to be out of date in some, perhaps many, important particulars by the time it is read, in book form, months or even years later. The question-and-answer section that follows is presented merely to suggest the kinds of questions that can arise in this area, and the circumstances in which answers may be given. In this, as in most aspects of mergers and acquisitions, there is no substitute for current counsel.

Can union contracts include provision for continuance of the agreement in case of merger or other corporate change?

They can, and they do. Many union contracts include successor clauses automatically requiring recognition by the merged company.

Suppose there is a firm termination date in the contract. Does the new employer have the right to ignore the agreement after that?

Only if he can prove that the union no longer covers a majority of the employees. And even then, this issue may have to be resolved by a costly Labor Board election.

Can unions have a direct voice in merger or acquisition negotiations?

For all practical purposes, they cannot, though there may be a rare exception in which a contract provides for this privilege. On the other hand, most union contracts have a "management rights" clause giving management an exclusive hand in the administration of the business (including the right to sell, transfer, or acquire property) as long as the collective bargaining agreement is not breached.

Is management obligated to bargain with unions on new employment conditions resulting from shifts in ownership or control?

Court and Labor Board rulings may require bargaining with the union. But this does not necessarily mean that management is obligated to make concessions demanded by unions unless there has been a violation of "rights" previously gained in collective bargaining.

Do any court rulings exist that indicate management's responsibilities and rights in mergers or similar action?

One, *Fibreboard v. United Steel Workers,* establishes the policy that bargaining units established by union contract cannot be destroyed by unilateral management decision. The issue arose when Fibreboard Paper Products Corp. of Emeryville, California, contracted out its maintenance work to an outside firm. The union had represented the company's employees for 22 years through a contract that automatically renewed itself every July 31 unless notice of intent to terminate or modify had been given no later than the previous May 26. The contracting-out decision, involving a saving of $225,000 annually, wasn't made known to the union until well after the date specified in the contract. The company said it would pay severance due under the contract, but would not renew the contract or require the new subcontractor to hire severed Fibreboard workers.

The union went to the NLRB. charging the company with refusal to bargain. At first the Board upheld Fibreboard, but then it agreed to a rehearing. It subsequently reversed itself, ruling that contracting-out of work was a change in employment conditions, subject to collective bargaining. In a milestone decision, the Supreme Court ultimately upheld this finding.

Does a company violate the law if it merges or subcontracts work as a way of avoiding a union agreement?

Yes. This was established several years ago in a case involving Town & Country, a house-trailer manufacturer of Lawton, Oklahoma, and the General Drivers, Helpers & Chauffeurs union. Almost immediately after the union notified the company that it represented a majority of the firm's drivers, the company subcontracted its hauling operations without consulting with the union. The NLRB ruled that the company had only one motive in subcontracting and discharging its drivers: to rid itself of the union. In a decision later upheld by the courts, the Board said that employers are required to bargain with a union before contracting out any job where the union represents a majority of the employees and jobs might be jeopardized by the move. Regardless of motive, said the NLRB, "the elimination of unit jobs . . . is a matter within the statutory phrase 'other terms and conditions of employment' and is a mandatory subject of collective bargaining within the Taft-Hartley Act."

The point of both these decisions *(Town & Country* and *Fibreboard)* is that, where unions are involved in mergers, companies must bargain on the basis of existing facts as well as in good faith. If in management's judgment a more economic operation will result from merger or acquisition, the union can do little to alter management's plans. If the merger is motivated by obvious anti-union considerations, management may find itself confronted with an order to "make whole all who suffer," and it is clear that an employer must observe contract conditions existing at the time of merger in any plant or plants of the affected companies.

Can the purchaser be cited where there is a finding of an unfair labor practice involved in a merger?

It can if it refuses to respect a labor contract it took over in the merger. Several years ago, Martin-Marietta, operating seven brick and construction materials plants through its United Brick division, sold the plants to Acme Brick Company, including one at Coffeyville, Kansas. Acme, for sound business reasons, began phasing out the Coffeyville plant without consulting with the union. At this point, the United Brick and Clay Workers, representing Coffeyville's employees, filed charges against both Martin-Marietta and Acme. The NLRB ruled that Martin-Marietta, as seller, had not committed an unfair labor practice and had no obligation to bargain. But Acme was found guilty of refusal to bargain because it had taken over the full inventory, handled the same products, employed the same workers, and had taken new orders to dispose of inventory.

Do seniority rights continue when a company moves to a new plant in another state?

The Supreme Court has ruled that they do in a case involving a plant operated by the Durkee's Famous Foods Division of the Glidden Corp. After 28 years in Elmhurst, New York, the plant was moved to a new location in Bethlehem, Pennsylvania. The Teamsters Union was notified. It sued for damages, claiming breach of contract because of failure of the company to recognize the employees' rehire and seniority rights covered by the contract in the old plant. The union won, establishing the right of continued seniority when plants are moved or merged.

Can there be any exceptions to this?

Only if the original union contract was very specific in limiting union recognition to the confines of a single geographic area. Thus, when Ross Gear & Tool Company of Detroit moves its plant to a new state, it said the union contract was no longer in effect. The reason: The contract said that Ross recognized the union only as the representatives of its employees in Detroit. Therefore, the union (UAW) could not claim continuance of seniority and other rights in the new plant. The courts upheld this argument.

What has the Supreme Court said about companies that close down a part of their business to avoid union bargaining?

If the closing is obviously intended to bypass a union's successful organizing campaign, then, says the Court, the company's action is illegal. The ruling was made in a case involving the Darlington Manufacturing Company, a subsidiary of Deering Milliken which operated 17 textile plants. When the union petitioned for an NLRB election, the company threatened to close the plant if the vote was successful. The vote was successful, and the company did put the plant up for auction.

The NLRB ruled that the action was illegal, since it violated provisions of the Taft-Hartley Act protecting workers' representation rights. The

Court of Appeals reversed this judgment, saying that "to go out of business, *in toto,* or to discontinue it in part, permanently at any time . . . was Darlington's absolute prerogative."

When the Supreme Court reviewed the case, it agreed that "an employer has the absolute right to terminate his entire business for any reason he pleases," but disagreed that "such right includes the ability to close part of the business no matter what the reason." The Court decision laid down three tests to judge whether or not an unfair labor practice had been committed in cases such as this:

1. The management has substantial interest in other plants which might benefit by the crackdown on unionization in the closed plant.
2. It can be shown that the closing was deliberately intended to discourage unions.
3. It can be seen that the closing will scare other workers in the remaining plants and make union organizers ineffective.

Can a company be sold without notifying the union in advance?

When sound economic reasons for the sale exist, union notification can be delayed. The *New York Daily Mirror* was in dire straits when it was put up for sale and ultimately bought by the *New York Daily News.* Only when the sale was firm did the company send telegrams to announce the action to four unions which were bargaining agents. Later, management met with union representatives and worked out settlements on the basis of existing contracts. It also cooperated in finding jobs for the union members.

The unions filed an unfair labor practice charge, claiming that the company had failed to bargain. The NLRB made it clear, as it had before, that the company had no "absolute right to sell its business without reference to union contracts." But it ruled that in this case, where "pressing economic necessity" forced the move, the company had acted fairly with the union. The Board pointed out that "the Unions and Respondents have had a long and effective bargaining relationship pursuant to which they had reached contractual settlement of the employees' severance pay and termination rights in the event of abolishment of unit jobs."

A company decides to cut out part of its line because it is unprofitable. Can it do this without consulting the union?

An NLRB case involving the Ador Corporation of Fullerton, California made it clear that such a step is perfectly proper. The company was in financial trouble and decided to discontinue a line of storm doors and windows, causing some layoffs. The union was not notified or consulted. When it complained, the NLRB ruled that the contract gave the employer the right to cut back when it had to without consulting with the union.

A company involved in union negotiations decides to sell one of its plants while the negotiations for a new contract are going on. Can the union claim foul?

It can insofar as it had wasted its time in negotiating the establishment of "phantom rates of pay." Said the NLRB: The company (Royal Plating and Polishing Co. of New York) should have told the union it was planning to sell off one of its plants for economic reasons. If it had, the union could have possibly suggested some alternative approaches to moderate effects of the closing on the employees. As it turned out, the company had to reimburse employees for loss of pay over a specified period.

Does a union contract continue in effect if the company is merged with a nonunion operation?

The Supreme Court has ruled that a union contract can survive merger of a unionized firm into a nonunion company. The case arose after Interscience Publishing (of New York), a unionized firm, was absorbed by nonunion John Wiley & Sons, Inc. Wiley claimed the union contract was washed out by the merger.

The Court ruled that the "disappearance by merger of a corporate employer that has entered into a collective bargaining agreement with a union does not automatically terminate all rights of the employees covered by the agreement, and that, in appropriate circumstances, present here, the successor may be required to arbitrate with the union under the contract." The Court also found that while ordinary contract law would not require a nonsignator to be bound by a contract, collective bargaining agreements are broader in scope because they are akin to "the common law of the plant."

The immediate issue was Wiley's obligation to arbitrate under the contract. The Court later, in another case, concluded that the entire contract, and not only the obligation to arbitrate, survives in mergers under specified conditions. The Court added, however, that in arbitrating grievances arising under the carried-over contract, the arbitrator is free to consider changed circumstances which might make adherence to the contract inequitable.

It has become clear that mergers and acquisitions do not eliminate bargaining rights unless there is a clause in the union contract to the contrary. Two conditions must exist for a successor company to take over bargaining obligations of a predecessor:

1. Management changes, but employees remain substantially the same.
2. Management remains, but there is a change in personnel and attitudes.

Is a company liable if new management replaces previous workers to avoid union recognition?

The NLRB has ruled that it is. Tennessee Products and Chemicals Corp. sold an insulation manufacturing plant to the newly formed Chemrock Corporation. The successor took over all the functions of the old company, even producing the same products on the same machines. It did not assume Tennessee Corp.'s contract obligations.

Workers of the old company represented by the Teamsters Union were let go and then informed that the new company would deal with them on an individual basis.

When the union complained, the NLRB ruled that the company had eliminated workers only to avoid dealing with the union. It was ordered to rehire them with back pay, and to bargain with the union.

Suppose a company buys another company's goodwill but does not assume its financial obligations. Is it required to bargain with the employees who had a contract under the previous ownership?

It is if it continues basically the same operation as the original company, using the same employees. This was established in a ruling on a company in Alabama (Maintenance, Inc.) which took over janitorial services for Federal agencies from a previous contractor but did not acquire its physical assets, etc. The fact that most of the old employees were hired by the new company meant that the union contract previously in existence was still effective.

Does a merging firm have to bargain with a union, if, in the process of merger, the union can no longer demostrate that it has a majority status among the employees?

It does not if it can show that the union is unable to obtain certification and as long as the new employer shows no hostility to the union. This ruling was established in the case of an Arkansas company, Mitchell Standard Corp., which for 17 years had had contracts with the union (United Furniture Workers). When the company was sold, the buyer said he would continue union recognition if the union could show it still had a majority. The union failed to do this and the NLRB ruled in favor of the company.

A purchasing concern is union-organized, but the seller is unorganized. Does the new owner have to extend a contract with his employees to employees of the unorganized firm?

Generally, it does not have to. In a California case, the courts overturned an arbitration award in favor of the union in such a case.

Can a purchasing firm lay off surplus employees resulting from a merger or acquisition?

Unless a union contract specifically forbids this, it can. But it must adhere to other provisions of the contract governing such things as seniority, termination pay, earned vacation pay, recall rights, etc.

Is the new employer obligated to upgrade benefits to the merged employees to meet those already enjoyed by his old employees?

He doesn't have to—there is no obligation. But from the point of view of good employee relations, he would be well advised to consider such equalization of benefits.

Do mergers affect existing coverage of contracts?

No. In a big merger there is no employer obligation to deal on a companywide basis if previous dealings have been on a plant-by-plant basis. Contracts do not have to be modified by new employers if the contracts have time to run after the merger. On the other hand, the new employer cannot unilaterally modify contract conditions or change the scope of a bargaining unit unless the union agrees.

How are seniority rights regarded after a merger or acquisition?

Most key arbitration awards in this area have held that, in an acquisition, employees of the purchased firm retain their seniority from date of hire. In one case in which employees of the seller and those of the purchaser were covered by different contracts, an arbitration board held that the seller's employees were entitled only to seniority from date of acquisition.

When plants are moved, maintenance of seniority usually depends on whether the contract's continuity is established.

One thing is clear where nonunion employees are involved. The NLRB has ruled that when a nonunion enterprise merges with a unionized one, the company is not required to enforce a contract provision that may require it to put the nonunion people at the bottom of the seniority list.

Is a successor company responsible for unfair labor practices committed by its predecessor?

No. The NLRB has upheld this doctrine even when the successor firm knew of the unfair labor practices at the time of merger or purchase. The only exception is when the new company is established simply to avoid penalties from unfair labor practices. The principle was set down in a case involving Atlanta Paper Company.

CONCLUSION

There is one obvious conclusion to be drawn from all this: Companies contemplating sale or merger may spare themselves needless grief if they serve adequate advance notice on the union and engage in good-faith bargaining. Employee and union opposition to a pending move can be softened by this enlightened approach. And it need not impose upon the purchaser or merged company any obligations beyond those spelled out in a contract.

Top managements of many major companies have given advance notice to employees, whether unionized or not, of pending changes in the corporate structure. Then they have gone ahead with their plans as originally blueprinted. The results have usually been satisfactory—and, unlike situations in which unions were kept in the dark, they have rarely been catastrophic.

VI

Postmerger Integration

"After marriage arrives a reaction, sometimes
a big, sometimes a little one; but it comes
sooner or later, and must be tided over
by both parties if they desire the rest
of their lives to go with the current."

RUDYARD KIPLING, *Plain Tales from the Hills*

Principles of
Postmerger Integration

J. FRED WESTON

"**O**NE TRANQUIL EVENING a month ago a dummy bomb came crashing through the window of a stately house in residential Vancouver, Canada. Attached to the missile was a message: 'Why do you have to get your hatchet men to do your dirty work?' The sender: Anonymous. The startled recipient: Harvey R. MacMillan, powerful Canadian industrialist and a controlling shareholder of Vancouver's MacMillan, Bloedel & Powell River, Ltd., the $305 million sales giant formed by the 1959 merger of MacMillan & Bloedel, Ltd., and Powell River Co. . . . Canadians had little difficulty guessing what was bothering Harvey MacMillan's unknown correspondent. Only that morning, the eleventh Powell River executive had handed in his resignation and stalked out of the merged company . . .

"At first it had seemed the ideal partnership. Powell River was known for its success in pulp and paper; in MacMillan & Bloedel, Harvey Mac-Millan had built up a major lumber concern. Combined, they could boast total assets of $3,000 million, rank as the seventh-largest forest product firm in North America, with most of the new company's sales in the U.S. . . .

"Just two weeks after the merger, this peaceful prospect exploded and the first Powell River executive quit the company. In the months that

---

Dr. J. Fred Weston is Professor of Finance at the University of California at Los Angeles.

followed, the sound of tramping feet grew louder as, one by one, five top Powell River men departed. . . . What had gone wrong in the 'perfect' merger?"

Not every merger which fails does so quite as dramatically as this one, described in an article which appeared in *Forbes* magazine a few years ago. But enough sobering news of the death or critical illness of other "perfect" mergers has appeared in the business press in recent years to make many managements take a cold, hard second look at the role of mergers in their companies' plans for diversification and growth.

In these reassessments, the *implementation* aspects of mergers have come increasingly to the fore, and particular attention is being paid to the problems and pitfalls of postmerger integration.

POSTMERGER PITFALLS

The growing and increasingly abundant literature on postmerger experiences suggests a number of potential pitfalls. Some involve bad planning of the merger. Often there was inadequate analysis of sales-to-capacity relationships. The company may have been sound at the time of purchase, but the subsequent deterioration in the industrial area should have been foreseen and taken into consideration. Related to this is the error of buying at the crest of sales and profits and paying on that basis. A small decline in the growth rate of sales and profits will render the purchase price excessive.

There may have been inadequate appraisal of the technical abilities either of the products or of the personnel of the acquired firm. Or the acquiring firm may have obtained the technical capability most appropriate for the defense market in which the acquired firm was operating, but inappropriate for the nondefense areas in which the acquiring firm is operating. The catalog could be broadly extended, but these examples are sufficient to exemplify the errors to be avoided.

Among the pitfalls related to postmerger relationships are those created by incompatible accounting systems, incompatible research organizations, or incompatible product-market lines. Another danger is failure to see how marketing organizations oriented to different customer areas can be related. Trouble may also arise from differing management philosophies based upon experience in industries with different degrees of richness of research and development activities.

Another error is the illusion on the part of firms with high price/ earnings ratios that, because they were using artificial money-stock with high P/E ratios to obtain the acquired company, only a superficial assessment of the acquired company need be made. "It wasn't real money anyhow." But the important fact is that, in order to maintain a high P/E ratio, a company must give strong indications that its earnings per share will continue to show the annual rate of increase that its high P/E ratio is based on. Thus the value of its common stock will not be sustained if the blessings conferred upon it by an optimistic investor community are not utilized in a profitable fashion.

THE IMPORTANCE OF INTEGRATION

Mergers can sometimes postpone the need for acquiring an understanding of the basic requirements of the economic environment within which the firm or firms are operating. However, mergers cannot permanently push aside the need for understanding. At some point there will be a reckoning and a necessity for facing up to the survival and growth implications of the product-market environment or environments in which the firm is operating.

This brief discussion will emphasize some aspects of postmerger integration of operations which have been relatively neglected, both in theory and in practice. First, the firm must take into account the need for effective long-range planning. The postmerger integration of operations must be within the framework of this long-range plan.

Second, there must be a clear understanding and application of the principles of organization, management, and planning. Effective coordination of functional operations must be achieved. Some writers have prescribed a time sequence for integrating functions as follows:

1. Accounting.
2. Research and development activities.
3. Production activities.
4. Marketing activities.
5. Personnel activities.

I doubt whether it is possible to justify such an inflexible priority pattern. It is more important to develop an effective timetable, regardless of the sequence. On the other hand, the timetable should not be frozen but used to provide control checkpoints.

FOUR BASIC PRINCIPLES

A review of a number of mergers, both successes and failures, suggests the applicability of the following principles for effective postmerger integration:

1. Unity.
2. Certainty.
3. Creativity.
4. Authority.

The principle of *unity* suggests that a group coalesces most effectively when it perceives a goal, a need, or a threat.

When a group sees a merger as a threat, forces may be joined to struggle against the integration and streamlining made possible by the merger. In contrast, the new management may demonstrate a competitive need to make operations more efficient in the attempt to secure full co-operation in increasing the viability of the firm, and hence of the essential workforce and organization of the firm. The management may also take the occasion of the merger to refocus and dramatize the new opportunities and potential goals of the reconstructed organization. If those in charge of postmerger activities effectively formulate the goals and clearly state the needs of the new enterprise, the emotions and energies of all segments of the organization can be focused positively rather than negatively.

The principle of *certainty* emphasizes the necessity for having a plan for blending the operations. It emphasizes the value of having a time-table for achieving specific objectives and decisions. While the plan may be modified, the principle of certainty states that people can adjust to bad news. However, they magnify and distort uncertain news. Uncertainties create anxieties and disrupt effective operations far beyond the consequences of bad news, if continued over an extended period.

This suggests that a definite timetable and plan be developed for making specific decisions and introducing specific organization, policy, and procedural changes. Thus, personnel will have a basis for understanding what changes will be made and when they will be carried out. This may represent bad news for some people, but it gives them definite knowledge as to when and to what degree they will be affected. The existence of a plan will also clearly delineate the extent to which people in the organization are going to be affected by the changes resulting from the merger. Without a definite timetable of this kind, the operations of the entire organization can go into a state of semiparalysis while many insecure executives are "waiting for the other shoe to drop."

The principle of *creativity* suggests that a change in which we participate enables us to express our desires and abilities and gives us a sense of accomplishment. A change that is imposed, however, is likely to be resisted. Thus, participation in the planning and execution of the postmerger blending process will give the employees a sense of creation of the new corporate body which the merger is in process of producing. Such changes will then be promoted with genuine enthusiasm by the broad group of executive personnel who have participated in the plans and programs for postmerger reorganization.

The principle of *authority* suggests that some blending and some discarding of nonessentials must be achieved, particularly in the concentric merger. To effect integration, someone must rule. A place of central and final decision must be clearly identified. Someone must settle the problems of merging management development. The merger might also provide a justification for getting rid of deadwood management personnel who should have been dealt with years before. If a merger is to be used to eliminate deadwood, someone has to wield the axe.

The need to integrate postmerger operations brings into focus the human aspects of business operations. Though humans are notoriously unpredictable, understanding and effective implementation of the four basic principles discussed here should go a long way toward assuring that an otherwise "perfect" merger does not fall apart in the postmerger integration phase.

Planning for
Postmerger Integration

JOHN L. HARVEY

ONCE A MERGER AGREEMENT has been reached, there begins a critical period during which a great deal of time and thought must be devoted to making the integration of the two previously separate entities as smooth and painless as possible. This is almost entirely a matter of "people integration," which in turn is largely a matter of communication. If people are kept adequately informed of the merger plans as they develop and if they are encouraged to contribute their special knowledge and experience to the integration process, the task of integration will be accomplished with a maximum of smoothness and a minimum of pain. Thus, for example, the marketing department should be asked to study the sales and distribution advantages of the merger and to explain them in terms that will be meaningful not only to marketing personnel but to other management and employee groups. Similarly, the engineering, production, accounting, and other departments should be asked to investigate and report on the implications of the merger in their respective areas.

In the pages that follow we identify briefly some of the more common problems to be avoided and precautions to be taken in planning for successful integration in the four key areas of (a) personnel, (b) marketing, (c) production and purchasing, and (d) accounting and financial control.

John L. Harvey, CPA, is administrative partner of the Pittsburgh office of Arthur Young & Company.

PERSONNEL

Perhaps the most serious integration problems have to do with the effects of the merger on management and other key personnel, and particularly on their compensation, their relative status in the company, and their future security. Accordingly, the treatment of salary and fringe benefit policies is probably the single most important consideration in planning for postmerger integration.

Responsibility should be specifically assigned to the top-ranking personnel executive to investigate all compensation and benefit policies affecting salaried personnel, including incentive bonus arrangements, stock option plans, profit-sharing plans, and retirement and pension programs. Beneficial hospitalization, major medical, or life insurance plans available to salaried personnel should also be reviewed. Once all the necessary information has been assembled, a plan must be worked out to merge the salaried employees of both companies and place them on as comparable a basis as possible without creating undesirable turnover. Following this, it will be necessary to establish, and to communicate effectively to all concerned, uniform policies and procedures for performance review and reporting.

As a general rule, the higher the level of management involved, the more serious the problems of integration are likely to be. Many of these problems, of course, will have been worked out during the period of negotiation. The composition of the board of directors, for example, is usually established during the initial planning stages. The creation of a management committee or an executive committee comprising representatives of both companies is a frequently used technique for making the process of assimilation as smooth as possible. Evidence of the successful integration of the top echelon is always reassuring to those below and generally helpful to morale. Another common, and often effective, technique for speeding up the integration process is the practice of transferring key personnel from one company to the other. This may also enable the acquiring company to place its own people in positions in the acquired company which will permit more effective control than could be achieved through any system of reporting.

It is desirable that the top executives of the two companies be familiar with one another on a social basis as well as on a business basis. Few mergers, in the author's experience, have been successfully consummated without the use of cocktails. Wives should always be included in these get-togethers.

As noted earlier, communication is the key to successful integration, and this can best be accomplished at the executive level through the liberal use of meetings, which should be held much more frequently during the integration stage than would otherwise be considered necessary or desirable. At these meetings all conflicts should be discussed openly in an effort to identify problems and work out mutually acceptable solutions. One of the most important "don'ts" in this area—and this, incidentally, applies to most other aspects of integration as well—is *don't change the original organization plan or other representation without first discussing the reasons for such a change with the appropriate personnel of the acquired company and securing their agreement.*

If key people in the acquired company are properly treated and have been kept adequately informed, they can generally be expected to work out well in the merged group. There are, however, exceptions to this as to any rule, and it is not unusual for such exceptions to go unrecognized until after the merger has been consummated, thus giving rise to the unpleasant necessity of letting people go. Experience suggests that there is little to be gained—and, in terms of general morale, a great deal to be lost—from a policy of immediately firing or even "freezing out" unwanted executives. A more sensible approach, which many companies have taken, is to give such an executive a number of special assignments. Assuming that he fails to handle these assignments adequately, it will then be clear to his associates that his discharge was occasioned by his own performance and does not reflect a general attitude toward the executives of the newly acquired company. In some cases, it may be possible to transfer such executives into positions which they would be capable of handling. Early retirement can also be a useful device for relieving unsatisfactory executives of their duties in a humane fashion.

It should be the responsibility of the industrial relations department to collect all pertinent data on labor contracts for all union and nonunion employees before the merger, so that a smooth integration can be accomplished in this vital area as well. This can be a very simple or a very difficult task, depending on the unions involved and the nature of the company's past relations with them.

MARKETING

If, as we have suggested, the compensation of executives and key employees is the most critical aspect of postmerger integration, nowhere is this more true than in the marketing function. In part this is a natural reflection of the vital importance of sales to any company, but it undoubtedly also has something to do with the "prima donna" attitude that is so common among successful salesmen.

Frequently, key sales personnel in a smaller company are able to achieve a level of compensation far out of proportion to that of their equally successful counterparts in a larger, more integrated organization. In fact, this situation is often a major stumbling block in initial merger negotiations. Although it may not be necessary or desirable to deal with this situation immediately after the merger is consummated, it is generally bad for morale to have any group overcompensated for any substantial period of time. On the other hand, of course, compensation cannot be sharply reduced without incurring some turnover—which, in the marketing area especially, could be disastrous. Generally, there has to be an exchange; something must be given in return for a reduced level of compensation. Some companies have found lump-sum cash payments useful for this purpose, while others have exchanged such benefits as pension plans, stock options, or increased insurance benefits to bring salesmen's salaries into line.

Often a combination of two companies is undertaken to permit a combination of their selling efforts. This means, of course, that both sales groups will be undertaking the sale of new products—a situation that could spell trouble unless proper steps are taken to train and motivate the salesmen. Most salesmen regard every new product with suspicion, and no salesman is anxious to jeopardize his existing customer relations. Special training must be undertaken to ensure that all salesmen understand and have confidence in the new products they are being asked to handle. One effective method of achieving this objective is to organize a special task force to clarify the problems, to work closely with the sales organization, to train salesmen in technical areas, and to help them understand the advantages of the expansion of their product lines.

When dealers, distributors, or other outside sales organizations are employed, much the same effort must be expended to train these groups to handle the new products. Often a merger may have as one of its advantages the combining of seasonal products to create a level year-round sales pattern. This, of course, can be of great benefit to any marketing organization, and to the extent that it occurs, should be emphasized as much as possible. Naturally, all distributorship agreements should be reviewed and modified as necessary in light of the changes resulting from the merger.

It can be very worthwhile to use the incident of merger as an occasion for calling on major customer accounts. An imaginative sales organization should be able to make good use of this opportunity to explain to the customer not only the reasons for the merger but the benefits that he (the customer) will derive from it.

PRODUCTION AND PURCHASING

It is difficult to generalize in any useful way about the integration of production operations. The problems and considerations involved will vary widely from one merger to another. The basic question of how much integration of production operations should be attempted will normally have been decided in the premerger negotiation and planning stages, and the basic considerations involved in that decision are discussed elsewhere in this volume.* The most difficult problems encountered in this area usually relate to the coordination of the two companies' production and sales activities. New procedures may have to be established for accurately estimating sales of each product under the new postmerger conditions, and new production schedules developed accordingly.

Integration of the purchasing operations of the two merged companies often leads to substantial cost savings as a result of standardization and the ability to purchase materials, equipment, etc., in larger quantities than were previously feasible for either company alone. Although such standardization is simple in theory and presents no difficult problems, it does require a great deal of pick-and-shovel work and an intimate knowledge of the products of both companies. An additional benefit which many merged companies have derived from purchasing standardization is the opportunity it affords to utilize numerical codes in place of written work-order descriptions, which in turn leads to significant economies in data processing.

ACCOUNTING AND FINANCIAL CONTROL

Here again, as we have noted in every area, people problems are paramount. The controller of the acquired company has always reported to his top management, perhaps for many years. He is now being asked to make himself independent of that management so that he may report objectively to a headquarters group that is new to him. The problem of motivating any controller to resist local management pressures and maintain his independence is difficult enough, but it is doubly difficult following a merger. Old loyalties are hard to break. The new management must utilize its full ingenuity to bring the controller to the realization that his own future depends primarily on how well he can serve his new masters. Yet he must remain motivated to serve the local operation. The success of management in this effort will be reflected both in the smoothness with

* See p. 10, "Planning for Mergers and Acquisitions," by John L. Harvey.

which the mechanics of accounting integration are achieved and, thereafter, in the reliance management can place on the accounting data generated by the newly acquired operation.

Obviously, any economies achieved through the integration of production and/or purchasing operations will have to be reflected in the cost accounting system. Where standard costs are used, these will have to be revised to reflect the new operating conditions.

If the newly acquired company is a small, owner-managed organization, it is almost axiomatic that its cost accounting system will be less than adequate—and possibly a great deal less than adequate. This may necessitate a major effort to develop a cost system almost from scratch. Even if an adequate cost system exists, it will have to be studied to ensure that its underlying principles are in conformity with those of the acquiring company's cost system. This does not necessarily mean that the cost methods of the acquired company should be adapted to conform with those of the acquirer. It can be a costly mistake to assume that the acquired company doesn't have its share of good ideas, and in many cases the best cost system will be achieved by combining the best features of both companies' systems.

One change in cost accounting which is virtually inevitable is the reallocation of overhead. This is always a touchy matter at best, and it must be handled in such a way that all departments will understand the rules of allocation. Naturally, the rules themselves must be sound. No product manager appreciates a charge for research and development when he is fully aware that no effort is being made to expand the application of *his* product. This is not merely bad accounting but bad psychology as well.

Although the integration of the marketing function may present the most difficult problems, the integration of accounting will probably involve the greatest amount of change. Here, again, the question arises, How much integration is desirable? Certain accounting functions must be centralized almost by their very nature. All financing, and hence the determination of over-all cash requirements and the consolidation of cash flow statements, must be handled at headquarters. Budgets must be controlled and combined by a central accounting department. Cash flow statements and budgets lead naturally to authorizations and budgets for capital expenditures, and these in turn encourage the establishment of uniform and centrally controlled fixed-asset records.

One of the most common aspects of accounting consolidation is payroll. Frequently a merger results in a consolidated payroll operation of sufficient size to permit the economic use of electronic data processing where it was not previously feasible.

Federal and often state and local tax work can also be combined and handled at corporate headquarters. This is a "must" if consolidated Federal income tax returns are filed, and may be desirable under any circumstances. Researching the same tax problem twice is a luxury no company can afford. Consolidation of state and local tax work depends, of course, on the locations in which the two companies operate. There should be only one group negotiating with each state and local tax authority, and if both companies have operations in the same state, county, or city, consolidation would seem to be indicated. Further centralization may permit a more efficient operation, but this may be offset by the loss of those intangible benefits that often seem to result from local, personal tax negotiations.

Insurance, whether or not it is under the jurisdiction of the accounting department, should be handled on a consolidated basis to assure uniform coverage and minimum premiums.

The extent of accounting centralization will determine the extent to which forms must be standardized. There will have to be uniformity in the reporting of cash flow, budgets, capital authorizations, payroll, tax information, and the other areas mentioned above as being desirable to consolidate. Further standardization may be deferred or not undertaken at all, depending on the situation. Here again it should be emphasized that standardization is not synonymous with adopting the procedures of the acquiring company. Good will and improved operations often result from combining the best features of both systems.

Standardization of reports is another area in which the extent of standardization considered desirable, either immediately or ultimately, will vary from one merger to another. One concept is, however, of the utmost importance: The information reported to top management from all segments of the combined operation must be comparable. Reporting below this level may derive benefits from uniformity, but it is less essential. As a general rule, the lower the level, the greater the diversity that is likely to be acceptable. This, however, refers only to the *use* of reports. If we turn to their preparation, the desirability of uniformity may increase sharply, especially where data are processed by machines.

Concerning the problem of furnishing comparable data from all operations to top management, we must take into consideration more than the need to have the same information available. The basic problem lies in establishing uniform definitions. What costs are capitalized and what costs are expensed? How is depreciation computed? What costs are included in inventory? Are they maintained on a LIFO, FIFO, or average-cost basis? What costs, such as research and development, are deferred? What liabilities are established for product guarantees? Are tax accruals established on the same basis? Are pension costs accounted for in the same manner? These are only a few of the literally hundreds of questions that must be asked and answered before steps can be taken to permit the development of figures which have that all-important characteristic, comparability. Not only must the accounting principles be uniform, but so, at least within broad headings, must the classification of accounts. Company A may include the salary of the vice president for sales under "Administrative expense"; Company B may classify it as "Selling expense." Such differences must be eliminated. It is in these areas that the accounting and finance departments will have to devote the greatest part of their efforts during the postmerger period.

One final thought on postmerger integration: In an effort to put through the deal, the management of an acquiring company will sometimes, with no intention to deceive, declare that there will be no change in the operation of the acquired company. "There will be different stockholders; that's all that's involved." This, of course, is transparent non-sense. Some change is inevitable. In the case of a sick company, the change may be drastic and sudden. More often the change will come gradually, over a period of several years. But either to represent or to believe that there will be *no* change may make the inevitable changes more difficult and create unnecessary problems during the critical postmerger period.

Integrating New Acquisitions:
One Company's Approach

JOHN W. SHERIDAN

I T IS NOW CLOSE to 20 years since American Machine & Foundry Company announced its intention to acquire sound, well-managed companies whose products would add breadth and diversity to its established line of equipment. Growth has always been a prime objective of AMF, but that announcement in 1950 anticipated and set the stage for a new kind of growth. The management of AMF had concluded that the company's profit potential would be enhanced through the acquisition of lines of general products to balance its traditional product lines of specialized tobacco and bakery industry equipment.

Since that time, AMF has acquired 35 companies in many different industries. In the process we believe we have learned a great deal about the successful integration of newly acquired companies—a result which depends as much, in our experience, on effective preacquisition efforts as on postacquisition activities.

PREACQUISITION ACTIVITY

Because of AMF's known desire to expand, the company is constantly receiving information from brokers, managements, and other outsiders about the availability of particular companies—in addition, of course, to

---

John W. Sheridan is Assistant Comptroller of American Machine & Foundry Company, New York.

solicitations made by AMF itself. In total, we average about 450 such offers a year. Few, however, get very far beyond the doors of our Business Development Division, for only 10 percent are actually considered to merit further investigation.

When an interesting prospect is selected, our initial approach is to request extensive data, principally financial, on the company being offered. We also, of course, obtain Dun & Bradstreet reports, make inquiries with bank contacts who are familiar with the company, and acquire other information from other sources. One of the first questions we want answered at this point is "Why is the company for sale?" Is it an estate problem on the part of the principal shareholders, is it a shortage of cash, is it a business turning downward, or is there management friction to be overcome? Our initial review of the financial and other data helps us to answer this question and, to a large extent, determines the degree of further interest that AMF will show. When considered appropriate, positive recommendations—including whether the acquisition should be regarded as a pooling of interests or a purchase—are made to our Executive Office in order to obtain authority to proceed and make an offer.

Our vice president in charge of the Business Development Division then meets with the management of the company and informs it of our interest. At this time he describes the organizational structure of AMF, discusses the benefits that we think AMF can bring to the company, and obtains any additional information that he feels is necessary. Our vice president is usually accompanied by the group executive from the appropriate AMF business group, whose responsibility it is to evaluate the potential integrational "fit" of this company as it relates to his particular group. He looks for historical growth, future growth potential, marketing fit, a knowledgeable organization in some depth, and manufacturing and other operational integration potential—in about that order. There is also some discussion of the asking price, and a counteroffer might conceivably be made at this time by us. Since most of our acquisitions are for shares of AMF stock, it is important that the caliber of the men to whom a large block of AMF shares are given is of the highest. We want only able men who can contribute materially to the joint enterprise.

Initial Problems

If this preliminary meeting is successful, it is the practice for a few members of our corporate staff who are knowledgeable in the areas of greatest interest or concern to visit the location in order that they may provide our Business Development Division with their findings and opinions in their specialized field or fields. An assistant comptroller, for example, is usually requested to visit a potential acquisition, not only to review the debit and credit elements of the balance sheet but to apply his broad business background to an evaluation of whether or not the company appears to be following sound business practices. His reports not only cover financial and internal control practices but also deal with marketing, production, physical plant appearance, exposure in tax areas, personnel policies, purchasing procedures, etc. Qualified men in other fields also visit the location for a brief survey, and their evaluations are, of course, weighed and assessed by our Business Development Division, which coordinates all acquisition activities.

At this point in time we are faced with certain initial problems, one of the greatest of which is restraining the enthusiasm of the AMF group executive. He, of course, is quite interested in the growth of his own business group, and sometimes he may be willing to pay what the other members of the evaluation team feel is too high a price for the potential to be realized.

Another problem is that the investigations which our people make at this stage of the negotiations are necessarily limited, both in scope and in depth. A substantial amount of the data which they obtain must be accepted on a good-faith basis, for it is too early in the negotiation process to attempt to verify the correctness of all the information obtained by detailed ferreting. With very few exceptions, however, we have not been seriously misled by companies that we have dealt with in these early conversations.

We have been fortunate too that our advance team of investigators comprises qualified men, long on knowledge of AMF, business in general, and business trends and values, and able negotiators who, representing AMF, have been able to "sell" our company to the acquisition candidate's management. This is a very important part of our negotiations, for it represents the first real exposure that the management of the acquisition candidate has to AMF's method of operating. If these contacts are not skillfully and tactfully handled, they could undoubtedly lead to many withdrawals.

There are also, of course, problems on the other side of the table. The management of an acquisition candidate is naturally quite anxious to know what its status will be if it becomes part of our company. Will individuals be deposed from their official positions? What limits on authority previously exercised will result from combining with AMF? Will there be any substantial impact of an adverse nature on their company's fringe benefits program? And, finally, how will the parent company go about monitoring the routine day-to-day operations of the newly acquired unit? We know from experience that these are the prime areas of concern to the managements of acquisition candidates, and we do our best to allay their fears by giving them a full understanding of how AMF operates, because, for the most part, local autonomy continues to be vested in the present management.

Detailed Investigation

Following these preliminary steps and acceptance by the Business Development Division of the various evaluations submitted, we then move into the investigatory phase, which involves a very detailed analysis of the financial, legal, administrative, marketing, and operational functions of the acquisition candidate.

In the financial area we require an audit by our independent public accountants. We also, of course, examine the tax files of the company, verify the adequacy of its insurance coverage, and check out the internal procedures followed.

In the legal area our general counsel review the various contractual agreements which exist, such as those pertaining to royalties, leases, etc. We also request counsel to give us an opinion as to whether or not the acquisition could place us in an unfavorable antitrust position. The Robinson-Patman Act requirements are carefully studied to ensure that our exposure is limited, the adequacy of patent protection is reviewed, and, of course, any current litigation files are thoroughly examined.

In the manufacturing area, we have specialists examine the plant operations in detail. Is the work done to rigid specifications, are engineering changes common, do the inspection and quality control procedures seem adequate? This group also examines the purchasing procedures to determine whether the most opportune methods of obtaining materials and equipment are being used and whether good inventory control is being maintained. They check the condition of the equipment and of the building itself to determine whether substantial new capital will be required to upgrade the equipment and whether repair and maintenance costs are likely to be significant. Packaging methods are also examined, and shipping procedures are reviewed. We are, of course, also interested in the development program of the company. Is their product subject to constant upgrading, or is it essentially the same product they made twenty years ago? Is there any attempt on the part of management to extend the company into newer fields?

Our marketing people obtain a very detailed analysis of the methods used in distributing the product, what promotional programs are used by the company to develop an increasing share of their market, the position of this particular company in its industry, what service and warranty programs (if any) exist, and what credit policies are followed.

Representatives of our personnel department also visit the location and review the union agreements that exist, the fringe programs provided, and the adequacy of personnel record-keeping, and evaluate as best they can the company's management capability, including the capability of support personnel. Labor relations are also reviewed to determine whether plant management is able to operate continuously or is subject to strike interruptions on a too-frequent basis.

Final Actions

Assuming that the over-all analysis based on the reports of these various specialists is indicative of a sound, well-managed company, capable of improvement, we now come to the final phase of our preacquisition activity. The problems at this juncture are basically in the area of human, customer, and public relations and have to do primarily with establishing the status of the acquired unit's personnel.

As mentioned earlier, the unit's autonomy is maintained to the greatest extent possible. However, certain employee benefit programs—particularly those relating to bonus plans and executive salaries—frequently are not compatible with our broad corporate program, and corrections have to be made. When such a situation exists, gradual adjustments can usually be negotiated. Key employees are assured of continued service so that we will be assured of retaining knowledgeable personnel.

In addition, the group executive must resolve the fears of the other people in the acquired unit, and this is generally accomplished through a series of meetings at which AMF executives discuss our company with local personnel.

One of the conditions usually included in our purchase contract requires securing approval from both our independent public accountants and the SEC to treat the acquisition as a pooling of interests. Since most acquisitions are made at a cost in excess of book value, it is generally more advantageous for us to "pool" the company acquired than to treat it as a purchase and create goodwill.

Frequently the company being sold may have to obtain stockholder approval. However, we rarely have any problem with dissenting stockholders, and at this point the acquisition is finally consummated.

POSTACQUISITION ACTIVITY

Once the acquisition has been made, we are faced with the problem of integrating the company as quickly as possible into the AMF business group to which it is best fitted. Naturally, there are certain limits on the acquired company's management, for AMF is publicly held and our Executive Office is responsible to many stockholders for all company actions. These restrictions are clearly enunciated in the corporate policy and procedures manuals which we provide to local management immediately.

In addition, the acquired company's actions are monitored through an Operating Management Board, which usually consists of five members of the Executive Office, plus the group executive. It is through this board that the extent and nature of the direction to be given to the particular acquired unit are determined. For the most part, our controls are of a financial nature and involve limits on capital spending, engineering projects, and advertising programs, as well as executive salary adjustments and, of course, the comparison of actual results with budget.

The board also serves to coordinate certain programs that might involve more than one of the business units of the particular group. For example, a tie-in advertising campaign that might involve using the products of two or more recreational units would be submitted to the board of the recreational group for review, and if considered feasible the necessary approvals to participate would be granted.

In connection with equipment appropriations, the Operating Management Board might first require that the requesting unit contact other affiliated members of the AMF family to determine if such equipment might be surplus at another location. Similarly, on new engineering programs it might be the feeling of the board that, although a proposed program has merit, greater capabilities exist in other units of AMF, and the project might well be routed to another unit of the company for preliminary study.

These actions, of course, are sometimes difficult to understand in a new unit, particularly if it has been a closely held company whose chief executive officer has for many years nurtured this child of his to maturity and now all of a sudden finds that other people are, in his words, "trying to tell him how to run his business." Through personal contact, however, the initial impact of having others participate with him in business decisions is mitigated considerably, and it has been our experience that, within a year, the benefits that a large company's resources can make available are usually clearly appreciated. For example, it also is recommended to the local management that, wherever possible, they avail themselves of the centralized purchasing opportunities which exist through AMF headquarters. This frequently can produce substantial manufacturing cost reductions and helps to bring about a further upgrading of consolidated earnings. The management is also made more fully aware of the various central staff divisions that exist and is encouraged to draw on them for help in solving various problems. All such assistance, incidentally, is provided on a "no charge" basis, for we discontinued allocating corporate G&A to the field units several years ago.

Legal Status

One of the major problem areas is in our own comptrollership operations. It is usually our decision whether the acquired unit will continue to operate as a corporate entity or as a division of the parent company. In making this decision we have to consider, among other things, the impact on the earned-surplus account of both the parent company and the newly created company. If a separate corporation is created, AMF frequently retains title to patents obtained and licenses the new company to use such patents. An intercompany royalty charge is normally made for the data provided.

Control

We find also that some of the companies we acquire do not have a modern accounting control system. Our tighter requirements in these areas are clearly defined in our comptrollers manual, a copy of which is sent to the local comptroller immediately after the acquisition is consummated. Few of these companies used flexible budgets, and there of course was no need to provide analytical financial commentaries to explain performance variances from either budget or last year, since there was no absentee management. The acquired companies' financial reports were generally prepared at a more leisurely pace than we demand, and our due date requirements frequently caused concern. Most units, however, have found that the report schedule is realistic and within three months were in line with the rest of our company.

Certain other control elements usually found in a major company, such as expenditure limits, property detail records, adequate inventory records, and short-term forecasts, have been lacking in some of the companies we have acquired.

Accounting

The acquired company's chart of accounts is never in agreement with ours, of course, and since our basic approach is to maintain a feeling of autonomy at each unit we do not insist on an immediate transfer to the AMF code structure. Instead, we overcome this problem through a series of instructions included in the comptrollers manual which describes the line content of our principal financial statements.

A simple example to illustrate this point is the matter of advances to employees for travel. We at AMF consider this to be a deferred expense; however, many companies record such advances on their statements as an account receivable. Our instructions stipulate that, for standardization reasons, the unit should reclassify any travel advance balances to the prepaid expense line of the balance sheet.

Other Areas

Other problems initially encountered relate to the transfer of financial responsibility to corporate headquarters. This may involve establishment of new banking arrangements, discharge of any existing debt, and placing the acquired unit on an imprest cash system. We also initiate an adjustment of fringe benefit programs, so that in time they will be more in line with broad AMF coverages, and we place the general insurance coverage under Executive Office control. This latter change is sometimes difficult to effect immediately because of the personal relations that may exist between local management and local insurance agents. We also advise the local management that its public accounting requirements will now be handled by our corporate auditors rather than their local firm, and we recommend that the use of other outside consultants be terminated, where practical, as soon as possible.

In the tax field there are normally no particular problems that are immediately faced, except possibly there having been certain minor instances of noncompliance with the tax laws—for example, failure to pay an excise tax or failure to qualify in certain states in which the company has been doing business. We correct these errors immediately in order to minimize AMF's exposure to future penalties.

Acquisitions by Purchase

One other major accounting problem which, prior to the introduction of the pooling-of-interests concept, required a considerable amount of effort to resolve had to do with the disposition of the difference between investment cost and equity acquired. In those instances where an excess was paid, it was necessary to determine the amounts that could be allocated to the various assets to which this excess was attributed and, after exhausting this distribution, to record any remaining excess as goodwill. The amortization of these amounts, of course, became a penalty against future operating income. Similarly, if the equity acquired was greater than the investment, we would have to make a determination as to which assets were overstated on the books and provide writedowns or reserves.

A corollary problem under a purchase arrangement was determination of the earned surplus of the acquired company at the date of aquisition, and it was frequently necessary to adjust the reported earned surplus at the acquisition date in order to roll back, or possibly even move forward, certain substantial adjustments that were made on the books of the acquired company.

Continuing Problems

The integration of all acquisitions has proved to be of substantial benefit to AMF. We know that we can bring more to a company in the way of growth and profits out of a given supply of assets, particularly where they are closely related, than would be likely with the former individual management operating on its own.

We cannot, of course, neglect the matter of continuing profit improvement. In itself this is not the problem of a particular acquisition, but it is a problem of the combined corporation. We try to accomplish this in many ways, such as the centralized purchasing procedure previously referred to. Through a series of reports, we keep a watchful eye on such items as return on assets employed and inventory investments, and we exercise strict control over travel, overtime, and communications costs. We stress new product developments and subsequent commercialization. When a unit is in difficulty, we may have a task force of Executive Office specialists visit the location in order to assist local management in taking corrective measures. We provide trade relations data through our corporate offices, as well as technical assistance in data-processing techniques. At the corporate level the exception technique is used to report to executive management those units that are substantially off budget and/or last year's performance.

Mutual Benefits

Thus far we have dwelt mainly on the problems. Needless to say, there are also many benefits that stem from acquisitions. The most obvious, surely, is growth for the parent and for the acquired company, and a broader horizon for the aspiring executives of both. If our homework has been done properly, we not only will grow in volume but also should grow at the net income level. Distribution costs frequently have been substantially improved when related to dollar of revenue, because we have achieved a broader base for the sale of our AMF lines, as well as the opening of new distribution outlets. The acquired company also benefits from lower insurance costs under the blanket coverage policies of AMF.

The management of the new unit also has available advice and help from specialists in our Executive Office in dealing with various day-to-day problems. For our own part, we at AMF also have learned many things from these organizations about improving our methods of operating, and we have "borrowed" many ideas and procedures from newly acquired units.

One final consideration is a matter of personal interest to the principal shareholders of the business that is being sold. Many acquisitions made by large companies in recent years have been of companies that are privately held. Usually the chief executive officer has been fairly well along in years and has been anxious to put his estate in order. The opportunity to exchange his holdings for those of a publicly owned company has frequently been a decisive factor in the decision to combine his company with ours.

SMALL-COMPANY ACQUISITIONS

The preceding discussion has related primarily to acquiring and operating a company as a continuing autonomous entity. Another practical consideration is the acquisition of smaller companies which complement existing product lines and the blending of such acquisitions into existing facilities.

The transfer of operations to an existing facility produces substantial reductions in fixed costs, tightens administrative control, and projects a better corporate image in the industry served—all of which tends to increase the profit margins obtained.

In the past three years we have had five transactions of this nature, and initial results have been most satisfactory. In two of these combinations we were able to add new lines to our existing products immediately, thereby reducing engineering development time on such products.

VII

Acquisitions Abroad

"As the Spanish proverb says, 'He, who would
bring home the wealth of the Indies,
must carry the wealth of the Indies with him'."

SAMUEL JOHNSON, quoted in Boswell's *Life* (1778)

Finding and Evaluating Acquisitions Abroad

GEORGE B. FINNEGAN

ONCE A U.S. COMPANY has decided to acquire operating facilities abroad, it must set up machinery to carry out this decision. The first step is to choose an organization form for those who will be concerned with all phases of the acquisition, so that the program will be using the best talent available in the most effective manner.

ORGANIZING THE ACQUISITION TEAM

The company that makes only occasional acquisitions does not need a full acquisition staff; a task force may be formed for each individual project. Men will be drawn from international operations to analyze the sales, manufacturing, and financial aspects of the acquisition; additional help may be requested from domestic operations to fill in gaps or to supplement the efforts of the international task force.

Where the overseas acquisition program is more active, the domestic acquisition staff, augmented by selected experts from international, may be used. This form combines the experience of a domestic staff engaged full-time in the problems of acquisition with the knowledge of those engaged full-time in international operations. As the program proceeds, the domestic staff will probably pick up many of the international experts'

George B. Finnegan is Vice President–Western Region of Business International Corporation. This chapter is based on a Business International survey of company practices in the subject area.

skills, and in time it may be able to relieve the smaller international staff of some of the burden. Having the two groups work together may also promote understanding between the company's domestic and international operations and lead to greater cooperation in other areas.

A third organizational form, for the company with a full-scale international acquisition program, is a permanent new business and development staff responsible for acquisitions as well as other forms of expansion abroad. This experienced group will conduct studies that may lead to acquisitions worldwide. Since it is acting on its own, however, care must be taken to dovetail its objectives with those of the corporation as a whole. There have been many cases of international and domestic planners going off in opposite directions. In other cases, the international planning staff has ended up in a war with the line officers.

No matter which of these forms is chosen, over-all corporate policies must be clearly understood by the men responsible for locating, evaluating, and negotiating each acquisition. These policies—including the percentage of equity required, the types of acceptable financing (cash or stock swap, etc.), the geographic areas in which to concentrate, whether or not to diversify, which product lines are being sought, what types of firms fit the over-all corporate goals—may differ significantly from the policies followed in domestic operations.

LAYING THE GROUNDWORK

Once clear policy guidelines have been established, the acquisition team must take the proper steps in the proper order. The first of these steps is to determine the requisites a prospective acquisition must meet. FMC Corporation, for example, looks for a company with future growth potential to which it can add technical and managerial competence and where it can expect a return on assets of 12 to 15 percent in developed countries. FMC insists that acquiring for added volume alone is not justifiable. General Foods, on the other hand, takes a slightly different approach by looking for an "operating base," a company with good management skilled in the food business, with an efficient distribution system compatible with GF's (where GF has no business facilities, its requirements for distribution systems are less strict) and the capability of absorbing GF's product lines. The feeling is that talented management can easily switch to producing and marketing GF products. On this basis, GF acquired a chewing-gum manufacturer in France and an ice-cream company in Brazil even though it had never been in those fields. A third case is that of Kaiser Aluminum and Chemical, which is looking for growth in its own fields rather than diversification. In fact, its foreign acquisition program was prompted by antitrust laws that prohibit additional expansion in the United States.

After deciding what it is seeking, how the acquisition is to be financed, and how it fits into the corporate goals, a company must decide whether to use its own staff or outside "finders" to look for prospects. Many companies feel that the best contacts can be made through banks, especially foreign banks, since, in the words of one international v.p., "They know when a company is ready for acquisition before its owners do." Other service organizations or the company's distributors, affiliates, and licensees may also furnish leads to acquisition candidates. The U.S. company's experience in the local market should also give it a good idea of who may be a prospect. Another effective approach is for the acquiring company to secure a list of the manufacturers of products in which it is interested and make direct inquiries (perhaps talking about a possible licensing tie-up on the first call). The most direct approach is one used by a convenience foods company: It goes to a supermarket, picks out the products that are of interest to it, and then looks up the makers. This, of course, may not work for other types of products, but it might be worth a try.

Another delicate problem is how best to present acquisition proposals to the board of directors in order to win its final approval. Some companies keep up a constant flow of information to the board during the acquisition process. Negotiations may be completed with unexpected rapidity, and a great deal of cash may have to be spent or a new capital issue made to pay for the acquisition. Preliminary board approval is always a good idea. When final approval is sought, many international executives feel that the people who actually worked on the project should make the presentation, since they have lived with the problems and are in the best position to answer the board's questions. If the information is passed up the line to an executive connected with the project only superficially, much may be lost in "translation."

All of this, of course, is in addition to the regular form of investment proposal that would be drawn up for a capital input, whether starting from scratch or through an acquisition. In this proposal, many firms include not only a projection of earnings, return on invested capital, and payout ratios, but the contribution the acquisition will make to the parent company's earnings on a per-share basis.

In setting corporate goals it is important to maintain flexibility. Indeed, the setting of arbitrary standards by the board in the United States can be particularly dangerous. For example, one U.S. company rejected an acquisition in Germany negotiated by its international officers because the German firm's earnings-to-sales ratio was well below that of the U.S. parent. A U.S. competitor then acquired this German firm and practically eliminated the products of the first U.S. company from the German market. As with all policies, the important goal is *total short-term and long-term sales and profits,* not necessarily arbitrary, inflexible ratios of earnings to sales or to net worth.

FINDING PROSPECTIVE ACQUISITIONS

If a company decides to make use of outside "finders," it will probably increase the number of firms from which it will ultimately make a choice, but it will also increase the number of problems associated with the acquisition. In addition, the company must not forget that using an outside agency will not eliminate the necessity for a well-thought-out program and will force the company to narrow down the type (or types) of acquisition that it is seeking. Otherwise, a very lengthy list may be presented that will cost a great deal to narrow down. On the other hand, if the finder is given a very narrow description of what is sought, flexibility is sacrificed, and solid candidates may be overlooked because they do not fit the acquiring company's description exactly enough. Many companies have found that the failure of outside finders to do their job adequately stems as much from poor preparation and direction on the acquirer's part as from shortcomings on the finder's part.

The two major limitations of outside finders cited by experienced acquirers are (a) that the finders cannot provide much that the company itself cannot provide in the way of know-how, contacts, and personnel, and (b) that the finders often make poor analyses of the firms they find. Usually the acquirer must make a more detailed analysis of the prospective acquisition and almost always it must evaluate the position of the prospective acquisition in relation to the industry—an area in which the finder cannot normally be expected to have the requisite knowledge. This is a real stumbling-block to the use of finders, since the additional analysis required can be quite costly and time-consuming. One international company reported that it received the names of more than a hundred acquisition prospects from a search firm, but, after spending countless hours evaluating the names, found that it could not use a single one. In this case part of the trouble was due to the failure of the company to give the finder enough direction during the search. In contrast, a company with an experienced acquisition staff that never uses outside finders found six suitable firms in Europe and acquired all of them—perhaps an unprecedented success that points up again the value of careful planning and preparation.

There are, however, definite advantages in using a finder, particularly for companies that do not have the manpower and the time for an extensive search. Another major benefit is that the finder allows the company interested in acquisition to remain anonymous during the search period. This prevents prices of acquisition candidates from rising when word leaks out that an American company is in the market. Negotiations, however, are almost never left in the hands of middlemen.

If finders are to be used, it is important first to establish a series of safeguards to protect the company from unwarranted claims. Most companies using finders have a standard form stipulating that, before any discussion can start, the agent or broker will agree that any and all compensation or fees must come from the seller and not from the acquirer. Often, only one or two persons in an acquiring company are permitted to discuss acquisition with any outsider to prevent later claims.

Even if the agent or broker signs an agreement that fees will be paid by the selling corporation, the acquirer must be careful to insure that these costs do not turn up in the selling price, and often an agreement on this point is also signed.

In general, companies experienced in acquisitions are split on the value of finders. Some will not use them under any circumstances. Others will consider interesting proposals, but stress that the broker must be removed from the picture as quickly as possible after he has brought the two parties together and that in no case should he be allowed to take part in the negotiations on either side.

There is more faith, however, in the competence and trustworthiness of professional service organizations or search firms with an established reputation, working only for the acquirer. Foreign search firms have been successfully utilized in canvassing the European acquisition market, and more U.S. companies today are recognizing their worth, since the obvious acquisition prospects in Europe were picked off some time ago and the search, for the most part, now centers on harder-to-find small public or family-owned firms.

In addition to European search firms (fee usually paid by seller) a number of U.S. search firms operate in Europe (fee usually paid by buyer). In the long run, the cost may be no greater and the job may be done more speedily and efficiently by a specialist who may already have a warehouse of companies for sale and be in a better position to find others than a nonspecialist. Very few search firms, however, have adequate experience in and knowledge of this work in Europe as a whole. Also, the purchaser may prefer to keep inquiries "in the family" and to hand the search assignment to a tried and trusted executive rather than to an outsider whose expenses will have to be met whether or not his recommendations are followed.

Although a search specialist may not be able to appraise prospective acquisitions in the light of the purchaser's special needs, this need not be a reason for not employing him; after he submits his report on a company, the purchaser's own experts can make a more detailed appraisal. Professional and amateur searchers alike suffer from the limited sources of information on European companies.

The lack of both search firms and information sources is, of course, much greater in less-developed parts of the world, and a combination of organizations may have to be called upon.

Whether or not it hires a finder, an acquiring firm should be prepared for the search to take at least one year. Judging by the charges of reputable search firms, the potential purchaser must reckon on at least $2,000, and perhaps as much as $5,000, a month to cover the search firm's expenses *(or* those of an executive and assistants assigned to the task). To this sum must be added the cost of trips by one or more executives to evaluate firms on the spot, perhaps other trips to negotiate and renegotiate, plus a commission of 1 to 3 percent to a search firm or third party on completion of sale. This commission varies according to the purchase price and according to whether or not it is paid to a firm that has done the search work. Some banks charge a fee, others do not. The same applies to attorneys, public accountants, management consultants, and others.

Most banks with international operations provide a limited finder service for clients. Banks have extensive business contacts and can sometimes bring together client companies (or clients of correspondents or associates) which have complementary acquisition interests. They can also provide leads and background information for client companies looking for acquisitions or buyers. The usual procedure is to keep bank officers in all branches—domestic and overseas—aware that this information is valuable, and to have any leads they develop channeled to a single office to attempt to match buyers and sellers. Banks will seldom if ever allow themselves to become involved beyond bringing the potential buyer and seller together. This clearinghouse operation is usually a noncharge client service, but some Swiss (and other) private banks charge for such services.

The investment banks may be good finders, particularly for their larger clients, and a number of investment banks operate as brokers, acquiring companies themselves and then reselling them.

A number of the large international accounting firms perform search activities for their clients, and in recent years several of them have established central merger and acquisition departments, staffed with specialists, to coordinate this activity. A number of the large management consulting firms also provide international search services.

EVALUATING PROSPECTIVE ACQUISITIONS

Probably the most crucial aspect of acquisition is the evaluation of the firm that is to be purchased. Ideally, every buyer has a thorough knowledge of what he is about to purchase. But ideals in acquisition are rarely met. Even small companies are tremendously complex and may have numerous hidden commitments or future liabilities that do not appear until long after the firm is actually acquired.

Still, a thorough evaluation is a necessity before any sort of price negotiation can take place. No buyer can know what a company may be worth until he is intimately familiar with all the good and bad points of the company. Similarly, a thorough evaluation should turn up and help solve many of the problems that will have to be faced after the acquisition is completed.

Some companies have what they call a "go/no-go" evaluation checklist—a short list of questions, the answers to which determine whether the company should proceed with a more detailed evaluation. Such checklists vary from one company to another, but essentially they point up obvious factors that might make any particular acquisition an unfortunate move. Usually, the "go/no-go" questions can be answered by mail, by an intermediary finder, or by a very quick inspection of the company. A typical "go/no-go" checklist, developed by FMC Corporation, is shown in the appendix at the end of this chapter.

The next step is to make certain that, if time and money are to be spent on a thorough evaluation, there is a fairly high probability that a deal can be arranged. The "go/no-go" checklist should include an estimate of the price the seller expects, and this estimate must be reasonable. But even more important, in order to be sure the company is not wasting its time, is the signing of a preliminary option. It may cost $50,000 or more to find and evaluate a prospective acquisition. If, after the money is spent, the candidate turns out not to be worth buying or refuses to sell at a reasonable price—or if someone else buys it before you do—considerable cost is incurred with no balancing gain.

Once the prospective acquisition has passed the "go/no-go" test and an option has been signed (where possible), a full-scale evaluation is begun. Different companies handle this in different ways. In general, at least two and often a team of four or five men from the buying company are involved. One leading company has a team made up of a man from the corporate legal staff, an accountant, a plant engineer, and a sales analyst. If possible, all should have foreign *and* acquisition experience. For companies that are expanding abroad or intent to expand abroad, it might be wise to set up a team that will work together on all the company's future acquisition evaluations. As in all things, there is no substitute for experience.

The first thing that the team (or individual) must do is to acquaint itself with the ground rules for business operation in the country in which the prospective seller operates. Acquiring another firm inside the United States is fairly simple compared with doing it in Germany or Australia or any other foreign market. The evaluators in the United States have plenty of knowledge of the way business is done in the United States and of its business law. But what may be fine in the United States may be illegal in another country, and vice versa.

Once the team has come to know business conditions and practices in the foreign country, it should, if possible, talk to other U.S. companies that have already acquired a firm there. Almost every U.S. acquirer in Italy, for example, has met a serious hidden tax liability problem, resulting from the fact that Italian companies rarely pay the taxes they are supposed to according to the letter of the law. Advice on how to handle this problem can be obtained from the U.S. company's auditors or corporate counsel, but the best advice may come from other U.S. companies that have faced the same problem.

At this point the team is ready to "invade" the offices and plants of the prospective acquisition. But here, too, problems arise. It is usually necessary to keep the evaluation secret. Should a team of U.S. executives wander into XYZ AG in Germany and begin checking inventory, receivables, union relations, or what have you, the secret would be in the business press very quickly. There are a number of precautions that can be taken. One used by some companies is to pretend that the team, or part of the team, is making an investigation only for the purpose of concluding a licensing agreement or some similar deal. In a case in Australia, the U.S. executives visited the plant only at night when no one else was around. The trouble with this sort of "flashlight tour," however, is that a lot of things are considerably less visible in darkness than in daylight. Of course, much of the necessary information can be obtained in corporate offices, and only an engineer need visit the plant or other physical facilities.

Most companies use some sort of checklist for evaluating acquisitions, both in the United States and abroad, and some of the available checklists are quite voluminous. Short or long, however, even the best checklist is of limited utility. Few selling companies are very cooperative in providing an evaluation team with the answers. After all, the deal may not go through and the investigating company may be a competitor some day soon. A company cannot reveal all its corporate secrets, and, more seriously, it may have hidden liabilities of which it is unaware. Even a simple matter like the basic financial statements may not be easy to secure. In many foreign countries, it is standard practice for a firm to have several sets of books: one for the tax collector, another for the stockholders, still another for the key officers, etc. Obviously, the tax books, developed over many years to minimize taxes, give a very poor picture of the firm's real assets and liabilities. Getting the most accurate set of books for the previous three to five years eases the problem of finding out what the various accounts really mean. Each account should be examined, and a detailed explanation of each asset and liability is necessary. The purchaser must get a complete breakdown of the accounts receivable to see if the accounts include items long past due that should have been written off. Inventory should also be broken down in great detail to see if any goods that are no longer usable or salable (particularly finished inventory) are included. Fixed assets must be analyzed. Machinery and equipment may be of much greater or much less value than book value. Some may have to be replaced immediately. Some perhaps can be written up in value. Land and buildings may also be of much greater actual value than original cost less depreciation, as shown in the balance sheet. Other assets that must be examined are those not included in the balance sheet or included at far below actual value—managerial capability, company organization and controls, and the quality of the marketing force.

The liabilities must also be analyzed with a fine-tooth comb (unless the buyer is planning to purchase only the assets of a firm). Most important in this regard are the contingent liabilities that are not in the balance sheet: possible or current legal actions; possible future tax liens on income that had been hidden prior to the acquisition; the cost of discarding, when necessary, workers, management, distributors, or licensees. These, plus whatever else the management of the prospective seller has promised, can be extremely costly after the acquisition has been completed. Other possible and important liabilities, not in the balance sheet, include antitrust factors and difficulties with labor unions.

Many of the problems with regard to hidden liabilities can be avoided by agreeing to purchase only the assets of a firm, or by including in the purchase agreement a statement that the only liabilities the acquirer assumes are those in the balance sheet on the day of takeover. Some companies also include in the agreement a clause giving them recourse to the seller, should certain specified contingent liabilities appear within a given time.

Still another mechanism that is often used is delayed payment of the purchase price until several months after the acquirer has taken over. The buyer then has an opportunity to check through all the operations, unencumbered by secrecy or the withholding of information by the seller. In one recent case in Australia, a U.S. acquirer paid 75 percent of the purchase price down, the rest one year later. In another case, a U.S. producer of refrigeration equipment paid 60 percent down, the rest after completion of a thorough audit by a certified public accountant.

Other important considerations for evaluating a possible acquisition are these: Is the candidate's plant set up for rapid and inexpensive expansion? Is there plenty of room in the plant for additional production lines? Can new products be introduced easily? What have the firm's profits really been according to the most conservative bookkeeping methods? What do local banks, the candidate's customers and suppliers, the government, and other firms that have dealt with it think of the firm? (Checking business opinion on the company can be one of the best checks of a prospective acquisition's future profit performance.) What would be the reaction in industrial and government circles to the proposed takeover?

The general conclusion of most companies is that there is no substitute for a thorough evaluation by the company that is to pay the price. Although some service firms (notably independent public accountants) provide evaluation services, their best use seems to be in assisting in an evaluation rather than replacing the buyer's own evaluation effort entirely. On the other hand, where small amounts of money are involved, independent accountants have been successfully used for the entire evaluation process.

The final steps in the evaluation process are to come to a conclusion as to just how much the buyer is willing to pay for the prospective acquisition. To do so he must answer three questions:

1. What is the basic earning power of the dollar value of the assets, both in and out of the balance sheet, of the selling firm?

2. What is the dollar value to the buyer of such non-asset factors as speed, drawing a lead on competitors, less investment risk, securing a trained labor force in a labor-tight market, and other advantages gained by not starting from scratch?

3. What is the cost of converting the acquired company into a fully functioning part of the buyer's worldwide operations—and in the process cleaning up all the acquisition's hidden and contingent liabilities?

In practice, of course, there are a number of mathematical formulas that may be used to estimate the proper price of an acquisition, as described elsewhere in this volume. In essence, however, the amount of items 1 plus 2 above, minus item 3, should come out as the approximate price the buyer is willing to pay for the selling firm.

Appendix:

"Go/No-Go" Acquisition Checklist

Acquisition is becoming a much more common route for companies that need to make up lost time in foreign markets. The checklist below was developed by FMC Corporation as an aid in making preliminary evaluations of prospective acquisitions. If the information gathered through the "Go/No-Go" checklist does not show a prospective acquisition to be worth pursuing, the matter is dropped without further expenditure of time or money. If the company passes the test, a more detailed evaluation is made at a later stage.

Asking Price

An indication of the asking price and the seller's basis for valuing the company.

Personnel

1. Brief résumé, including title, age, year employed, background, and experience of key management personnel available to continue with the business. Similar data, if practical, for sales and engineering personnel.

2. Listing of annual salary, bonus, and any other compensation received by the foregoing key management groups.

3. Tabulation of over-all company employment, showing number of personnel in each principal department on fixed salary, indirect hourly and direct hourly wages. If practical, develop an organization chart to show scope of executive and departmental responsibility.

4. Summary outlining any management bonus, salesmen's bonus, general profit sharing, medical and life insurance, or retirement programs covering the company's employees. Copies of contracts, if available.

5. Current average hourly shop wage rate.

Financial

1. Copies of audited balance sheets and operating statements of past five years, with interim statement to date.

2. Current order backlog with comparable figures for at least one prior year.

3. Breakdown of dollar and/or unit sales for at least two years, preferably five, on the following bases:

(a) by product or major product groups, and including parts and service

(b) by geographic territory

(c) by method of distribution

(d) by month

(e) by principal users accounting for roughly 80 percent of sales.

4. Breakdown of gross profits by products or major product groups for at least two years, pereferably five. If on standard costs, outline standards procedure.

5. Breakdown of cost of sales for at least two years, preferably five, to clearly indicate direct labor, material, factory overhead, and any other charges which are normally made to cost of sales. Detail on factory overhead, if available.

6. Breakdown of charges under selling and advertising, engineering, and general administrative expenses. If engineering expense is normally a part of factory overhead, these charges will have been included under item 5 above.

7. Brief statement of depreciation policies, bad-debt write-offs, and inventory obsolescence practices. Date of latest physical inventory.

8. Schedule of insured value of buildings, equipment, and inventories.

9. Comment on any unusual charges such as royalties received, interest payments, capital gains, etc., under other income and other deductions.

10. Schedule of all company loans or debentures outstanding, including name of lender, interest payments, payment requirements and restrictions. Comment on any warrants or stock options outstanding.

11. Statement of preferred and common stock authorization as well as the date and state of incorporation. Review directors' meeting minutes as well as corporate charter and by-laws for items of significance.

12. Distribution of the stockholders constituting at least 85 percent of the voting shares outstanding.

13. Statement on the latest year for which statements have been reviewed by tax authorities. Include the settlement amounts paid during the past five years.

14. Schedule of any important contractual agreements not elsewhere covered, such as employment contracts, material purchase contracts, or any other commitments that may be of continuing obligation to the firm.

15. Brief summary of all litigation during the past five years which resulted in any substantial loss to the company. Include all litigation still pending.

16. Management's best estimate of annual sales and operating profits during the next five years. Indicate any new products which are expected to significantly contribute to the company's sales volume. Include estimate of major capital requirements for equipment and facilities that will be needed to realize management's forecast of future operations. Also indicate any industry indices which have some correlation to the company's general business activity.

Marketing

1. Outline of sales organization and methods of distribution.
2. Salesmen's compensation arrangement.
3. Tabulation of geographic sales coverage showing territorial coverage; number of sales, service, or other personnel assigned; and names and addresses of manufacturers' representatives, agents, disributors, jobbers, or dealers.
4. Copies of standard sales agreements used with manufacturers' representatives, agents, distributors, jobbers, or dealers.
5. Schedule of discounts extended to various levels of distribution.
6. List of major competitors, with estimate of the market portion held by each.
7. Complete set of current product catalog literature, with price lists of the past five years.

Engineering

1. Brief résumé of the name, title, age, service, and technical training of engineering department personnel.
2. List of principal company products which have been contributed by this engineering group.
3. Market introduction date of each important product line.
4. Outline of any significant development programs under way.

Patents

1. Listing of issued patents and applications, including number, expiration date, and identification of product covered.
2. Brief summary of the significance of these patents.
3. Name and address of patent counsel.
4. Schedule of all royalty agreements, including name of licensor or licensee, royalty rate, prepayments made, term of agreement, and product covered.

Facilities

1. Description of plant facilities, machinery, and equipment.
2. Layout or sketch of the physical factory arrangement.
3. If significant, indicate the source and tonnage of raw steel supplies, as well as iron, steel, and nonferrous castings and forgings.
4. Copy of any recent appraisal report on plant and equipment.

How to Make an Overseas Acquisition You Can Live With

ROBERT M. PRINCE

A CQUISITION has long been considered an important method of expanding or diversifying a company's operations in the United States, and in recent years it has come into increasing favor as a means of entering or expanding foreign markets. Today, the development of such regional groups as the European Economic Community makes it increasingly necessary for any international-minded company to operate from within the tariff walls abroad. In order to compete successfully with foreign corporations, more and more firms are turning to acquisitions as one of the fastest, least expensive, and often most advantageous ways of increasing their operations in foreign markets.

Before launching an overseas acquisition program, management would be well advised to take a good look at three important elements—people, places, and practices. In addition to the considerations present in a domestic acquisition, these factors must be reckoned with if a foreign venture is to succeed.

PEOPLE

The first major difference between acquisitions here and abroad is the fact that the people involved will come from cultures that are often quite

---

Robert M. Prince is Assistant to the President, Dow Chemical International, Midland, Mich.

different from our own, and their customs, manners, and mores must be taken into consideration if friction and misunderstanding are to be avoided.

A great deal has been written about cultural differences in various countries, and we will not go into detail in describing them here. On the whole, there is little difference in doing business at the executive level from one country to another. Business men the world over have the same desires and motivations and react to certain business conditions in pretty much the same way. The problem starts when we fail to recognize the differences that do exist in business customs or procedures.

The "go get 'em" type of approach, when used in the preliminary discussions with any acquisition candidate, will in most countries assure you of a speedy exit, though accomplished with courtesy and tact on the part of your host.

The foreign business man, particularly when being courted by an American with the acquisition gleam in his eye, usually wants to spend a good deal of time getting better acquainted on a purely personal basis before settling down to statistical studies of his business.

One European executive stated that any American being sent into his company to work with him as an understudy should have a "sense of history." He didn't mean someone with knowledge of the historical details of his country's past; he meant a person who would have an instinctive feel for the business and political activities of the country and the people with whom he would be in day-to-day contact. An academic view of history is important for this purpose, but more important is the understanding of how and why the historical pattern has developed and is continuing to develop.

The people you use for your foreign activities, both before and after the acquisition, should understand the mores and customs of their counterparts in the foreign business world. You can instill many of your own methods of business with the full cooperation of your foreign associates if you first take time to develop an understanding and appreciative relationship. Time spent in the beginning is worth thousands of dollars in the end and can develop a more permanent and secure investment position than any other single factor.

Understanding doesn't stop with executive-level communication, though this is where the acquisition program must start. During the negotiations for the acquisition and in the postacquisition period, relations with the minority shareholders, financial institutions, government leaders, and labor representatives are of great importance. They, too, have customs

that are different from ours. But they are also identical in having the same ultimate goal—namely, benefit to their particular group.

If you aren't familiar with these matters to the point where you are comfortable and satisfied with your strategy of foreign business relations, then hire someone with the necessary experience; call on the professional talents of people who can guide and assist you in this area, or plan to spend some time in a relaxed but thorough get-acquainted visit in the business community of the area in which you have picked your prospect.

PLACES

The place in which the acquisition will be made is the second major consideration in acquiring a foreign business. For the most part, overseas acquisitions will be centered in Europe, since this is the major area in which business development has reached a maturity at which acquisition is feasible. With some exceptions, countries in Latin America and the Orient have not developed economically to the point where acquisition candidates of the size and scope normally of interest to the U.S. business man can be found. In those areas—exclusive of Japan—the substantial business activities are usually branches of or joint ventures with large U.S. or European companies.

Investment Climate

It is important to recognize the local differences in the investment climate. Over the past years there have been marked changes in certain areas of Europe—in most cases, in a direction that creates more difficulty for the acquisition-minded U.S. company.

A few years ago, for example, the purchase of control of a local industry almost anywhere in Europe, in many cases approaching 100 percent, did not arouse any antagonism. Today, however, the acquiring company must begin to accept the idea of less than 100 percent ownership, particularly in areas of business substantially involving the public interest, and recognize that 50 percent or less participation will be a normal condition rather than an exception.

This comes about quite naturally because of the prosperity of industry abroad. There is less need for new capital and less desire by substantial shareholders to part with their investment. In addition, the business community in many countries is concerned about American competition in the form of acquisitions, and local business men are designing their own acquisition policies to prevent a company from falling into the hands of American owners. Finally, and possibly most important of all, many

European governments have increased their industrial take-over regulations and established procedures and practices that require some form of government approval before an acquisition may be made.

Monetary Restrictions

The monetary restrictions of the country must always be reviewed. The investigation should include the past history of monetary restrictions, at least for the last few years, since past policy may well be indicative of future trends. An easing of restrictions may be purely temporary and possibly cannot be continued in light of local conditions or worldwide monetary problems. Such easing may even be a "come-on" to foreign investors and not intended to be maintainable. Enthusiastic economics is no substitute for fiscal facts of life.

Restrictions on repatriating capital, paying dividends and interest, and paying royalties or license fees will be a limitation in many countries. A good rule of thumb is that the restrictions will be greater in those countries that are less economically developed.

PRACTICES

When you come down to the specifics of evaluating acquisition candidates, the first thing to remember is that you cannot assume any similarity between foreign practices and our own in the fields of accounting, marketing, corporate organization, or financing. Naturally, some similarities do exist, and in some companies the American methods have been injected— many times by nationals who are American-trained.

Keep in mind that the existing dissimilarities do not come about accidentally but have historical business and fiscal roots. Accordingly, while you expect your foreign associate to follow many of our established practices, the changes must not be so precipitous as to cause internal turmoil and insecurity within the very group of key personnel on whom you are depending for management and growth.

Temperate action and, again, adequate time will accomplish most of the necessary adjustments. We Americans do not have all the answers, so be willing to learn from the man who has been on the spot in an environment different from ours.

Stock Powers and Rights

Stock powers and rights can differ materially from those with which we are familiar. In some situations, for example, you can vote only 3 percent of your shares, no matter how many you own. Ownership of 51 percent of the stock may not ensure real corporate control; the laws of the country must be thoroughly checked to see what powers minorities have in excess of those usual to our practice. Investigation may also reveal a variety of subtleties we would be unlikely to expect—for example, delegation of all the powers of the directors to a single individual, the use of proxy directors or alternates, and the unenforceability of voting trusts.

In most corporations, the directors do not vote the dividend. This is done by the shareholders, if they wish to follow the recommendation of the directors. Annual reports to shareholders are in no way as complete as those you're familiar with; by themselves they are of no real value in providing a complete background for a financial history.

Reserve Practices

The declared dividend will usually be almost 100 percent of the net profit for the year shown in the report to shareholders. This should not be a matter of concern to you if you are able to analyze the reserve practices of the company in the current and prior years. This can be one of the most important items on your agenda.

There is no particular uniformity in reserve practices, with the possible exception of the so-called legal reserve—a required "set-aside," usually out of pretax profits, at a rate of 5 percent of such profits up to a minimum accumulation equal to 20 percent of the paid-in capital.

In addition, out of after-tax profits, other reserves can be set aside for contingencies, currency revaluation or exchange losses, uninsured losses, and so forth. These are a form of undistributed profits if not ultimately used.

These sums should not be confused with reserves for employee benefits, statutory or voluntary. Reserves for severance payments, sick benefits, retirement, and so on are not available to shareholders, so they are not a part of real net worth. As a matter of fact, these reserves are too often technically insufficient to meet the basic requirements of the statutory or contractual obligation if the company should come upon bad times. Moreover, they are seldom of the funded variety. Instead of having liquidity, they have been reinvested in the company and are held in the form of buildings, machinery, and investments in subsidiaries or affiliates. In other words, these are frozen reserves, and current payments for benefits are paid out of operations.

What happens if a general business depression strikes? If you do not have the funds to pay severance obligations, do you keep excess employees on the payroll and increase your losses? Do you pour more capital into the company at a time when this is the last thing you want or are able to do? In such a situation, will the government of the country step in and take over your business to ensure that the statutory obligation to the employees is met? As a result, will the government manage the business until the money advanced by it is repaid?

These are some of the possibilities that should be given careful consideration. At the same time, take a long look at the trends toward increasing social benefits and obligations in many parts of the world and pick the countries, the companies, and the risks with this in mind.

Depreciation Practices

Depreciation practices also have a good deal of flexibility. Although the tax laws of a country allow certain maximum rates for scheduled items of equipment, buildings, and sometimes land, this does not mean that the company will take the maximum allowable deduction. A management philosophy of maintenance of dividend payments might override the concept of a conservative approach to depreciation and obsolescence. You may well find that assets have been underdepreciated for a period of years and, in a sense, dividends have been paid out of capital. You then have a sort of partial liquidation. Inventory practices may also reflect the same philosophy, particularly in the area of obsolescence and, conversely, undervaluation.

The other side of the coin is the case where, in an inflationary economy, or due to currency devaluation, the asset values of the company have been written up to better reflect the so-called "true" or "plus" value. We see this practice in some companies in the United States, but the item is usually designated separately as "appraisal surplus." This is not always the case abroad. Accordingly, a thorough analysis of the surplus and reserve accounts must be made to make certain that appraisal surplus is not carried as a form of shareholders' surplus or in equity reserves—and to determine whether dividends have ever been paid from such a surplus.

Subsidiaries and Affiliates

In Europe, Americans do not have a monopoly on the idea of growth by acquisition. The European industrial giants, particularly in the Common Market area, are also acquisition-minded, with money and talent to expand their facilities for production and marketing.

The concept of the joint venture in Europe has also reached a sophisticated stage of development. This, of course, is not of recent origin, but such arrangements are probably more prevalent today than they were fifty years ago.

For this reason, in analyzing an acquisition candidate, one must always make a study of the company's shareholdings in subsidiaries and affiliates. The spiderweb of corporate interrelationships is, in some cases, extremely complex—and these affiliations can present hazards as well as some occasional benefits.

You might find, for example, that some of these associates are actually in control of sources of basic raw materials used by your candidate. They may control important marketing outlets for a large segment of your productive capacity. And if your candidate operates under license agreements from any of these affiliates or associated companies, you might find that such agreements are subject to termination or are limited in duration where there is a change in the control of the licensee.

On the plus side, it should not be overlooked that your new acquisition, through its associated activities in other corporations, will provide you with new and potentially profitable business connections, including sales outlets, material supply contracts, and even locally important financial connections.

Many companies have a substantial number of investments in subsidiaries and affiliates in addition to their prime activity. These are usually carried on the books under the designation of "participations," not "investments." Since the practice of making consolidated statements is not very prevalent, it will be necessary to analyze the financial statements of each of the participations to determine their real value and, just as important, the intercorporate transactions that would be eliminated in a consolidation.

You must also determine whether the value of the participation on the parent books is original cost of the stock or the present net equity value of the shares. Obviously, a losing affiliate or subsidiary requires an adjustment on the parent's books where there is no consolidation.

Because of the prevalence of participations in the corporate structure of foreign companies, another item that must be investigated is the extent to which guarantees of any debts of a subsidiary or affiliate have been made by the parent, or vice versa. Many times such guarantees will be carried as a supplement to the balance sheet (where required by law); other times they will not be shown at all, except possibly in the text of the report to shareholders.

In addition to this practice, you may find that substantial advances have been made to subsidiaries and affiliates. Such advances can be in the form of money, material, or equipment, and the amount of the advance will often be carried as a current receivable and not as an additional investment. Obviously, this affects the current position of the parent and the percentage profitability of the subsidiary operation.

Capitalized Costs

In evaluating net worth and operating profitability, attention should also be given to the capitalization of costs that we would normally consider expenses. These may be lumped in with other deferrals such as prepayments, and they can be overlooked unless the entire account is specifically discussed.

One item frequently treated in this way is deferred research. In some countries, the tax laws require that, where research has been productive of a commercial product, the past costs of the research for that development must be set up as a deferred asset, regardless of the profitability of the product. In other cases, a company will follow such a deferral practice even though it is not required by law.

AFTER THE ACQUISITION

It is easier to make an acquisition or merger than it is to operate with it after the marriage. Again, knowledge, understanding, and time are the primary requirements. Too many people from the acquiring company trying to do too much in too short a time can destroy all the good will that was stored up during the acquisition activity and can bring about serious morale problems in the acquired company.

It is well to include in the first analytical team used for the study of the acquisition candidate those people who will be directly a part of the future management or coordinating group in the post acquisition period. They can gain much needed knowledge and understanding of their future associates, and you can judge the ability of these men to work with and adapt themselves to the foreign environment and customs. Your negotiators will usually be top executives, but the manager-designate should at least sit in as an observer at all final negotiations to better understand the terms of agreement—both the formal, written agreements and the equally important oral understandings that will affect operations in the future.

Early involvement of the people who will actually be involved in the operation of the acquisition will often make it possible to anticipate many of the problems that inevitably arise after any acquisition. When these problems are dealt with early—if possible, even before the acquisition is consummated—they can often be avoided or at least prevented from growing to serious proportions.

One of the major areas in which problems arise is in operating and control procedures. The parent company will often require some kind of changes in, for example, the accounting procedures of the acquired firm in order to unify the practices of parent and subsidiary and make it possible to evaluate performance. Such changes may well be resisted—and there are often good reasons for following procedures that meet the specific requirements of the local situation, even when they depart from the practices of the parent company. These problems should be investigated early, so they can be settled with a minimum of disruption of both companies' operations.

Personnel problems also loom large after an acquisition. The employees of the foreign firm, both managers and workers, are naturally apprehensive about the changes that their new owners may be planning, and morale may slump dangerously while they worry about what the future holds in store. Not only does efficiency suffer, but valuable men may start leaving for new positions elsewhere—a loss that can seriously weaken the company.

Again, it is important to face these problems as early as possible. Employees of the acquired company should be given the facts about their new status and the effect that new ownership will have on their work, their responsibilities, and their authority. Most people prefer facts, even when they are unpleasant, to uncertainty; the sooner the effects of the acquisition are understood, the sooner the company can adjust to them and settle down to work.

Every effort should be made to assure employees that the changes that are made will contribute to the efficiency and success of the company as a whole and to their individual well-being.

———————

An acquisition, and particularly a foreign acquisition, requires compromises and accommodations on both sides. Summing up, we can say that there are three general requirements for any acquisition program abroad: time, knowledge, and understanding. Take time, develop knowledge, and achieve understanding. The result will be an acquisition you can live with.

American Acquisitions Abroad: A View from the Other Side

NICHOLAS A. H. STACEY

THERE IS A GROWING FEELING that some U.S. companies have been less successful in carrying out their European expansion plans by acquisition than they should or could have been. This dictum applies especially to larger corporations mounting their first European venture. The causes of this lack of success are various, but the main obstacles to profitable acquisitions are: the absence of adequate information regarding local conditions; lack of knowledge of the right type of corporation available for purchase; erroneous assumptions about the price to be paid for an acquisition; the exhibition of a degree of unduly hard bargaining in negotiations with Europeans, which American corporations would not deign to adopt in their domestic dealings; and, surprisingly enough, procrastination in decision making once the discussions for a possible acquisition are under way. The agility which characterizes the domestic operations of American business frequently seems to take leave of its officers when overseas expansion plans are being translated into action.

The large, overseas well-established and experienced U.S. corporation is largely exempt from such corporate frailities, but most of the others are subject to it in varying degrees. What are the causes of this confusion and inertia which are time and money wasting and give some

Nicholas A. H. Stacey is Director of Chesham Amalgamations & Investments Ltd. of London. This chapter is derived from his recent book, *Mergers in Modern Business,* Hutchinson & Co., London.

American business men a bad image? They are worth analyzing if profitable acquisitions overseas are considered an important part of the corporation's over-all expansion and diversification plan. The real hazard in the overseas acquisition stakes perhaps is not that in the end U.S. companies will disdain from acquiring overseas subsidiaries, but rather that they will acquire the wrong ones. In so doing, the managements of American corporations are unlikely to blame themselves; in their post mortems they will find it simpler to pillory the unreliable and impossible foreigner. "The American dream" will have been shattered—the task of bestowing the fruits of American enterprise on the foreigner stymied.

How are U.S. corporations currently going about formulating and implementing their Western European expansion plans by acquisition? Quite properly, an internal study is first prepared identifying the type of expansion desired; the long-range corporate planning staff, inside the corporation, will pinpoint basic objectives. Slowly, the corporate profile of the desired acquisition becomes clearly drawn. The plan emerges, tentative provision for investment funds is made—all that is needed now is to find the optimum choice—the overseas company itself—which conforms to requirements and is available to be acquired. The chase for the proposition is about to begin. At this stage, a surprising vacuum develops in the corporation's operations as events unfold. While many details of the corporate plan for overseas expansion have been laid with great care and sophistication in Boston, Cleveland, or New York, its physical execution is frequently attempted with the utmost primitivism in Birmingham, Frankfurt, or Lyons.

NO DIVISION OF SPOILS

Even the acquisition part of the plan itself often suffers from the major defect of imprecise definition. Inadequate attention is devoted to selecting the type of overseas corporation most desirable for a specific purchaser with a definite purpose in mind. For instance, should the American corporation purchase a firm in Britain, France, or Germany? And should this business be a listed (quoted) public company, or a private company owned by a family or by a handful of people managing the firm? Just because public companies are almost invariably larger than private companies, there are many sizable firms among the latter suitable for acquisition. Yet American corporations will tend to go for public companies rather than for the private variety—this mainly because by sitting in their transatlantic head offices and relying largely on the findings of desk research, U.S. managements will have scant opportunities for identifying suitable private companies in distant lands across the Atlantic. Yet the acquisition of public companies by overseas buyers is always attended by more clatter and badinage—and sometimes by proxy battles and a little xenophobia—than that of private companies. Perhaps it should be added that the reaction pattern of Americans to foreigners attempting to gain control of a U.S. corporation is not different from that of Europeans.

Another frequent error in the implementation of corporate acquisition plans for overseas expansion is the seeming insensitivity of much of American business to the climate of opinion in the host country finally selected as the base of operations. If an overseas corporation decides to register a new company, buy a plot of land, erect suitable buildings, equip the factory with plant and machinery, recruit labor, and start producing, then new benefits will accrue to the economy of the host country; and, in exchange, profits will be—as they should—remitted to the United States. If, on the other hand, an American corporation bids for a public company in Europe and makes it a wholly owned U.S. subsidiary, then the investing community in the host country will be denied participation in the expanding fortunes of the acquired company.

One possible, if narrow, interpretation of such a step, is to construe that for the incoming American company, the acquired firm is purely a predatory exercise and the intention is simply to exploit a situation. Therefore, much good will can be generated by leaving a part of the equity capital in the hands of the investors in the host country. But good will is only one aspect—and perhaps not the most important one—of the "good neighbor" policy so ardently professed by American corporations. An overseas public company in which a majority interest has been acquired by a U.S. corporation but which still remains a public company confers substantial advantages on the majority shareholder. Money can be raised locally for expansion, at a time, perhaps, when it is less propitious to raise funds in the States; and by maintaining its native identity, such a company is in a more advantageous position to obtain government orders. Thus, the partnership element with local investors should not be abrogated lightly by the U.S. corporation buying all the shares in a publicly quoted company overseas. After all, control lies with the incoming American side, irrespective of whether 100 percent, 75 percent or 51 percent of the shares are owned. Moreover, the profits of the overseas acquisition can be consolidated in the American parent's accounts if over 50 percent of the shares are owned by the American corporation.

HOW NOT TO SUCCEED

Although it is less complicated from every point of view to purchase a private limited company in England, in Germany, or, for that matter, anywhere in the world, the American corporation is in more serious difficulties when it comes to finding a suitable one to buy. For the greater part, the corporate planner of the U.S. company must rely on desk research to identify overseas private companies in various industrial sectors apparently suitable for acquisition. Much detailed information is usually available about public companies, but meaningful information on private companies is scarce—particularly financial information. Financial and trade intelligence can, of course, be picked up about private companies, but only through listening posts in their country of location. Thus, the corporate planner working thousands of miles away has well-nigh insurmountable difficulties in identifying the right kind of private company which should be acquired, unless he is prepared to spend a longish time in the country which has been selected for expanding the operations of his firm.

THE PRESIDENT'S TALE

Although the board of the American corporation may have approved the plan to expand overseas by acquisition, this is quite some way off from finding a workable *modus operandi* for carrying out the operation. For the corporation embarking on this exercise for the first time, there is little doubt that the president, or the specially nominated "vice president for overseas expansion," will personally want to attend to the business. Often, American corporation chief executives arrive in Europe single-handed to "do a deal" when in identical circumstances on their home ground they would take their time over a decision and not budge without a battery of advisers and attorneys!

It is hard to credit it, but there are U.S. company presidents who advertise in European newspapers in advance of their arrival in one of the capital cities—asking those who have companies for disposal to write or to contact them at their hotel. On arrival, the president finds a bunch of letters from improbable people, a fact he discovers perhaps too late, and sets about interviewing them one after another. If this relatively inexperienced—in overseas acquisitions—American business man is not taken for a ride by some smart local talent, this can be put down to good fortune rather than perspicacity. Often, he sustains some little financial loss, fails to find a worthwhile proposition during his whirlwind tour, and then leaves the country feeling cheated, disappointed, and half determined not to go any further in expanding overseas; at least not in that country. His first promising corporate excursion has proved abortive, and from this sample of one he may even go as far as deducing a general theory. This is how misconceptions arise!

Then there is the very informality of American business men to consider. Admirable and endearing though this is in personal relationships, in other circumstances it may prove an occupational hazard and redound to their disadvantage when attempting "direct action." The president of an American corporation can easily contact the president of another on the phone, arrange to meet him at the country club or accost him during a cocktail party, and put to him the simple question "How much do you want for your stock?—We think you're a good buy!" Perhaps such a direct assault is not out of the ordinary in the working day of the American corporate chief—but such disarming frankness can, and does, put a stop to promising corporate acquisitions in Western Europe. Whether right or wrong, prudent or foolish, this approach eliminates the last vestiges of the "comedy of corporate manners"—which is just as important in France, for example, as in Britain or any other country.

To know what is "good form" for Americans abroad is not automatic on becoming president of even a large corporation; it has to be learnt. Ability to employ it eases problems of business negotiations before an acquisition and reconciles problems of business coexistence afterwards.

THE CORPORATE PLANNER'S TALE

Chances of success in overseas acquisitions improve materially if first the corporate planner is sent on a fact-finding tour. However, his mission is not enviable and his task weighty. Unless he has some general experience of the conditions and the people in the country where the acquisition is planned, his visit is bound to fall short of the ideal. His odyssey will resemble that of the now extinct type of British employee who went to work in India around the turn of the century: He sailed in a British ship, on arrival stayed at the British enclave, entertained at the British club, and worked in a British firm. On returning from India twenty-five years later, he knew of the country only a little more than when he arrived. Substitute the word "American" for "British" and the same hazards confront the American business visitor—except even more so!

Invariably the corporate planner is given the choice of finding alternative locations. This means that instead of being able to spend his scheduled two weeks in Britain—where at least a common language divides us—to investigate the position, he may be forced to allocate his time among two or more countries where the language difficulties and local customs really assail him. Thus, instead of concentrating his efforts on the examination of plausible propositions prepared for him in advance by local organizations, he must start from first base, which is time-consuming, and will return to home base without accomplishing his mission. As a result, sometimes he will get frowns from his superiors for not achieving the impossible—that is, for not bringing back a fully worked-out sound proposition. In this way overseas expansion by acquisition is once more shelved in some corporations.

CORPORATE DECEIT

Logic would dictate that to carry out a successful plan of expansion by overseas acquisition, local talent must be harnessed to the objective. Why American business executives should consider themselves "universal geniuses" who can "clinch a deal" in any country by just their commanding presence on the local scene has for long been a source of puzzlement on the eastern approaches of the Atlantic. The motivating sentiment behind such faulty thinking is the often firmly held view of innate superiority—the American business man's descent, so to speak, from a higher industrial civilization to a "comparatively backward" one. And, when the plans go astray, "the fault, dear Brutus, is not in our stars, but in ourselves, that we are underlings."

The same North American corporate braves who investigate with such consummate vigor any slight change in their product's domestic market shares, scrutinize the copy platform of their competitors or the distributive mutations of competitive merchandise in the smallest detail, often join the race in the overseas acquisition stakes without having done their homework. Far from having instructed a local organization in the chosen country to assist their officers and executives, they may not even have advised their American bankers of their intentions.

ARE EXECUTIVES INHIBITED?

There are further obstacles, mainly psychological, in finding and keeping alive suitable acquisition propositions—particularly for U.S. businesses. Even assuming that the U.S. corporation has collaborated with a reputable local organization overseas to discover a "good buy" and to "keep one warm," the much-vaunted speed of action with which American executives are supposed to be endowed fails to appear. Yet, in the acquisition game, time is of the essence.

This is what in fact happens. The European "finder"—be it a professional marriage broking institution or a bank—will send a detailed letter to its U.S. principals alerting them to a business opportunity. In seven cases out of ten, the letter remains unanswered. In due course, either another letter or a cable is sent as a follow-up—and here again the U.S. side often just sends an acknowledgment. The much-expected speedy action—whether or not the proposition is suitable, and, if in the affirmative, whether a plenipotentiary will be sent to examine it in detail—only rarely materializes. The practical upshot of such procrastination is that the potential vender—approached, processed, and convinced of the advantages of teaming up with the U.S. client—sells to someone else, as his instincts to join up with someone have been aroused.

One of the explanations for the delay is, simply, that U.S. business men don't like writing letters—much of American business being carried on by telephone. Another is that some think a proposition in another country cannot be as urgent as the most banal business transactions on their own doorstep. After all, has not the U.S. entrepreneur read repeatedly and heard incessantly how sleepy and sluggish these English, French, or Italian so-called business men have become? A frequent source of failure, therefore, is the voluntary devaluation of the urgency of foreign business. Naturally, this does not often apply to the executives of substantial U.S. international corporations with experience of and respect for methods of business in other countries.

Protracted haggling with foreigners, agreeable to negotiating their firms, may be a way of acting out the legendary strong-man business lore, long redundant but perhaps still hankered after by some American business men; but this is a false premise and no longer valid; the bull-in-the-china-shop tactic is not advisable any more in "world business"—especially not in a seller's market for companies, a condition long enjoyed in Western Europe. A last-minute peremptory demand for lowering the purchase price or reducing the value of the goodwill element in the business, or offering to pay less by discounting likely growth as a result of "private meditative research" can wreck a promising deal. Indeed, it could even be said that the untimely intercession of the buying company's president in negotiating a corporate acquisition may lead to a hardening of the price. And it should be noted that emotionally satisfying price chiseling can ensue only in the case of overpriced propositions—which from the outset must be approached with great caution. In corporate acquisitions, bargains must be suspect.

WORKING TOGETHER

The moral, it seems, is that American corporations wishing to acquire overseas companies should consider "not going it alone" in exploring and in negotiation for them. They would be better advised to instruct a local organization experienced in corporate acquisitions—both from the financial as well as the industrial side. Some European professional firms are capable of undertaking a thorough-going research program for their American principals, if so instructed, and this prepares the groundwork for the corporate planner, allowing him to complete quickly his investigations abroad.

Provided the necessary brief is received from the U.S. corporation it is possible not only to identify the "best buy" in corporate acquisitions, but also to take soundings about its availability before anyone sets out from the United States on an expensive mission. Thus, American firms can save valuable executive time and ensure a greater likelihood of successful acquisitions if they choose the right kind of professional help in the country selected for their expansion. They will also receive advice about a miscellany of local conditions which they would be hard put to discover unaided.

EXPANDING HORIZONS

European industry is poised once more on the threshold of further expansion. Because local markets are fast giving place to world markets, and because the size of enterprise is steadily rising, European companies are increasingly becoming international—both in outlook and in composition. Multinational corporations are being formed, and the joint ownership of firms between companies of various nationalities is steadily rising. International companies wishing to secure a foothold in Europe must purchase participations in or acquire a company for themselves in the Common Market or the European Free Trade Area.

What is vital is that American corporations wishing to join in the expansion of European business should stake a claim within the next decade, before the structure of European trade and industry has solidified into a new mold. It will, of course, be possible to gain entry afterwards, but the terms of doing so may be more onerous. What American business needs, to evolve a viable and worthwhile program of corporate acquisitions in Western Europe, is not more economics or better planning, but stronger boots!

VIII

How Not To

"Wedlock, indeed, hath oft comparèd been
To public feasts, where meet a public rout,—
Where they that are without would fain go in,
And they that are within would fain go out."

SIR JOHN DAVIES, *Contention Betwixt a Wife, etc.*

How Not to Sell Your Company

ROBERT L. CHAMBERS

THE MAN I am most envious of is the president of a profitable, growing company who—

- ☐ owns his company or has completely compatible co-owners;
- ☐ has adequate capital not only for current operations but also to finance a growth program that will challenge his young and capable executive team;
- ☐ has solved all his personal estate problems as well as those of other principal stockholders.

Undoubtedly such a man averages no more than four hours a day at his office, the balance spent either on the golf course, with his family, or traveling in foreign lands. His brow is unfurrowed, his shoulders erect, his hair jet black. Such a man should consult a psychiatrist if he entertains the slightest thought of selling his company.

The problem is that some of us have furrowed brows *and* estate problems *and* inadequate capital *and* dissident stockholders. So we finally come to the conclusion that having some large corporation's eggs in our company's nest might not be too bad an idea.

WORDS TO THE WISE

Those of us who have made this decision usually have learned a few things not only about the opportunities but also about the pitfalls and hazards involved in selling a company.

Robert L. Chambers is President of Bartlett-Snow-Pacific, Inc., New York.

The best way to start is with an actual case history illustrating what can happen if one sells the wrong way. . . .

A typical young "growth" company started scratching in 1947, and by its last complete fiscal year had worked up to $8 million worth of sales of a consumer durable in a highly competitive hard-goods market!

Only a few key executives of the company were stockholders, with the bulk of the stock owned by the three founders. Because the company had pulled itself up by the proverbial bootstraps, it had not paid dividends. Accordingly, all three owners had their eggs singularly contained. The principal problems were these:

☐ **the owners' estate valuation and ability to pay estate taxes;**

☐ **insufficient capital to provide the growth that is required to retain young top-management personnel;**

☐ **extreme economic vulnerability due to the necessity of carrying heavy inventories of a product that is subject to wide seasonal and cyclical fluctuations.**

Because they thought that each succeeding year would be a "better year for valuing the company," they postponed decision. When in 1958 they finally decided to take the big step, economic conditions were not very favorable.

And now appeared the president of a glamor company actively expanding by mergers and acquisitions. In a matter of a few hours he had "analyzed" the company, made an offer, and answered the owners' "questions as to the future." The price was excellent—better than the owners had expected. So they sold. What's the mistake? Where's the lesson?

If you have personal or family pride in your organization, probably money is not your sole consideration in releasing the reins of responsibility. Such things as perpetuating the company, continuing its contribution, and protecting its employees from undue hardship will be part of your decision.

The three owners of this subject company certainly realized that changes would be required if they were to adjust to a new organization and new policies as their company changed into a division of a large corporation. But although they were ready to cooperate, they were hardly prepared for what actually happened.

The day after the sale became final, the president—now the new boss—showed up. "Dismiss the treasurer," he ordered.

"Why?"

"Because this is the job to which every firm pensions the old trusted employee; we won't need him."

He continued his stroll through the office. "Cancel the contract for all IBM equipment."

"Why?"

"Because I once had a plant with IBM, and it was a headache."

"But we only adopted IBM after investigating other systems for controlling costs, invoicing, sales analysis, and so forth. And it is integral with our complete accounting and cost system."

"I think that we will cancel the contract all the same."

Each step he took through the plant equaled another step in dissecting the company. No requests for opinions, no heeding of existing policies and programs. Just slice here, squeeze there, and liquidate whenever possible.

Not too slowly the significance of this technique became apparent: by liquidating inventory, squeezing receivables, selling part of the fixed assets, the purchaser can often free sufficient cash to pay the cost of a company acquisition. If the company has sales momentum—perhaps a nationally known trade name—"what's left" after the squeezing and slicing can be operated with a skeleton crew and an abnormal margin obtained. When this program finally catches up with itself—as it surely must—"what's left" can be liquidated, and the original buyer walks away with a profit.

Less than two years later, the company in this case history, which was once a leader in its industry, was a corporate skeleton. The qualified engineers, merchandisers, financial experts, all had left for jobs in other companies. Although the owners did not cry on their way to the bank, they had many remorseful hours since making that fateful decision to sell.

Such events have eliminated many a productive economic unit and have wreaked hardship on numerous people. And in the process the public concept of "free enterprise" has certainly suffered.

But what are the alternatives? Have you any way of predicting the consequences of selling your company?

STEPS TO A SAFE SALE

Let us start with the thesis that you recognize some of the advantages of selling: better estate valuation, diversifying risk, ending divergent objectives of the owners, and so on. But let us assume that up to the present you have not put your company "on the market." Here are some specific suggestions as to how to avoid the "worse-than-death" results experienced by the owners mentioned in the preceding case history:

1. *Don't wait too long!* Mañana may never come. When your company's future is sunniest is probably the best time to seek the association which will provide a useful umbrella when circumstances threaten rain. Undoubtedly a young, rapidly-growing company which is doubling its net worth every year will be hesitant to sell—perhaps advisedly so. But the sophisticated buyer will generally recognize the potential and arrange purchase terms which permit the sellers to realize a substantial percentage of these anticipated earnings.

2. *If you decide to "associate," make your decision with resolve.* Flirtation without intent to consummate a marriage can be a dangerous practice. You will not be subpoenaed for breach of promise, but you may get a tarnished reputation which might discourage a serious suitor.

3. *Don't be careless and haphazard in making your plans to sell.* I have been amazed at how naïvely many presidents go about the job of selling their companies. These same men would approach a production or merchandising problem with all the planning, assignment of responsibility for action, and follow-up that has ever been recommended in the *Harvard Business Review.* But when it comes to selling their company, they approach the job with less thought and finesse than their greenest salesman shows when he makes his first sales call.

4. *Don't fall for a letter from a "business broker" stating that a large company is "keenly interested in talking with you."* While there are reputable, responsible professionals in this field, there are also some deplorable sharpers who can catch many an unwary and unsophisticated president. An example may make this clear:

One day four years ago I had a phone call from a man in Chicago who explained that a large company was most eager to acquire my own. Could he get some figures to present to them? I thought I was being very cautious in telling him we would never talk without knowing the identity of his principal. Soon he was on the line again with the statement that it was our arch-competitor who was interested. I thereupon called the vice president of the competitor and said, "I understand you are interested in purchasing our company." He replied, "No, but I understood you are interested in selling to us." Obviously the broker in Chicago was playing both of us against the middle—and he was waiting in the middle.

5. *Do some deep thinking on your own first.* Very frequently the president starts by "having a chat" with his banker or lawyer. While these may both be very helpful people in normal operations, most likely neither of them is a "professional" in terms of selling companies. And most frequently both are faced with a conflict of interests—they do not want to lose an account! While there are always exceptions, the advice they give may even be harmful to the potential seller.

So rather than beginning by chatting with your banker or lawyer, or taking potluck on a business broker, consider the advantages of the following procedure:

(a) Carefully analyze your own objectives. For example, if you want not only to sell out but to get yourself clear out, your course of action should be different than if you wish your company and your presidential responsibilities to continue.

If it is a "clear out" decision, your principal objective may be the maximum cash price now. I doubt if you will accede to an indefinite payout if someone else will be calling the shots. Once again you should determine to what degree you hope to protect the jobs of old employees, and perhaps the company monument you or your father has built.

If your decision is to "stay in," then your course of action must be more carefully planned.

(b) Having determined your objectives, the next step is to plot your strategy. Reflect for a moment on the psychology of a potential buyer.

Many companies are willing to buy if the acquired company is a "great bargain." If you are willing to give $1.50 for each $1.00 paid, then your selling job will be relatively easy.

A merger or acquisition is a "natural" if the result is $2 + 2 = 5$. The most prudent companies can be interested in your operation if the combination of yours and theirs makes a total greater than the sum of the units. This is the type of buyer situation a potential seller should strive to find.

6. *Look for a merger that will make the total greater than the sum of the individual company parts.* Let me illustrate the $2 + 2 = 5$ situation by referring to a Midwest company which I happen to know. It is an old-line machine-tool producer with a dominant position in its industry. Previous management operated under a "save the cash" policy, with the result that today the company has a surplus of unused liquid assets, no debt, and a listing on the New York Stock Exchange. Most important, it has made the policy decision to grow through acquisition.

What type of companies should the Midwest company acquire in order to make $2 + 2 = 5$? Here are a few:

☐ **A young, undercapitalized growth company which could use some of the Midwest company's cash in order to exploit its market more rapidly.**

☐ **A moderate-size company producing electrical components similar to the Midwest company's own industrial switches and solenoids. By combining products of both companies a wider product line and better distribution might be achieved.**

☐ **A company with a major new technological development, but without the funds to carry it to completion, which could take advantage of the Midwest company's cash and facilities, and could at the same time make a substantial contribution to the parent's research and development program.**

☐ **A company with a surplus of competent young management with creative capacity greater than justified by the market it presently serves.**

7. Carefully plot the strategy of "approaching" likely buyers. It is axiomatic that you do not want your company to be known as "shopped," and you must take steps to avoid this. But first you must obtain all possible information about the companies you think are the most logical buyers. Published balance sheets, proxy statements or prospectuses filed with the SEC, Dun & Bradstreet and trade association summaries are all good sources. Then, when you have settled on candidate No. 1, and you know the company from A to Z, including why it needs you, you are ready to take positive action. Here there are two alternatives:

(a) It is generally more desirable to be pursued than pursuing. To achieve this coveted position, however, you must accomplish the delicate maneuver of seeing that cupid's dart reaches your target. And for this you need some common line of communication, which you probably will be able to get from the results of your investigation—for example, the bank, your CPA, your attorney, your major customer or supplier, the executive secretary of the trade association, or even a friend.

When your line of communication has been discovered, you can place the responsibility formally or informally. It might be only a side comment, "You know, Sam, if United and ourselves were wearing the same hat, we could both earn twice our profit." Or, "Has Bill Buyer ever mentioned that he would be interested in acquiring Universal?" If your common acquaintance runs true to form, he will see that you soon hear from Bill Buyer. (But use this technique only if you are certain this "good friend" will not subsequently surprise you or the buyer with a bill for a "finder's fee.") With your bank or your accountant you are probably safe—and indeed you need not be so indirect. Simply ask them to make certain you are pursued.

(b) Another completely different approach may be appropriate if you are sufficiently sure of your ground. Let us assume that you have made certain that the potential buyer has the desire and the funds to make an acquisition of your company. Then you personally should arrange to meet the chief executive officer. Under such circumstances, it is better to be frank than coy. Briefly explain why you are motivated to such a decision, why you have chosen his company first, and why this marriage was "made in heaven." It is perfectly appropriate to request and receive confidential treatment of your offer and facts. If you do not have such confidence in the company in which you are interested, you probably should not be considering it anyway.

8. *If it is important to you that your company continue, be sure you devote sufficient time to discussion of future operating plans.* Make certain you know what the potential buyer anticipates as the particular orbit of your company—and you!

The buyer's words are not enough. To be really safe, you should check deeds. Ask permission to talk with heads of other companies that this company has purchased. To be thorough you should converse not only with presidents who have stayed with the new parent but also with some who have left. And do not be satisfied with talking only to former company presidents—talk to employees all up and down the line—to anyone in a position to know the company intimately.

Don't be too disappointed if after long negotiations you discover some questionable characteristic of a would-be purchaser; just be thankful you found out before you took the leap. You will be better prepared next time. And there *will be* a next time—for the field is full of eligibles.

In short, on an important matter like this, care is more important than time.

How to Succeed in Business
Without Really Buying

B. R. WAKEFIELD

MANY COMPANIES have neither the need nor the desire to acquire other businesses. As increasing attention is paid to the subject of mergers and acquisitions in the business press, however, it is becoming more and more difficult for a company's management to come right out and admit that it is not interested in this particular avenue of growth. Stockholders and other interested parties, after all, are likely to regard any company that does not have a diversification-through-acquisition program as somewhat stodgy and old-fashioned, to say the least.

The following program, which has been tested in practice by companies of various sizes in a wide range of industries, is suggested for any company that is not really interested in acquisitions but wishes to appear to be avidly pursuing numerable opportunities for the enrichment of sales and earnings.

STAFFING THE PROGRAM

Choosing the right man to head up your acquisition program is all-important. Select a senior management official who is about to retire—or, better yet, one who has already retired—to serve as your Director of Diversification. Ideally, the individual chosen should have a background

---

B. R. Wakefield is Vice President–Acquisitions and Mergers of Bangor Punta Corp., New York.

in purchasing, personnel, or some other department in which he is not likely to have developed any particular knowledge or experience in the area of mergers and acquisitions.

The main responsibility of the Director of Diversification is to appear as frequently as possible at stockholder meetings and other public functions. Considerable care should be taken, however, to ensure that he does not actually say anything on these occasions.

DEVELOPING ACQUISITION CRITERIA AND POLICIES

The most effective acquisition criteria and policies for a program of this sort are either (a) so general that any company which has been in operation for more than six months will qualify or (b) so restrictive that no company will qualify. Merely to set a minimum requirement of 40 percent return on sales and assets, however, may not be sufficient. For greatest effectiveness this criterion should be supported by a maximum purchase price of 4 times earnings.

COMMUNICATING WITH THE PUBLIC

Communication with the public, through the business press and other media, is a vital part of any acquisition program, and this one is no exception. Prepare a series of standard statements that can be uttered on appropriate occasions by important executives or directors of the company—for example, "We have three acquisitions on the fire right now, and several more on the back burners." If, as sometimes occurs, the speaker is pressed for further information, he should point out that negotiations are at an extremely delicate stage at the moment and it is impossible to identify the other parties.

ADVERTISING

Advertisements in the "Business Opportunities" columns of *The Wall Street Journal* and other business publications can be quite useful, but the wording of such ads must be carefully considered in terms of your specific objectives.

If, for example, you are interested in developing a large file of replies, which can be shown to anyone who is interested in the actual workings of your acquisition program, you will want to use something like the following:

On the other hand, you may prefer to save yourself the time and expense of having to read, acknowledge, and file replies, in which case the following approach is recommended:

In addition to saving you a great deal of time and expense, since it can virtually be guaranteed that no one will answer such an ad, this approach has the advantage of advertising your company as a forward-thinking, aggressive acquirer.

By following these four simple steps, any company should be able to project a modern and progressive image, while at the same time allowing management to devote all its attention to running the present business.

A Sure Guide to Unsuccessful Mergers

JOHAN BJORKSTEN

MANY OTHERWISE PROMISING MERGERS have foundered because the participants were so busy eyeing the balance sheets—or the current ratio of assets to liabilities, product styles, fixed assets, book value vs. market price of the stock being exchanged, and so on—that they overlooked what was more basic than all of these considerations: whether the products and processes of the company being acquired were already or soon-to-be obsolete. Only competent scientific research could have told them that.

REASONS FOR MERGERS

Generally speaking, most mergers and acquisitions take place for one or more of the following reasons:

1. *To secure new products.* In one industry synthetic fibers brought into the market a veritable flood of new products, from nylon stockings to house insulation. Innumerable producers have endeavored to adapt these new fibers to new products—or, alternatively, to acquire other companies that have done so successfully.

2. *To offset a threatened loss of market.* When the diesel locomotive outmoded the steam locomotive, it hurt not only the soft-coal industry, but thousands of producers of steam locomotive parts, boiler additives, and so forth. Such companies had to seek new markets, new products,

---

Dr. Johan Bjorksten is President of Bjorksten Research Laboratories, Madison, Wis.

or both. Today many tobacco companies, faced with the prospect of more stringent anti-cigarette measures in the future, are anxious to diversify into other markets through the merger route.

3. *To increase the rate of growth.* For example, hand tools such as hammers, saws, screwdrivers, and the like have a market demand closely related to population growth. But those producers who are not satisfied to stay even with market demand seek other products (and companies) to supplement their present line—e.g., power tools or industrial tools.

4. *To improve cyclical and seasonal stability.* The coal dealer buys out the ice dealer in order to wipe out seasonal peaks and valleys. In similar fashion, the manufacturer of electric refrigerators seeks a company which produces a line of electric space heaters, humidifiers, and dehumidifiers.

5. *To improve the effectiveness of the marketing effort.* A manufacturer of business office supplies, whose salesmen call on office supply dealers, endeavors to buy a company which produces rubber cement, or mimeograph paper, or plastic briefcases. The reason is obvious: The same salesmen calling on the same customers will have more items to sell.

6. *To employ excess working capital.* Some manufacturers have excess capital, and acquisitions permit them to diversify with relative safety, variety, and stability.

7. *To change from a holding company to an operating company.* A private holding company that wants to convert itself into an operating company for tax purposes can do so most painlessly by acquisition.

In almost every instance above the major focus of interest is *new products.* Merger mistakes are rarely made in the area of finance—unless fraud is involved. Examination of production methods and facilities and valuation of machinery, equipment, and plant soon add their weight. The sales and distribution picture is often easily ascertainable—although the outlook for the future may not be so easy to project. But who knows whether there are not scientific changes in materials or processes that will weaken the attractiveness of, or make obsolete, the basic products of the acquired company in the near future?

COSTLY OVERSIGHTS

Overlooking the scientific development of new competitive materials and new processes is only one of the faults that sometimes lead to unhappy merger results. Another costly oversight is failure to consider those new developments in chemistry, physics, metallurgy, plastics, and so on which are now still in the pre-patent stage but which, when in full bloom, may completely wipe out the market for the acquired company's chief product. Patents may be developed for new scientific processes which chop production costs radically, make machinery and equipment obsolete, and undermine many of the older processes.

For example, a major manufacturer of electronic-organ parts decided that diversification was a sound move. With the help of its major bank, this manufacturer acquired a well-run electronics company on the West Coast which specialized in electronic circuitry. This West Coast producer had a new process in its lab—a method for imparting electrical conducting properties to hard-surface plastic or glass materials. This was done by specially treating the glass or plastic and then scratching a circuit on its surface with a mechanical stylus. The result was a sort of primitive printed circuit which had excellent potentiality for savings in material and labor costs.

About two years after this costly acquisition, the parent manufacturer discovered that new chemical techniques were available which would produce uniform circuits on plastics and glass, outmoding the entire process of scratching such circuits with a mechanical stylus. Actually, the clues to this chemical development were all in the scientific literature of the industry at the time of the acquisition—but no one had been asked to look.

How can this sort of sad but common error be avoided? The answer lies in understanding how scientific innovations are detected in every industry. Many branches of the various scientific disciplines run along parallel paths. For example, high-temperature research may be going on simultaneously in the laboratories of companies in the manufacture of metals, petroleum, plastics, glass, rubber, gases, diesel engines, adhesives, ceramics, and so forth. In addition, fundamental research on high temperature is going on in various university laboratories, both in the United States and abroad. While all of these research efforts may run along parallel paths, they do not necessarily converge except under special circumstances.

A specialist—chemist, physicist, metallurgist, pharmacologist, engineer —in any one of these areas often remains oblivious to developments in the other areas. They are, after all, not part of his province, which is complex enough. But scientific consulting organizations *must* keep abreast of all areas in order to meet the wide and varying demands of their clients.

Sure Guide to Unsuccessful Mergers / 311

When the continued success of a prospective acquisition is dependent upon a technical or scientific product or process, it is impossible to make a sound evaluation of the acquisition without extensive research into many parallel scientific areas. This may sound impossible, yet it is precisely the business of most independent research organizations. Failure on the part of an acquiring company to make such an evaluation has more than once resulted in a serious corporate decline.

THE NEED FOR RESEARCH

The likelihood of making acquisition mistakes is especially strong among large companies which are buying a scattered selection of smaller companies operating in many diverse fields in which technical products or processes are involved. That this approach is quite common today is evidenced by a recent report of the Federal Trade Commission, which indicated that conglomerate acquisitions were on the rise in many manufacturing industries. Among such acquisitions reported was the purchase of a canning-machinery concern by a diesel engine manufacturer; the acquisition of a bottle producer by a manufacturer of precision parts for aircraft; and the merger of a vacuum cleaner manufacturer with an oil burner manufacturer. All of these products, of course, involve highly intricate technical and scientific know-how.

Within recent years large companies in the dairy-products field have purchased organizations in such unrelated lines as fisheries, sardine canning, and brewing. Leading integrated petroleum corporations have acquired companies manufacturing chemical sprays, cotton presses, and shipbuilding materials.

The variety of actual conglomerate mergers, consolidations, and acquisitions that have taken place in recent years is truly astounding. We find such bizarre and unique combinations as a manufacturer of asbestos products taking over a company producing heavy forgings; a manufacturer of floor-finishing machinery becoming interested in a department store; an assembler of motor trucks taking over a chain of supermarkets.

Some of these companies have taken the plunge because they had a lot of cash in the corporate till and were in a hurry to grow. Others have wanted to leap out of stagnant industries in one jump. Still others have chosen to diversify in order to escape their own industry's bust-or-boom cycle. And a few have decided to move into new fields because they might run afoul of antitrust laws if they acquired firms in their own industry.

No one who has any real knowledge of the science or technology upon which many of these businesses are based can read about the extensive combinations of such very diverse lines of business without wondering what the result will be in the years ahead. Where major, top-flight companies undertake conglomerate activities in which scientific knowledge (among other things) is imperative, it is far more costly to plunge ahead without scientific advice than it is to secure such advice beforehand.

A large plywood manufacturer, for example, had been selling certain plywood grades to manufacturers of private airplanes; the plywood was used for interiors. The plywood manufacturer's bankers recommended that the company acquire a small chemical firm that had developed a process for producing a certain material which combined resistance to high temperatures with a high degree of transparency. It seemed most suitable for aircraft windshields, and could be sold by the plywood manufacturer's sales staff as readily, the banker thought, as they sold the plywood to the aircraft companies.

So the plywood manufacturer acquired the chemical company. An additional six-figure investment by the plywood company enabled the chemical subsidiary to install new equipment for producing the material in volume. When the chemical subsidiary was ready to submit samples to the civilian aircraft engineers, however, the parent company discovered, to its considerable dismay, that researchers in another field had developed an equally transparent material which was resistant to still higher temperatures—and which could be produced at a lower price.

This development had been foreshadowed in research papers in the learned journals of this field, which were available to any knowledgeable technical investigator at the time the plywood company bought the subsidiary. Apparently, however, the purchaser had not known where to look. And thus another golden opportunity for expansion turned into a monument to scientific oversight.

There are no sure guides to a successful merger. But there is one sure guide to an *un*successful merger: Pay no attention to the scientific possibilities that might undermine a company's basic products, processes, or markets.

Index

National Gypsum Co., 168
National Labor Relations Board, 226, 228, 231–233, 235
"Negative goodwill," 15
Net worth, 13
New York Central Railroad, 227
New York Daily Mirror, 233
New York Daily News, 233
New York Stock Exchange, 134
Nonconvertible preferred stock, *see* Preferred stock
Nontaxable transactions, *see* Tax-free transactions

Objectives, definition of, 4, 10–12, 303, 309–310
Organizing for mergers and acquisitions, 5, 25, 267, 306
Overseas acquisitions, *see* International acquisitions
Overseas borrowing, 109

Packaging methods, integration of, 25
Park & Tilford, 51
Partnerships, 180
Part pooling–part purchase, 87
Patents, 13, 17, 26, 150, 179, 186–187, 279
P/E ratio, *see* Price/earnings ratio
Penn-Olin Chemical Co., 53
Pennsalt Chemicals, 53, 121
Pennsylvania Railroad, 227
Pension costs, 14, 32, 82, 192, 270
Pension plans, 23, 190–208
Personal holding company, 163, 310
Personnel considerations, 11, 22, 26, 104, 209–237, 277, 280, 288
"Phantom" assets, 205
"Phantom" pay rates, 234
Philadelphia National Bank, 52
Pillar Rock Packing Co., 170
Pillsbury Mills, 51
Planning for mergers and acquisitions, 10–29, 192, 217, 246–253, 293
Pooling of interests, 86–91, 103, 111, 176, 258
Postmerger integration, 19–24, 224, 239–263, 287–288
Powell River Co., 241
"Practical merger," 65
Preferred stock, 113, 168

Present-value concept, 98–100
President, role of, 3–9, 292
Press relations, 29, 307
Price, determination of, 15, 133–142, 171, 277
Price/earnings ratio, 5, 12, 96, 106, 111, 112, 118–132, 135, 242
Privately owned companies, 96, 133, 290
"Private offering" exemption, 70–71
Process industries, average P/E ratios in, 120
Procter & Gamble Co., 55
Product extension mergers, 55, 60
Production considerations, 11, 21, 250
Profit-sharing plans, 23, 190–208, 225
Property, plant, and equipment, 13, 20, 43
Proxy solicitation, 28, 67–69
Purchase versus pooling of interests, 86–91, 103, 176, 261

Qualified retirement plans, 190–208

Ralston Purina Co., 71
Radiation, Inc., 140
R & D, *see* Research and development
Real estate, 149, 152, 179
Recapitalization, 109
Receivables, 42
"Reg A" exemption, 70–71
Registration under Securities Act, 65–67
Remaining useful life, *see* Economic useful life of assets
Reorganizations, *see* Tax-free transactions
Repair and maintenance costs, accounting treatment of, 81
Research, need for technical and scientific, 312
Research and development, 11, 82, 121
Reserve for bad debts, 183
Reserve practices in other countries, 284
Residual securities, 91, 112
Retained cash flow, 111, 112
Retirement plans, qualified, 190–208
Richmond Television Corporation, 185
Risk, 13, 101–103
Robinson-Patman Act, 257
Ross Gear & Tool Company, 232
Royal Plating and Polishing Co., 234
Royalties, 163
Ruhe, Karl, 187